THE

African-American

ADDRESS

BOOK

THE

African-American

ADDRESS

BOOK

Tabatha Crayton

A PERIGEE BOOK

Every effort has been made to provide the most current mailing addresses.
Addresses, however, do change, and neither publisher nor author is
responsible for misdirected or returned mail.

We regret that when this book went to press, it was too late to include the
names of the recently elected United States public officials.

A Perigee Book
published by
The Berkley Publishing Group
200 Madison Avenue
New York, NY 10016

Copyright © 1995 by Tabatha Crayton
Cover design by James R. Harris
Text design by Stanley S. Drate/Folio Graphics Co., Inc.

First edition: February 1995

Library of Congress Cataloging-in-Publication Data

Crayton, Tabatha.
The African-American address book / Tabatha Crayton. — 1st ed.
p.   cm.
"A Perigee book."
ISBN 0-399-52148-8 (pbk.)
1. Afro-Americans—Societies, etc.—Directories.   I. Title.
E185.C877   1995
973'.0496073'025—dc20   94-30205
CIP

Printed in the United States of America
3   4   5   6   7   8   9   10

Thanks go to:

My dad, Spurgeon Crayton; his wife and my buddy, Claudia Crayton; my grandmother, Caroline O'Neal; my sisters, Marcia and Noreen; my brother, Chip; my niece, Ashley; my godmother, Ruby Moore; brother-in-laws, uncles, aunts and cousins, and some very special friends: Eudora, Alarice, Chan, my agent, Alice, and my editor, John, and his assistant, Genny. And to Michael Levine, the creator of *The Address Book*.

Thanks,

Tabatha

Author's Note:

To make this directory as useful as possible, I tried to supply telephone numbers wherever possible for businesses, associations and organizations. Unfortunately, they were not always readily available. Please excuse the inconsistency.

TLC

CONTENTS

INTRODUCTION

"Wherever I have knocked, a door has opened. Wherever I have wandered, a path has appeared. I have been helped, supported, encouraged, and nurtured by people of all races, creeds, colors, and dreams."
—*Alice Walker*, In Search of Our Mother's Gardens, *1983*.

The old saying that the whole is greater than the sum of its parts couldn't be more appropriate for this book. In the more-or-less mechanical process of building this collection, name by name, *The African-American Address Book* became a celebration of achievement in the black community and revealed the scope and influence of the people listed in these pages.

Not only will you find the famous and notorious—athletes, artists, religious and political leaders, movie stars and headline makers—but also literally thousands of individuals and organizations who have made a continuing contribution to and impact on America and the world.

Even in the high-tech world of cellular phones, faxes, and e-mail, there's still nothing as powerful and empowering as the letter. Michael Levine, in his introduction to the original *The Address Book*, reported that for every letter that politicians get they assume that there's a hundred other folks out there who think the same way as the writer but didn't bother to write . . . ask any seasoned elected official about the power of a letter-writing campaign!

For the first time, this book brings together the movers, shakers and opinion makers from the African-American community. These are the people who make the music, play the games, run the corporations—and whose opinions are heard far and wide. These are the people you'll want to reach to ask for help or advice, to commend or criticize. . . .

The reasons for writing are as many as there are people willing to pick up a pen—getting financial assistance for college, selling a product or service, making a complaint, asking for an autographed photo, building a grass roots movement, joining an association, getting a job or offering condolences or congratulations when the occasion warrants.

Americans love to move, so it's likely that you'll find some of the addresses to be out of date—many of your letters will be forwarded, some will come back to you. This shouldn't happen too often and it's expected that the book will be updated regularly. Don't hesitate to write if you see errors or omissions. If your name is in this book and your address is inaccurate, please contact the publisher c/o: *The African-American Address Book*, c/o Perigee Books, 200 Madison Avenue, New York, NY 10016.

THE MEDIA

PERSONALITIES AND NEWSMAKERS

Allen, Byron
300 W. Alameda Ave., #2977
Burbank, CA 91523

Alleyne, Sonia
c/o Black Elegance
75 Park Ave. South
New York, NY 10016

Arnez, Nancy
Professor of English
Howard University
2400 6th St. NW
Washington, DC 20059
Journalist

Barras, Jonetta
PO Box 21232
Washington, DC 20009

Berry, Bertrice
c/o William Morris Agency Inc.
151 El Camino Dr.
Beverly Hills, CA 90212

Boston, Kelvin
c/o Polaris Communications, Inc.
PO Box 32522
Detroit, MI 48232

Bradley, Ed
c/o CBS-TV
555 W. 57th St.
New York, NY 10019

Brown, Jamie Foster
PO Box 4148
Washington, DC 20018

Brown, Tony
c/o Tony Brown Productions
1501 Broadway, #2014
New York, NY 10036

Canning, Lisa
c/o Night Beat
6735 Yucca St.
Los Angeles, CA 90028

Chambers, Veronica
c/o New York Times Magazine
229 W. 43rd St.
New York, NY 10036

Clayton, Xerona
c/o TBS Inc.
1 CNN Center
Atlanta, GA 30348

1

Cole, Harriette
c/o Essence Magazine
1500 Broadway
New York, NY 10036

Cose, Ellis
c/o New York Daily News Inc.
220 E. 42nd St.
New York, NY 10017

Curry, George
c/o Emerge Magazine
175 Varick St.
New York, NY 10003

Fee, Debi
c/o Fresh Magazine
PO Box 91878
Los Angeles, CA 90009

Ferguson, Kate
63 Grand Avenue, #230
River Edge, NJ 07661

George, Nelson
c/o Village Voice
36 Cooper Sq.
New York, NY 10003

Gillespie, Marcia Ann
c/o Ms Magazine
230 Park Ave.
New York, NY 10169
Editor

Grant, Gwendolyn Goldsby
c/o Essence Magazine
1500 Broadway
New York, NY 10036

Gumbel, Bryant
c/o NBC-TV
30 Rockefeller Plaza, #304
New York, NY 10020

Gumbel, Greg
c/o CBS-TV
51 W. 52nd St.
New York, NY 10019

hampton, dream
205 Lexington Ave.
New York, NY 10016

Harper, Vaughn
c/o WBLS-FM
3 Park Ave.
New York, NY 10016

Horner, Cynthia
c/o Right On! Magazine
355 Lexington Ave.
New York, NY 10017

Hunter-Gault, Charlayne
356 W. 58th St.
New York, NY 10019

Jack the Rapper
c/o Ma Ma Productions
142 2nd Ave., #306
New York, NY 10003

Jackson, Hal
c/o WBLS-FM
3 Park Ave.
New York, NY 10016

Jemison, Mae
c/o The Jemison Group
830 Apollo La.
Houston, TX 77058
*Astronaut, Physician, Chemical
  Engineer*

Jones, Lisa
c/o Village Voice
36 Cooper Sq.
New York, NY 10003

Jones, Sam
c/o Black Entertainment
  Television
1700 N. Moore St., #2200
Rosslyn, VA 22209
Sports commentator

King, Rodney
c/o Steve Lerman
9100 Wilshire Blvd.
Beverly Hills, CA 90212

Lampel, David
c/o WBLS-FM
3 Park Ave.
New York, NY 10016

Levy, Victor
c/o CBS-TV
524 W. 57th St.
New York, NY 10019

Madgett, Naomi L.
16886 Inverness St.
Detroit, MI 48221

Martin, Carol
c/o CBS-TV
524 W. 57th St.
New York, NY 10019

Mason, B. J.
820 S. Michigan Ave.
Chicago, IL 60605

McCall, Nathan
c/o Washington Post
1150 15th St. NW
Washington, DC 20071

McDowell-Head, Lelia
PO Box 43208 V St. NW
Washington, DC 20010

McEwen, Mark
c/o CBS-TV
524 W. 57th St.
New York, NY 10019

Neal, Charlie
c/o Black Entertainment
  Television
1700 N. Moore St., #2200
Rosslyn, VA 22209
*Talk show host, sports
  commentator*

Nelson, Havelock
c/o Billboard Magazine
1515 Broadway
New York, NY 10036

Oliver, Stephanie Stokes
c/o Essence Magazine
1500 Broadway
New York, NY 10036

Page, Clarence
Chicago Tribune
435 N. Michigan Ave.
Chicago, IL 60611

Powell, Kevin
PO Box 1196
New York, NY 10113-0910

Quarles, Norma
1 CNN Center
PO Box 30348
Atlanta, GA 30348

Rasberry, William J.
c/o Washington Post
1150 15th St. NW
Washington, DC 20071

Rashad, Ahmad
c/o NBC-TV
30 Rockefeller Plaza
New York, NY 10019
Sportscaster

Red Alert
c/o WRKS-FM
1440 Broadway
New York, NY 10018
DJ

Roker, Al
c/o NBC-TV
30 Rockefeller Plaza
New York, NY 10019
Weatherman

Rowan, Carl T.
1101 7th St. NW
Washington, DC 20036

Salaam, Yusef A.
167 W. 136th St.
New York, NY 10030

Shaw, Bernard
111 Massachusetts Ave. NW,
3rd Floor
Washington, DC 20001

Simmons, Sue
c/o ABC-TV
75 W. 66th St.
New York, NY 10032

Simpson, Carole
1717 DeSales St. NW
Washington, DC 20016

Simpson, Donnie
c/o Black Entertainment
Television
1700 N. Moore St., #2200
Rosslyn, VA 22209
Vee jay, show host

Smith, Bev
c/o Black Entertainment
Television
1700 N. Moore St., #2200
Rosslyn, VA 22209
Talk show host

Stuart, Rachel
c/o Black Entertainment
Television
1700 N. Moore St., #2200
Rosslyn, VA 22209
Talk show host

Sutton, April
c/o Black Entertainment
Television
1700 N. Moore St., #2200
Rosslyn, VA 22209

Tate, Greg
c/o Village Voice
36 Cooper Sq.
New York, NY 10036

Tatum, Art
c/o Amsterdam News
2340 Frederick Douglass Blvd.
New York, NY 10027

Taylor, Susan L.
c/o Essence Magazine
1500 Broadway
New York, NY 10036
Editor-in-chief, author

Villarosa, Linda
c/o Essence Magazine
1500 Broadway
New York, NY 10036

Wattleton, Faye
435 N. Michigan Ave.
Chicago, IL 60610
*TV journalist, former head of
    Planned Parenthood of America*

Wilkins, Roger
229 W. 43rd St.
New York, NY 10036

Williams, A. B.
c/o Black Entertainment
Television
1700 N. Moore St., #2200
Rosslyn, VA 22209
Television show host

Williams, Montel
c/o William Morris Agency
151 El Camino Dr.
Beverly Hills, CA 90212
Talk show host

Williams, Wendy
c/o WRKS-FM
1440 Broadway
New York, NY 10018

Winfrey, Oprah
PO Box 909775
Chicago, IL 60690
Talk show host, actor, producer

BROADCAST GROUPS AND STATIONS

Radio Networks

American Urban Radio Networks
463 7th Ave.
New York, NY 10018
212/714-1000

Black Entertainment Television
1700 N. Moore St.
Rosslyn, VA 22209

**Inner-City Broadcasting
  Corporation**
801 2nd Ave.
New York, NY 10017
212/661-3344

**National Black Network
  Broadcasting Corporation**
463 7th Ave., 6th Floor
New York, NY 10018
212/714-1000

**Sheridan Broadcasting
  Corporation**
411 7th Ave., #1500
Pittsburgh, PA 15219
412/281-6747

Willis Broadcasting Corporation
1645 Church St., #400
Norfolk, VA 23510
804/622-4600

Radio Stations
(Listed geographically by state)

ALABAMA

WAGG-AM
424 16th St. N.
Birmingham, AL 35203
205/254-1820

WAPZ-AM
Rt. 6, PO Box 43
Wetumpka, AL 36092
205/567-2251

WATV-AM
PO Box 39054
Birmingham, AL 35208
205/780-2014

WAVE-AM
1408 3rd Ave. W
Birmingham, AL 35208
205/786-9293

WBIL-AM
PO Box 666
Tuskegee, AL 36083
205/727-2100

WBIL-FM
PO Box 666
Tuskegee, AL 36083
205/727-2100

WEUP-AM
PO Box 1198
Huntsville, AL 35814
205/837-9387

WGOK-AM
PO Box 1425
Mobile, AL 36633
205/432-8661

WJLD-AM
1449 Spaulding Ishkooda Rd.
Birmingham, AL 35211
205/942-1776

WMGJ-AM
815 Tuscaloosa Ave.
Gadsden, AL 35901
205/546-4434

WOOF-AM
PO Box 1427
Dothan, AL 36302
205/792-1149

WORJ-FM
PO Box 1259
Ozark, AL 36360

WOXR-AM
Drawer E
Talladega, AL 35160
205/362-9041

WQIM-FM
PO Box 604
Prattville, AL 36067
205/365-0390

WRAG-AM
PO Box 71
Carrolton, AL 35447
205/367-8136

WSLY-FM
PO Box 400B
York, AL 36925
205/392-4787

WTQX-AM
1 Valley Creek Circle
Selma, AL 36701
205/872-1570

WTSK-AM
142 Skyland Blvd.
Tuscaloosa, AL 35405
205/345-7200

WXAL-AM
Highway 80 E
Drawer X
Demolis, AL 36732
205/289-1400

WXVI-AM
PO Box 4280
Montgomery, AL 36104
205/263-3459

WZMG-AM
PO Box 2329
Opelika, AL 36803
205/745-4656

WZZA-AM
1570 Woodmont Dr.
Tuscumbia, AL 35674
205/381-1862

ARKANSAS

KCAT-AM
PO Box 8808
Pine Bluff, AR 71611
501/534-5000

KCLT-FM
307 Hwy 49
PO Box 2870
West Helena, AR 72390
501/572-9506

KXAR-AM
PO Box 320
Hope, AR 71801
501/777-3601

CALIFORNIA

KACE-FM
161 N. La Brea Ave.
Inglewood, CA 90301
213/330-3100

KBLX-AM
601 Ashby Ave.
Berkeley, CA 94710
510/848-7713

KBLX-FM
601 Ashley Ave.
Berkeley, CA 94710
510/848-7713

KDIA-AM
100 Swan Way
Oakland, CA 94621
510/633-2548

KEST-AM
185 Berry St., #6500, Bldg 2
San Francisco, CA 94107
415/978-5378

KFOX-FM
123 W. Torrance Blvd.
Redondo Beach, CA 90217
213/374-9796

KGFJ-AM
1100 S. La Brea Ave.
Los Angeles, CA 90019
213/930-9090

KGGI-FM
2001 Iowa Ave., #200
Riverside, CA 92507
714/684-1991

KJAZ-FM
1131 Harbor Bay Parkway, #200
Alameda, CA 94501
510/769-4800

KJLH-FM
3847 Crenshaw Blvd.
Los Angeles, CA 90008
213/299-5960

KJOP-AM
15279 Hanford Armoba Rd.
LeMoore, CA 93245
209/584-5242

KKBT-FM
6735 Yucca St.
Hollywood, CA 90028
213/466-9566

KKGO-FM
PO Box 250028
Los Angeles, CA 90025
310/478-5540

KMAX-FM
3844 E. Foothill Blvd.
Pasadena, CA 91107
213/681-2486

KMJC-AM
4875 N. Harbor Dr.
San Diego, CA 92106-2304
619/224-1556

KPOO-FM
PO Box 11008
San Francisco, CA 94101
415/346-5373

KRML-AM
PO Box 22440
Carmel, CA 93922
408/624-6431

KSDS-FM
1313 12th Ave.
San Diego, CA 92101
619/234-1062

KUOR-FM
1200 E. Colton Ave.
Redlands, CA 92374
909/792-0721

COLORADO

KEPC-FM
5675 S. Academy Blvd.
Colorado Springs, CO 80906
719/540-7489

CONNECTICUT

WKND-AM
544 Windsor Ave.
Windsor, CT 06095
203/688-6221

WNHC-AM
112 Washington Ave.
New Haven, CT 06473
203/234-1340

WYBC-FM
165 Elm St.
New Haven, CT 06520
203/432-4118

DISTRICT OF COLUMBIA

WHUR-FM
Howard University
529 Bryant St. NW
Washington, DC 20059
202/806-3500

WJYE-FM
5321 1st Pl. NE
Washington, DC 20011
202/722-1000

WKYS-FM
4001 Nebraska Ave. NW
Washington, DC 20016
202/686-9300

WMMJ-FM
400 H St. NE
Washington, DC 20002
202/675-4800

WOL-AM
400 H St. NE
Washington, DC 20002
202/675-4800

WPFW-FM
702 H St. NW
Washington, DC 20016
202/783-3100

WUST-AM
815 V St. NW
Washington, DC 20001
202/462-0011

WYCB-AM
National Press Building
529 14th St. NW, #228
Washington, DC 20045
202/737-6400

FLORIDA

WANM-AM
300 W. Tennessee St.
Tallahassee, FL 32301
904/222-1070

WAPN-FM
1508 State Ave.
Holly Hill, FL 32017
904/677-4272

WAVS-AM
4124 S.W. 64th Ave.
Davie, FL 33314
305/584-1170

WCGL-AM
4035 Atlantic Blvd.
Jacksonville, FL 32207
904/399-0606

WEDR-FM
PO Box 551748
Opalocka, FL 33055
305/623-7711

WEXY-AM
412 W. Oakland Park Blvd.
Ft. Lauderdale, FL 33311-1712
305/561-1520

WHJX-FM
10592 E. Balmoral Circle, #1
Jacksonville, FL 32218
904/696-1015

WJHM-FM
37 Skyline Dr., #4200
Lake Mary, FL 32746
407/333-0072

WLIT-AM
3033 Rivera Dr., #200
Naples, FL 33940-4134
803/248-9040

WPOM-AM
6667 42nd Terr. N
West Palm Beach, FL 33407
407/844-6200

WPUL-AM
2598 S. Nova Rd.
Daytona Beach, FL 32119
904/767-1131

WRBD-AM
4431 Rock Island Rd.
Fort Lauderdale, FL 33139
305/731-4800

WRFA-AM
800 S.E. 8th Ave.
Largo, FL 34649
813/581-7800

WRXB-AM
1700 34th St. S
St. Petersburg, FL 33711
813/327-9792

WSVE-FM
4343 Spring Grove Rd.
Jacksonville, FL 32209
904/269-3693

WSWN-AM
PO Box 1505
Belle Glade, FL 33430
407/996-2063

WTMP-AM
5207 Washington Blvd.
Tampa, FL 33619
813/626-4108

WTOT-AM
PO Box 569
Marianna, FL 32446
904/482-3046

WTWB-AM
PO Box 7
Auburndale, FL 33823
813/967-1570

WVIJ-FM
3279 Sherwood Rd.
Punta Gorda, FL 33980
813/624-5000

WYFX-AM
400 Gulf Stream Blvd.
Delray Beach, FL 33444
407/737-1040

WZAZ-AM
2611 Werd Radio Dr.
Jacksonville, FL 32204
904/389-1111

GEORGIA

WAOK-AM
120 Ralph McGill Blvd., #1000
Atlanta, GA 30365
404/898-8900

WFAV-FM
PO Box 460
Cordele, GA 31015
912/273-1404

WFXM-FM
369 2nd St.
Macon, GA 31208
912/742-2505

WGML-AM
PO Box 615
Huntsville, GA 31313
912/368-3399

WGOV-AM
PO Box 1207
Valdosta, GA 31603
912/242-4513

WGUN-AM
2901 Mountain Industrial Blvd.
Tucker, GA 30084-3073
404/491-1010

WHCJ-FM
PO Box 31404
Savannah, GA 31402
912/356-2399

WHGH-AM
PO Box 2218
Thomasville, GA 31799
912/228-4124

WIBB-AM
369 2nd St.
Macon, GA 31208
912/742-2505

WIGO-AM
1532 Howell Mill Rd.
Atlanta, GA 30318
404/352-3943

WJGA-FM
100 Brownlee Rd.
Jackson, GA 30233
404/775-3151

WKIG-AM
226 E. Bolton St.
Glenville, GA 30427
912/654-3580

WKZK-AM
PO Box 1454
Augusta, GA 30903
706/738-9191

WLOV-AM
823 Berkshire Dr.
Washington, GA 30673
706/678-2125

WLOV-FM
823 Berkshire Dr.
Washington, GA 30673
706/678-2125

WPGA-FM
Drawer 980
Perry, GA 31069
912/982-2980

WQVE-FM
PO Box 434
Camilla, GA 31730
912/294-0010

WRDW-AM
1480 Eisenhower Dr.
Augusta, GA 30907
404/667-8001

WRDW-FM
1480 Eisenhower Dr.
Augusta, GA 30907
404/667-8001

WROM-AM
PO Box 5031
Rome, GA 30162
706/234-7171

WSAI-AM
206 E. Factors Walk
Savannah, GA 31401
912/947-1450

WSNT-AM
PO Box 150
Sandersville, GA 31082
912/552-5182

WSNT-FM
PO Box 150
Sandersville, GA 31082
912/552-5182

WTHB-AM
PO Box 1584
Augusta, GA 30903
706/279-2330

WTJH-AM
2146 Dudson Dr.
East Point, GA 30364
404/344-2233

WVEE-FM
120 Ralph McGill Blvd., #1000
Atlanta, GA 30605
405/549-1470

WXAG-AM
2145 S. Milledge Ave.
Athens, GA 30605
404/549-1470

WXRS-AM
PO Box 1590
Swainsboro, GA 30401
912/237-1590

WYZE-AM
11 11th Blvd. SE
Atlanta, GA 30312
404/622-7802

ILLINOIS

WBCP-AM
PO Box 1023
Champaign, IL 61820
217/359-1580

WBEE-AM
15700 Cambell Ave.
Harvey, IL 60426
708/331-7840

WCFJ-AM
1000 Lincoln Highway
Ford Heights, IL 60411
708/758-8600

WESL-AM
149 S. 8th St.
East St. Louis, IL 62201
618/271-1490

WGCI-FM
332 S. Michigan Ave., #600
Chicago, IL 60614
312/984-1400

WJPC-AM
820 S. Michigan Ave.
Chicago, IL 60605
312/247-6200

WLNR-FM
820 S. Michigan Ave.
Chicago, IL 60605
312/247-6200

WLUV-FM
2272 Elmwood St.
Rockford, IL 61103
815/877-9588

WPNA-AM
408 S. Oak Park Ave.
Oak Park, IL 60302
708/524-9762

WSBC-AM
4949 W. Belmont Ave.
Chicago, IL 60641
312/282-9722

WVAZ-FM
800 S. Wells St., #250
Chicago, IL 60607
312/360-9000

WVON-AM
3350 S. Kedzie Ave.
Chicago, IL 60623
312/247-6200

WXKO-FM
PO Box 465
Pama, IL 62557
217/562-3949

INDIANA

WLTH-AM
3669 Broadway
Gary, IN 46402
219/884-9409

WPZZ-FM
645 Industrial Dr.
Franklin, IN 46131
317/736-4040

WSLM-FM
PO Box 385
Salem, IN 47167
812/883-5750

WWCA-AM
487 Broadway, #207
Gary, IN 46402
219/886-9171

IOWA

KBBG-FM
527½ Cottage St.
Waterloo, IA 50703
319/234-1441

KIGC-FM
William Penn College
North Market and Trueblood
  Aves.
Oskaloosa, IA 52577
515/673-1095

KTFC-FM
PO Box 102-A
Sioux City, IA 51106
712/252-4621

KANSAS

KEYN-FM
2829 Salina Ave.
Wichita, KS 67204
316/838-7744

KQAM-AM
2829 Salina Ave.
Wichita, KS 67204
316/838-7744

KENTUCKY

WCKU-FM
651 Perimeter Dr., #102
Lexington, KY 40517
606/269-9540

WLLV-AM
515 S. 3rd St.
Louisville, KY 40202
502/581-1240

WLOU-AM
2549 S. 3rd St.
Louisville, KY 40208
502/636-3535

WQKS-AM
905 S. Main St.
Hopkinsville, KY 42240
502/886-1480

WRLV-AM
PO Box 550
Salyersville, KY 41465
606/349-6125

WTCV-AM
PO Box 685
Greenup, KY 41144
606/473-7377

LOUISIANA

KBCE-FM
PO Box 69
Boyce, LA 71409
318/793-4003

KFXYZ-FM
3225 Ambassador Caffery Pkwy.
Lafayette, LA 70506-7214
318/898-1112

KGRM-FM
Drawer K
Grambling, LA 71245
318/247-2344

KJCB-AM
413 Jefferson St.
Lafayette, LA 70501
318/233-4262

KOKA-AM
PO Box 103
Shreveport, LA 71161
318/222-3122

KQLX-FM
7707 Waco St.
Baton Rouge, LA 70806
504/926-1106

KRUS-AM
PO Box 430
Ruston, LA 71273
318/255-2530

KTRY-AM
PO Box 1075
Bastrop, LA 71220
318/281-3656

KTRY-FM
PO Box 1075
Bastrop, LA 71220
318/281-3656

KXLA-AM
PO Box 990
Rayville, LA 71269
318/728-6990

KYEA-FM
516 Martin St.
West Monroe, LA 71291
318/322-1491

KZZM-AM
311 Alamo St.
Lake Charles, LA 70601
318/436-7277

WBOK-AM
1639 Gentilly Blvd.
New Orleans, LA 70119
504/943-4600

WQUE-AM
1440 Canal St., #800
New Orleans, LA 70112
504/581-1280

WQUE-FM
1440 Canal St., #800
New Orleans, LA 70112
504/581-1280

WTKL-AM
2777 Rosedale Rd.
Port Allen, LA 70767
504/383-4920

WWOZ-FM
PO Box 51840
New Orleans, LA 70151
504/568-1239

WXOK-AM
7707 Waco Dr.
New Orleans, LA 70806
504/927-7060

WYLD-AM
2228 Gravier Ave.
New Orleans, LA 70119
504/882-1945

WYLD-FM
2228 Gravier Ave.
New Orleans, LA 70119
504/882-1945

MARYLAND

WANN-AM
PO Box 631
Annapolis, MD 21404
301/269-0700

WBGR-AM
3000 Druid Park Dr.
Baltimore, MD 21215
410/367-7773

WESM-FM
University of Maryland Eastern
   Shore
Backbone Rd.
Princess Anne, MD 21853
301/651-2816

WJDY-AM
1633 N. Division St.
Salisbury, MD 21801
301/742-5191

WWIN-AM
200 S. President St., 6th Floor
Baltimore, MD 21202
410/332-8200

WWIN-FM
200 S. President St., 6th Floor
Baltimore, MD 21202
410/332-8200

WXTR-FM
5210 Auth Rd.
Marlow Heights, MD 20746
301/899-3014

MASSACHUSETTS

WILD-AM
90 Warren St.
Boston, MA 02119
617/427-2222

WLVG-AM
670 Cummins Way
Boston, MA 02126-3243
617/576-2895

WUMB-FM
University of Massachusetts
Boston Harbor Campus
Boston, MA 02125
617/929-7919

MICHIGAN

WCHB-AM
32790 Henry Ruff Rd.
Inkster, MI 48141
313/278-1440

WCXT-FM
220 Polk Rd.
Hart, MI 49420
616/873-7129

WDZZ-FM
1830 Genesee Tower
Flint, MI 48503
313/767-0130

WFLT-AM
5317 S. Averill St.
Flint, MI 48506
313/239-5733

WGPR-FM
3146 Jefferson Ave. E
Detroit, MI 48207
313/259-8862

WGVU-FM
301 W. Fulton St.
Grand Rapids, MI 49504-6495
616/771-6666

WJLB-FM
645 Griswold St., #633
Detroit, MI 48226
313/965-2000

WJZZ-FM
2994 E. Grand Blvd.
Detroit, MI 48202
313/871-0591

WKSG-FM
850 Stephenson Highway
Troy, MI 48083
313/792-6600

WKWM-AM
PO Box 828
Kentwood, MI 49508
616/676-1237

WLLJ-AM
PO Box 393
Cassopolis, MI 49031
616/445-2543

WMTG-AM
PO Box 1310
Dearborn, MI 48126
313/846-8500

WNMC-FM
1701 E. Front St.
Traverse City, MI 49684
616/922-1091

WQBH-AM
Penobscott Building, #2056
Detroit, MI 48226
313/965-4500

WTLZ-FM
126 N. Franklin St., #514
Saginaw, MI 48607
517/754-1071

WXLA-AM
101 Northcrest Rd., #4
Lansing, MI 48906
517/484-9600

MISSISSIPPI

WACR-FM
1919 14th Ave. N
Columbus, MS 39713
601/328-1050

WALT-AM
PO Box 5797
Meridian, MS 39302
601/693-2661

WAML-AM
PO Box 367
Laurel, MS 39440
601/425-4285

WBAD-FM
PO Box 4426
Greenville, MS 38704
601/335-9265

WESY-AM
PO Box 5804
Greenville, MS 38704
601/385-9405

WJMG-FM
1204 Grave Line St.
Hattiesburg, MS 39401
601/544-1941

WKKY-FM
PO Box 1919
Mccomb, MS 39648
601/475-4108

WKRA-FM
PO Box 398
Holly Springs, MS 39635
601/252-1110

WKXG-AM
PO Box 1686
Greenwood, MS 38930
601/453-2174

WKXI-AM
PO Box 9446
Jackson, MS 39206
601/957-1300

WLTD-FM
Drawer N
Lexington, MS 39095
601/834-2295

WMIS-AM
20 E. Franklin St.
Natchez, MS 39120
601/442-2522

WMLC-AM
PO Box 949
Monticello, MS 39654
601/587-7997

WNBN-AM
1290 Hawkins Crossing Rd.
Meridian, MS 39301
601/483-7930

WOKJ-AM
1850 Lynch St.
Jackson, MS 39203
601/948-1515

WORV-AM
1204 Grave Line St.
Hattiesburg, MS 39401
601/544-1941

WQFX-AM
PO Box 789
Gulfport, MS 39502
601/863-3626

WQFX-FM
PO Box 789
Gulfport, MS 39502
601/863-3626

WQIS-AM
PO Box 151
Laurel, MS 39441
601/425-1491

WRDC-AM
114 T. M. Jones Hwy
Boyle, MS 38730
601/843-1400

WRJH-FM
PO Box 145
Brandon, MS 39043
601/825-5045

WRKN-AM
PO Box 145
Brandon, MS 39043
601/825-5045

WTYJ-FM
20 E. Franklin St.
Natchez, MS 39120
601/442-2522

MISSOURI

KATZ-AM
1139 Olive St.
St. Louis, MO 63101
314/241-6000

KATZ-FM
1139 Olive St.
St. Louis, MO 63101
314/241-6000

KCXL-AM
2420 E. Linwood Blvd., #10
Kansas City, MO 64110
816/333-2583

KMJM-FM
PO Box 4888
St. Louis, MO 63108
314/361-1108

KPRS-FM
11131 Colorado Ave.
Kansas City, MO 64137
816/763-2040

KPRT-AM
11131 Colorado Ave.
Kansas City, MO 64137
816/763-2040

KSTL-AM
814 N. 3rd St.
St. Louis, MO 63102
314/621-5785

NEBRASKA

KBWH-FM
5829 N. 60th St.
Omaha, NE 68104
402/571-3714

NEVADA

KCEP-FM
330 W. Washington Ave.
Las Vegas, NV 89106
702/648-4218

NEW JERSEY

WIMG-AM
1737 Princeton Ave.
Lawrenceville, NJ 08648
609/695-7701

WNJR-AM
1 Riverfront Plaza, #345
Newark, NJ 07102
201/642-8000

WUSS-AM
PO Box 7539
Atlantic City, NJ 08401
609/345-7134

NEW YORK

WBLK-FM
712 Main St., #112
Buffalo, NY 14202
716/852-5955

WBLS-FM
3 Park Ave.
New York, NY 10016
212/545-1075

WDKX-FM
683 Main St.
Rochester, NY 14605
716/262-2050

WLIB-AM
801 2nd Ave.
New York, NY 10017
212/661-3344

WPNR-FM
c/o Utica College
Burnstone Rd.
Utica, NY 13502
315/792-3069

WRKS-FM
1440 Broadway
New York, NY 10018
212/642-4300

WUFO-AM
89 La Salle Ave.
Buffalo, NY 14214
716/834-1080

WWRL-AM
41-30 58th St.
Woodside, NY 11377
718/335-1600

NORTH CAROLINA

WAAA-AM
4950 Indiana Ave.
PO Box 11197
Winston-Salem, NC 27116
919/767-0430

WARR-AM
PO Box 577
Warrenton, NC 27589
919/257-2121

WBMS-AM
310 Davis St.
Wilmington, NC 28401
919/763-4633

WBXB-FM
PO Box O
Edenton, NC 27932
919/482-2224

WCLY-FM
64 Maywood Ave.
Raleigh, NC 27603
919/821-1550

WCPS-AM
3403 Main St.
Tarboro, NC 27886
919/823-2191

WDJB-FM
PO Box 509
Windsor, NC 27983
919/794-3131

WDKS-FM
PO Box 2008
Fayetteville, NC 28302
919/484-2107

WDUR-AM
PO Box 650
Durham, NC 27702
919/596-2000

WEAL-AM
1060 Coatewood Ave.
Greensboro, NC 27405
919/272-5121

WEGG-AM
PO Box 608
Rose Hill, NC 28458
919/289-2031

WGIV-AM
520 Highway 20 N
Concord, NC 28025
701/342-2644

WGSP-AM
4209 F. Stuart Andrew Blvd.
Charlotte, NC 28217
704/527-9477

WGTM-AM
PO Box 3837
Wilson, NC 27893
919/243-2188

WIDU-AM
Drawer 2247
Fayetteville, NC 28302
919/483-6111

WIZS-AM
PO Box 1299
Henderson, NC 27536
919/492-3001

WKJA-AM
PO Box 591
Bellhaven, NC 27810
919/964-9290

WOKN-AM
522 E. Martin St.
Raleigh, NC 27601
919/833-3874

WOKN-FM
PO Box 2006
Goldsboro, NC 27530
919/734-4213

WOOW-AM
304 Evans St.
Greensville, NC 27834
919/757-0365

WPEG-FM
520 Highway 29 N
Concord, NC 28025
704/333-0131

WRSV-FM
PO Box 2666
Rocky Mount, NC 27802
919/442-9776

WRSV-FM
1001 Parkview Dr.
Elizabeth City, NC 27909
919/335-3517

WSMX-AM
PO Box 16049
Winston-Salem, NC 27115
919/761-1545

WSRC-AM
PO Box 1331
Durham, NC 27702
919/477-7999

WTNC-AM
PO Box 1920
Thomasville, NC 27360
919/472-0790

WVOE-AM
Rt. 3, PO Box 328
Chadbourn, NC 28431
919/654-5621

WWLE-AM
5106 Wrightsville Ave.
Wilmington, NC 28403
919/791-9083

OHIO

WABQ-AM
8000 Euclid Ave.
Cleveland, OH 44103
216/231-8005

WBBY-FM
PO Box 14
Westerville, OH 43081
614/891-1829

WBGU-FM
31 W. Hale
Bowling Green State University
Bowling Green, OH 43403
419/372-8800

WCKX-FM
510 E. Mound St.
Columbus, OH 43215
614/464-0020

WIZF-FM
7030 Reading Rd., #316
Cincinnati, OH 45237
513/351-5900

WJMO-AM
11821 Euclid Ave.
Cleveland, OH 44106
216/795-1212

WJMO-FM
11821 Euclid Ave.
Cleveland, OH 44106
216/795-1212

WJTB-AM
105 Lake Ave.
Elyria, OH 44035
216/327-1833

WMMX-AM
PO Box 1110
Fairborn, OH 45324
513/878-9000

WNOP-AM
1518 Dalton Ave.
Cincinnati, OH 45214
513/241-9667

WNRB-AM
PO Box 625
Niles, OH 44446
216/652-0106

WSLN-FM
40 Slocum Hall
Ohio Wesleyan University
Delaware, OH 43015
614/369-4431

WVKO-AM
4401 Carriage Hill La.
Columbus, OH 43220
614/451-2191

WVOI-AM
6695 Jackman Rd.
Toledo, OH 43613
419/243-7052

WZAK-FM
1729 Superior Ave.
Cleveland, OH 44114
216/621-9300

OKLAHOMA

KPRW-AM
4045 N.W. 64th St.
Oklahoma City, OK 73116
405/848-9870

KTOW-FM
886 W. 21st St.
Sand Springs, OK 74063
918/245-0254

KXOJ-AM
PO Box 1250
Sapulpa, OK 74067
918/224-2620

PENNSYLVANIA

WADV-AM
PO Box 940
Lebanon, PA 17042
717/273-2611

WAMO-AM
411 7th Ave., #1500
Pittsburgh, PA 15219
412/471-2181

WCXJ-AM
7138 Kelly St.
Pittsburgh, PA 15208
412/243-3050

WDAS-AM
Belmont Ave. and Edgely Dr.
Philadelphia, PA 19131
215/878-2000

WDAS-FM
Belmont Ave. and Edgely Dr.
Philadelphia, PA 19131
215/878-2000

WJSM-FM
PO Box 87
Martinsburg, PA 16662
814/793-2188

WLIU-FM
c/o Office of Student Activities
Lincoln University
Lincoln, PA 19352
215/932-8300

WPLW-AM
201 Ewing Ave.
Pittsburgh, PA 15205
412/922-0550

WUSL-FM
440 Domino Lane
Philadelphia, PA 18128
215/483-8900

SOUTH CAROLINA

WASC-AM
PO Box 5686
Spartanburg, SC 29304
803/585-1530

WBSC-AM
Drawer 629
Bennettsville, SC 29512
803/479-7121

WCIG-FM
PO Box 1005
Mullins, SC 29574
803/464-9252

WGSW-AM
2410 Kateway Rd.
Greenwood, SC 29646
803/223-5945

WHYZ-AM
PO Box 4309
Greenville, SC 29608
803/246-1441

WKQB-AM
PO Box 10164
Charleston, SC 29411
803/744-1779

WNCJ-AM
314 Rembert Dennis Blvd.
Moncks Corner, SC 29461
803/761-6010

WOIC-AM
PO Box 565
Columbia, SC 29202
803/796-9975

WPAL-AM
1717 Wappo Rd.
Charleston, SC 29417
803/763-6330

WQIZ-AM
PO Box 10164
Charleston, SC 29411
803/744-1779

WQKI-AM
PO Box 777
St. Matthews, SC 29135
803/874-2777

WSSB-FM
PO Box 1915
Orangeburg, SC 29117
803/536-8196

WSSC-AM
PO Box 1468
Sumter, SC 2951
803/778-2355

WTGH-AM
1303 State St.
Cayce, SC 29033
803/796-9533

WVBX-AM
Drawer W
Georgetown, SC 29442
803/546-5141

WVGB-AM
806 Monston St.
Beaufort, SC 29902
803/524-4700

WWKT-FM
PO Box 525
Kingstree, SC 29556
803/382-2361

WWWZ-FM
PO Box 30669
Charleston, SC 29417
803/556-9132

WYNN-AM
PO Box F-14
Florence, SC 29501
803/662-6364

WYNN-FM
PO Box F-14
Florence, SC 29501
803/662-6364

TENNESSEE

KRNB-FM
PO Box 11839
Memphis, TN 38111
901/323-0101

WABD-AM
PO Box 2249
Clarkville, TN 37042
615/431-4984

WBMK-FM
2108 Prosser Rd.
Knoxville, TN 37914

WDIA-AM
112 Union Ave.
Memphis, TN 38103
901/529-4300

WEMG-AM
2108 Prosser Rd.
Knoxville, TN 37914

WHRK-FM
112 Union Ave.
Memphis, TN 38103
901/529-4300

WLOK-AM
PO Box 69
Memphis, TN 38101
901/527-9565

WMDB-AM
3051 Stokers La.
Nashville, TN 37218
615/255-2876

WNAH-AM
44 Music Square E
Nashville, TN 37203
615/254-7611

WNOO-AM
108 Hendricks St.
Chattanooga, TN 37406
615/894-1023

WQQK-FM
PO Box 8085
Nashville, TN 37207
615/227-1470

WTBG-FM
PO Box 198
Brownsville, TN 38012
901/772-3700

WVOL-AM
PO Box 8085
Nashville, TN 37207
615/227-1470

TEXAS

KADO-AM
303 W. Broad St.
Texarkana, TX 75501
214/793-4671

KALO-FM
7700 Gulfway St.
Port Arthur, TX 77642
409/963-1276

KAZI-FM
4700 Loyola La., #104
Austin, TX 78723
512/926-0275

KBWC-FM
711 Wiley Ave.
Marshall, TX 75670
214/938-8341

KCOH-AM
5011 Almeda St.
Houston, TX 77004
713/522-1000

KFKY-FM
2727 Inwood Rd.
Dallas, TX 77535
214/352-3975

KGBC-AM
PO Box 11138
Galveston, TX 77553
409/744-4567

KHVN-AM
PO Box 7116
Fort Worth, TX 76111
817/640-7900

KSAQ-FM
217 Alamo Plaza, #200
San Antonio, TX 78205
512/271-9600

KSII-AM
217 Alamo Plaza, #200
San Antonio, TX 78205
512/271-9600

KYOK-AM
3001 LaBranch St.
Houston, TX 77004
713/526-7131

KZEY-AM
PO Box 75712
Tyler, TX 75712
214/593-1744

UTAH

KDAB-FM
385 24th St.
Ogden, UT 84401
801/393-8611

VIRGINIA

WANT-AM
PO Box 6747
Richmond, VA 23230
804/353-9113

WARR-AM
553 Michigan Dr.
Hampton, VA 23669-3899
919/257-2121

WCDX-FM
2809 Emerywood Pwy., #300
Richmond, VA 23294
804/672-9300

WCLM-AM
4719 Nine Mile Rd.
Richmond, VA 23223
804/236-0532

WFTH-AM
5021 Brooks Rd., #100
Richmond, VA 23227
804/262-8624

WGCV-AM
10600 Jefferson Davis Highway
Richmond, VA 23237
804/275-1234

WHOV-FM
Hampton University
Hampton, VA 23668
804/727-5407

WILA-AM
PO Box 3444
Danville, VA 24543
804/792-2133

WKBY-AM
PO Box 105A
Chatham, VA 24531
804/432-8108

WMYK-FM
645 Church St., #400
Norfolk, VA 23510
804/622-4600

WOWI-FM
645 Church St., #201
Norfolk, VA 23510
804/627-5800

WPAK-AM
800 Old Plank Rd.
Farmville, VA 23901
804/392-8114

WPLZ-FM
PO Box 1510
Petersburg, VA 23805
804/672-9300

WTOY-AM
2614 Cove Rd. NW
Roanoke, VA 24017
703/362-9558

WZAM-AM
168 Business Park Rd.
Virginia Beach, VA 23462
804/473-1194

WASHINGTON

KKFX-AM
2815 2nd Ave., #500
Seattle, WA 98121
206/728-1250

KLUJ-AM
PO Box 513
Walla Walla, WA 99362
509/529-8000

KRIZ-AM
PO Box 22462
Seattle, WA 98122
206/251-5151

WISCONSIN

WAWA-AM
12800 W. Bluemond Rd.
Elm Grove, WI 53122
414/785-1021

WGLB-AM
900 E. Green Bay Rd.
Saukille, WI 53080
414/284-2666

WLUM-FM
2500 N. Mayfair Rd., #390
Milwaukee, WI 53226-1409
414/771-1021

WMVP-AM
4222 W. Capitol Dr., #1290
Milwaukee, WI 53216
414/444-1290

WNOV-AM
3815 N. Teutonia Ave.
Milwaukee, WI 53206
414/449-9668

WSUN-FM
PO Box 219
Kewaunee, WI 54216
414/388-4852

WYMS-FM
5225 W. Violet St.
Milwaukee, WI 53208
414/475-8389

MAGAZINES

About . . . Time
283 Genesee St.
Rochester, NY 14611
716/235-7150

Accents Magazine
c/o Mod Expo
404 17th St.
Brooklyn, NY 11215
718/768-9855

Ace Magazine
1360 Fulton St.
Brooklyn, NY 11216
718/789-0900

Africa News
PO Box 3851
Durham, NC 27702
919/286-0747

Africa Report
833 United Nations Plaza
New York, NY 10017
212/949-5728

Africa Today
c/o Graduate School of
   International Studies
University of Denver
Denver, CO 80208
303/753-3678

African American Heritage
c/o Dellco Publishing Co.
8443 S. Crenshaw Blvd., #103
Inglewood, CA 90305
213/752-3706

African American Literary Review
5381 La Paseo, #105
Forth Worth, TX 76112
817/429-6150

African Progress Magazine
c/o Africa Adventurer Club
30 E. 42nd St.
New York, NY 10017

African Voices
305 7th Ave., 11th Floor
New York, NY 10001-6008
212/206-7475

Afro-Hispanic Review
c/o Romance Languages
  Department
#120 Arts and Sciences
University of Missouri
Columbia, MO 65211
314/822-4874

**AIM: America's Intercultural
  Magazine**
PO Box 20554
Chicago, IL 60619
312/874-6184

American Visions
2101 S St. NW
Washington, DC 20008
202/357-1946

Beauty Trade
15 Columbus Circle
New York, NY 10022
212/757-7589

Being Single
PO Box 49402
Chicago, IL 60649
312/955-1100

Black American Literature Forum
Parsons Hall 237
Indiana State University
Terre Haute, IN 47809
812/237-2968

Black Angels
PO Box 14785
Oakland, CA 94614
510/530-7928

Black Beat
233 Park Ave.
New York, NY 10003
212/780-3500

Black Books Bulletin
7525 S. Cottage Grove
Chicago, IL 60619
312/651-0700

Black Books Round-Up
c/o The Black Scholar: Journal of
  Black Studies
PO Box 2869
Oakland, CA 94609
510/547-6633

Black Careers
c/o Project Magazine Inc.
PO Box 8214
Philadelphia, PA 19101-8214
215/387-1600

Black Church Magazine
PO Box 2216
Baltimore, MD 21203
410/338-1523

Black Collegian
1240 S. Broad St.
New Orleans, LA 70125
504/821-5694

Black Confessions
233 Park Ave.
New York, NY 10003
212/780-3500

Black Elegance
475 Park Ave. South
New York, NY 10016
212/689-2830

Black Enterprise
130 5th Ave.
New York, NY 10011
212/242-8000

Black Excellence
400 12th St. NE
Washington, DC 20002
202/543-5090 or 202/543-9112

Black Family
c/o Kent Enterprises Inc.
11800 Sunrise Valley Dr., #320
Reston, VA 22091
703/860-1343

Black Film Review
2025 Eye St. NW, #213
Washington, DC 20006
202/466-2753

Black Gold National
6750 S. Oglesby St.
Chicago, IL 60649
312/363-3061

Black Hair Care
c/o Harris Publications
1115 Broadway, 8th Fl.
New York, NY 10010
212/807-7100

Black Hair Digest
63 Grand Ave., #230
River Edge, NJ 07661
201/487-6124

Black Health
c/o Altier & Maynard
   Communications Inc.
6 Farmingville Rd.
Ridgefield, CT 06877
203/431-3454

Black Issues in Higher Education
10520 Warwick Ave., #B8
Fairfax, VA 20230
703/385-2981

Black Lace
PO Box 83912
Los Angeles, CA 90051
213/410-0808

Black Lifestyles
1185 S. Victoria Ave.
Los Angeles, CA 90019
213/939-3785

Black News Digest
c/o U.S. Department of Labor
Office of Information & Public
   Affairs
200 Constitution Ave. NW
Washington, DC 20210
202/606-7828

Black Orange
PO Box 59
Lake Forest, CA 92630
714/830-1390

Black Radio Exclusive
6922 Hollywood Blvd., #110
Hollywood, CA 90028-6363
213/469-7262

Black Romance
233 Park Ave.
New York, NY 10003
212/780-3500

Black Scholar
PO Box 2869
Oakland, CA 94609
510/547-6633

Black Secrets
233 Park Ave.
New York, NY 10003
212/780-3500

Black Tennis Magazine
PO Box 210767
Dallas, TX 75211
214/670-7618

Black Tress Magazine
c/o Harris Publications
1115 Broadway, 8th Fl.
New York, NY 10010
212/807-4700

Black Writer
PO Box 1030
Chicago, IL 60690
312/924-3818

BLK
6709 La Tijera Blvd.
Los Angeles, CA 90045
310/410-0808

Bronze Thrills
233 Park Ave.
New York, NY 10003
212/780-3500

Callaloo
c/o Johns Hopkins University
   Press
701 W. 40th St., #275
Baltimore, MD 21211
301/338-6983

Career Focus
Communications Publishing
   Group Inc.
3100 Broadway, #225
Kansas City, MO 64111
816/756-3039

Caribbean Review
9700 S.W. 67th Ave.
Miami, FL 33156
305/284-8466

The CeCe Guide
PO Box 91494
Washington, DC 20012
301/422-CECE

Chocolate Singles
PO Box 333
Jamaica, NY 11413
718/978-4800

Christ-Centered Singles
GPO Box 7720
New York, NY 10116
212/730-6422

Christian Index
Christian Methodist Episcopal
   Church
PO Box 665
Memphis, TN 38101
901/345-1173

Class Magazine
c/o R-E John Sandy
   Communications
900 Broadway, 8th Floor
New York, NY 10003
212/677-3055

Clubdate Magazine
13726 Kinsman Rd.
Cleveland, OH 44120
216/752-8410

Confrontation/Change Review
Economic Research Center Inc.
1107 Lexington Ave.
Dayton, OH 45407
513/275-6879

Corporate Headquarters
c/o HQ Publications
516 North Ave. E
Westfield, NJ 07090
201/233-8837

Creole
PO Box 91496
Lafayette, LA 70509
318/269-1956

Crisis
260 5th Ave., 6th Floor
New York, NY 10001
212/481-4100

Dawn
2002 11th St. NW
Washington, DC 20001
202/332-0080

Dollars and Sense
1610 E. 79th St.
Chicago, IL 60649
312/375-6800

Ebony
820 S. Michigan Ave.
Chicago, IL 60605
312/322-9200

EM: Ebony Man
820 S. Michigan Ave.
Chicago, IL 60605
312/322-9200

Ember
7305 Woodbine Ave., #528
Markham, Ontario, L3R 3V7
Canada
416/773-2889

Emerge
1700 N. Moore St., Ste. 2200
Arlington, VA 22209
703/875-0430

Essence
1500 Broadway, 6th Floor
New York, NY 10036
212/642-0600

Esteem
5733 Windridge Dr.
Cincinnati, OH 45243
513/244-9768

**Everybody's: The Caribbean-
    American Magazine**
1630 Nostrand Ave.
Brooklyn, NY 11226
718/941-1879

Feelin' Good
1142 Manhattan Ave., #112
Manhattan Beach, CA 90266-5398
213/649-3200

Final Call
734 W. 79th St.
Chicago, IL 60620
312/602-1230

Freedomways Quarterly
799 Broadway
New York, NY 10003
212/477-3895

Fresh
c/o Ashley Communications
PO Box 91878
Los Angeles, CA 90009
818/885-6800

Harmony Magazine
PO Box 81
Pratt Station
Brooklyn, NY 11205
718/875-7448

Health Quest
200 Highpoint Dr., #215
Chalfont, PA 18914
800/416-3232

Heart and Soul
c/o Rodale Press Inc.
33 E. Minor St.
Emmaus, PA 18908
215/967-5171

Hip Hop Fashions
475 Park Ave. South
New York, NY 10016
212/689-2830

Horn of Africa
PO Box 803
Summit, NJ 07901
201/273-1515

Hype Hair
63 Grand Ave., #230
River Edge, NJ 07661
201/487-6124

Image
11012 Ventura Blvd.
PO Box 350
Studio City, NY 91604
818/506-6418

In a Word
c/o Society of the Divine Word
199 Seminary Dr.
Bay St. Louis, MS 39520

International Review of African Art
4005 Crenshaw Blvd., 3rd Floor
Los Angeles, CA 90008-7071
213/294-7071

Intimacy/Black Romance
233 Park Ave.
New York, NY 10003
212/780-3500

Jazz Times
7961 Eastern Ave., #303
Silver Spring, MD 20910
301/588-4114

Jet
820 S. Michigan Ave.
Chicago, IL 60605
312/322-9200

Jive
233 Park Ave.
New York, NY 10003
212/780-3500

Journal of African Civilizations
347 Feldon Ave.
Highland Park, NJ 08904
201/828-4667

Journal of Black Studies
Sage Publications, Inc.
2111 W. Hill Crest Dr.
Newbury Park, CA 91320
805/499-0721

Journal of Negro History
PO Box 20
Morehouse College
Atlanta, GA 30314
404/215-2620

Lincoln Review
1001 Connecticut Ave. NW, #1135
Washington, DC 20036
202/223-5112

Link Magazine
PO Box 32722
Detroit, MI 48232

Living Blues
Center for the Study of Southern
    Culture
University of Mississippi
University, MS 38677
601/232-5993

Mahogany
1520 Roster Rd., #1000
Fort Worth, TX 76134-3604
817/551-5551

The Message
c/o Review and Herald
    Publishing Association
55 Oak Ridge Dr.
Hagerstown, MD 21740
301/791-7000

Minority Business Review
250 Fulton Ave., #507
Hempstead, NY 11550

Minority Employment Journal
5777 W. Century Blvd., #1245
Los Angeles, CA 90045
310/338-8444

National Black Monitor
231 W. 29th St., #1205
New York, NY 10001
212/967-4000

National Scene
22 E. 41st St.
New York, NY 10017
212/862-3700

Negro Educational Review
West Bay Annex, Box 2895
Jacksonville, Florida 32203
904/646-2590

Negro History Bulletin
1407 14th St. NW
Washington, DC 20005
202/667-2822

New People
PO Box 47490
Oak Park, MI 48237
315/541-6943

New Research Travel and Conventioneer
11717 S. Vincennes Ave.
Chicago, IL 60604
312/881-3712

New Visions
16360 Broadway
Maple Heights, OH 44137
216/581-7070

New Word Magazine
PO Box 627
Grand Central Station
New York, NY 10017
718/636-1404

The New York Christian Times
1061 Atlantic Ave.
Brooklyn, NY 11238
718/638-NEWS

NSBE Journal
National Society of Black
   Engineers
1240 S. Broad St.
New Orleans, LA 70125
504/822-3533

Our Texas
PO Box 4463
Dallas, TX 75208
214/946-5315

Persuasive Hair
PO Box 361319
Decatur, GA 30036-1319
404/987-8165

Pittsburgh Renaissance
1516 5th Ave.
Pittsburgh, PA 15219
412/369-0980

Players
8060 Melrose Ave.
Los Angeles, CA 90046
213/653-8060

Pre K-Today Magazine
730 Broadway
New York, NY 10003

Professional Magazine
Career Communications Group
729 E. Pratt St., #504
Baltimore, MD 21202
410/224-7101

Quarterly Black Review of Books
341 Madison Ave., 18th Floor
New York, NY 10017
212/883-1010

Rap Masters
63 Grand Ave., #230
River Edge, NJ 07661
201/536-0755

Rap Pages
9171 Wilshire Blvd., #300
Beverly Hills, CA 90210
213/858-7100

Rap Sheet
PO Box B-H
Los Angeles, CA 90064
310/399-7550

Reggae Report
PO Box 330-315
Coconut Grove, FL 33133

Research in African Literature
c/o University of Texas Press
PO Box 7819
Austin, TX 78712
512/471-8716

Review of Black Political Economy
Bldg. 4051
New Brunswick, NJ 08903
201/932-2280

Right On!
233 Park Ave. South
New York, NY 10003
212/949-6850

Roots
c/o Bongo Productions
PO Box 65856
Los Angeles, CA 90065
818/659-3061

Routes
521 W. 23rd St.
New York, NY 10011-1105
212/627-5241

Rumble, Inc.
PO Box 22151
Sacramento, CA 95822
916/427-8705

Score Magazine
PO Box 292494
Nashville, TN 37229
615/360-9444

SENGA
7501 Morrison Rd.
New Orleans, LA 70126
504/242-6022

Shade
636 Broadway
New York, NY 10012
212/533-0051

Shooting Star Review
7123 Race St.
Pittsburgh, PA 15208-1428
412/731-7039

Shoptalk Publications
8825 S. Greenwood St.
Chicago, IL 60619
312/978-6400

Sister 2 Sister Magazine
PO Box 41148
Washington, DC 20018
202/635-3879

Sisters
National Council of Negro
    Women Inc.
1211 Connecticut Ave. NW
Washington, DC 20036
202/659-0006

**Sophisticates Black Hair and
    Styles Guide**
1165 N. Clark St., #607
Chicago, IL 60615
312/266-8680

The Source
594 Broadway, #510
New York, NY 10012
212/274-0464

Spice Magazine
Starlog Communications
475 Park Ave. South
New York, NY 10016
212/689-2830

Superfly Magazine
250 W. 57th St.
New York, NY 10019
212/977-4647

Today's Black Hair Trends
PO Box 18867
Washington, DC 20036-8867
301/369-7455

Trend
13 Cuttersmill Rd., #176
Great Neck, NY 11201
718/225-0347

Two Hype
63 Grand Ave.
River Edge, NJ 07661
201/487-6124

Unique Hair and Beauty
9171 Wilshire Blvd., #300
Beverly Hills, CA 90210
310/858-7155

Upscale Magazine
PO Box 10798
Atlanta, GA 30310
404/758-7467

U.S. Black Engineers
729 E. Pratt St., #504
Baltimore, MD 21201
410/222-7101

Vibe
205 Lexington Ave.
New York, NY 10016
212/522-7092

Voice of Missions
475 Riverside Dr., #1926
New York, NY 10115
212/870-2258

Washington View Magazine
1101 14th St. NW, #1050
Washington, DC 20005
202/371-1313

Western Journal for Black Studies
Washington State University
Pullman, WA 99163
509/335-8681

Word Up
63 Grand Ave., #230
River Edge, NJ 07661
201/487-6124

Yes Magazine
144 North Ave.
Plainfield, NJ 07060
908/754-3400

Yo
PO Box 88427
Los Angeles, CA 90009
818/885-6800

Young Sisters and Brothers (YSB)
1700 N. Monroe St., #2200
Rosslyn, VA 22209
703/875-0430

NEWSPAPERS

ALABAMA

Birmingham Times
PO Box 10501
Birmingham, AL 35204
205/251-5158

Birmingham World
312 N. 17th St.
Birmingham, AL 35203
205/251-6253

Green County Democrat
PO Box 598
Euraw, AL 35462
205/372-3373

Inner City News
PO Box 1545
Mobile, AL 36633-1545
205/452-9329

Mobile Beacon
PO Box 1407
Mobile, AL 36617
205/479-0629

Montgomery-Tuskegee Times
PO Box 9133
Montgomery, AL 36108
205/264-7149

News Times
156 S. Broad St.
Mobile, AL 36602
205/432-0356

Shoals News Leader
PO Box 427
Florence, AL 35631
205/766-5542

Speakin' Out News
PO Box 2826
Huntsville, AL 35804
205/551-1020

Tuskegee News
PO Box 60
Tuskegee, AL 36083
205/727-3020

ARIZONA

Arizona Informant
1746 E. Madison St., #2
Phoenix, AZ 85034
602/257-9300

ARKANSAS

Arkansas State Press
PO Box 164037
Little Rock, AR 72216
501/371-9991

Arkansas Weekly Sentinel
PO Box 4520
Little Rock, AR 72214
602/257-9300

Statewide Mediator
500 E. Markham St., #300
Little Rock, AR 72201
602/243-1857

CALIFORNIA

Bakersfield News Observer
1219 20th St.
Bakersfield, CA 93301
805/324-9466

Bayou Talk
PO Box 1344
West Corunay, CA 91793
714/247-1316

Berkeley Tri City Post
PO Box 1350
Oakland, CA 94612
510/763-1120

California Advocate
452 Fresno St.
Fresno, CA 93706
209/268-0941

California Voice
1366 Turk St.
San Francisco, CA 94115
415/931-5778

Carson Bulletin
PO Box 4248
Compton, CA 90224
213/774-0018

Central News Wave
2621 W. 54th St.
Los Angeles, CA 90043
213/290-3000

Firestone Park News
PO Box 19027A
Los Angeles, CA 90019
213/291-9486

Herald Dispatch
PO Box 19027A
Los Angeles, CA 90019
213/291-9486

Inglewood Tribune
PO Box 4248
Compton, CA 90244
213/774-0018

Los Angeles Metropolitan Gazette
PO Box 93275
Pasadena, CA 91109
818/360-4175

Los Angeles Scoop
6309 Crenshaw Blvd.
Los Angeles, CA 90043
213/753-5931

Los Angeles Sentinel
3800 Crenshaw Blvd.
Los Angeles, CA 90008
213/299-3800

Lynwood Journal
PO Box 4248
Compton, CA 90224
213/774-0018

Mesa Tribune Wave
2621 W. 54th St.
Los Angeles, CA 90043
213/290-3000

Metro Reporter Group
1366 Turk St.
San Francisco, CA 94115
415/931-5778

Monterey Sentinel
PO Box 1309
Seaside, CA 93955
408/899-2305

Oakland Tri-City Post
PO Box 1350
Oakland, CA 94612
510/763-1120

Precinct Reporter
1677 W. Baseline St.
San Bernardino, CA 92411
714/889-0597

Richmond Post
PO Box 1350
Oakland, CA 94612
510/763-1120

Riverside Black Voice
3585 Main St., #201
Riverside, CA 92501
909/682-6070

Sacramento Observer
3540 4th Ave.
Sacramento, CA 95817
916/452-4781

San Bernardino American News
1583 W. Baseline St.
San Bernardino, CA 92411-0010
714/889-7677

San Diego Voice & Viewpoint
1729 N. Euclid Ave.
San Diego, CA 92105
619/266-2233

San Fernando Gazette Express
14621 Titus St., #228
Van Nuys, CA 91402
818/782-8695

San Francisco New Bayview Newspaper
4401 3rd St.
San Francisco, CA 94124
415/695-0713

San Francisco Post
PO Box 1350
Oakland, CA 94612
510/763-1120

Seaside Post News-Sentinel
PO Box 670
Seaside, CA 93955
408/394-6632

Southeast News
PO Box 19027A
Los Angeles, CA 90019
213/291-9486

Southwest Topics
2621 W. 54th St.
Los Angeles, CA 90043
213/290-3000

Sun-Reporter
1366 Turk St.
San Francisco, CA 94115
415/931-5778

Watts Star Review
PO Box 19027A
Los Angeles, CA 90019
213/291-9486

Wilmington Beacon
PO Box 4248
Compton, CA 90224
213/774-0018

COLORADO

Denver Weekly News
PO Box 569
Denver, CO 80201
303/839-5800

CONNECTICUT

Hartford Inquirer
PO Box 1260
Hartford, CT 06143
203/522-1462

DISTRICT OF COLUMBIA

Metro Chronicle
1143 National Press Bldg.
Washington, DC 20045
202/347-1114

Washington Afro-American Tribune
2519 N. Charles St.
Baltimore, MD 21218
410/554-8200

Washington Capital Spotlight
2112 New Hampshire NW
Washington, DC 20009
202/745-7858

Washington Informer
3117 Martin Luther King Jr. Ave. SE
Washington, DC 20032
202/561-4100

Washington News Observer
811 Florida Ave. NW
Washington, DC 20032
202/232-3060

FLORIDA

Black Miami Weekly
6025 N.W. 6th Ct.
Miami, FL 33127
305/754-8800

Broward Times
1001 W. Cyprus Creek Rd., #111
Fort Lauderdale, FL 33309
305/351-9070

Bulletin
PO Box 2650
Sarasota, FL 34230
813/953-3990

Capital Outlook
PO Box 1335
Tallahassee, FL 32301
904/681-1852

Daytona Beach Times
427 S. Martin Luther King Jr.
  Blvd.
Daytona Beach, FL 32114
904/253-0321

Florida Sentinel-Bulletin
PO Box 363
Tampa, FL 33601
813/248-1921

Florida Sun Review
PO Box 2348
Orlando, FL 32802
407/423-1156

Fort Pierce Chronicle
1527 Ave. D
Fort Pierce, FL 33450
407/416-7093

Jackson Advocate
6172 Pettiford Dr.
Jacksonville, FL 32209
904/764-4740

Miami Times
900 N.W. 54th St.
Miami, FL 33127
305/757-1147

Orlando Times
4403 Vineland Rd., #B-5
Orlando, FL 32811
407/841-3052

Palm Beach Gazette
PO Box 18469
West Palm Beach, FL 33416
407/844-5501

Pensacola Voice
213 E. Yonge St.
Pensacola, FL 32503
904/434-6963

Star News
PO Box 40629
Jacksonville, FL 32203
904/766-8834

Weekly Challenger
2500 9th St., #C
St. Petersburg, FL 33705
813/896-2922

Westwide Gazette
PO Box 5304
Ft. Lauderdale, FL 33310
305/523-5115

GEORGIA

Albany-Macon Times
813 Forsyth St.
Albany, GA 31202
912/432-7070

Atlanta Daily World
145 Auburn Ave. NE
Atlanta, GA 30335
404/659-1110

Atlanta Inquirer
PO Box 92367
Atlanta, GA 30314
404/523-6086

Atlanta Tribune
875 Old Roswell Rd., #C-100
Roswell, GA 30076
404/587-0501

Atlanta Voice
PO Box 2123
Atlanta, GA 30312
404/524-6426

Augusta Focus
PO Box 1282
Augusta, GA 30903
706/724-7855

Columbus Times
PO Box 2845
Columbus, GA 31993
404/304-2404

Cordele Southeastern News
PO Drawer 489
Cordele, GA 31015-8022
912/273-6714

Fort Valley Herald
PO Box 899
Fort Valley, GA 31030
912/825-7000

Herald
PO Box 486
Savannah, GA 31402
912/232-04505

Macon Courier
1055 Walnut St.
Macon, GA 31201
912/746-5605

Metro County Courier
PO Box 2385
Augusta, GA 30903
706/724-6556

Savannah Tribune
PO Box 2066
Savannah, GA 31402
912/233-6128

ILLINOIS

Chatham Citizen
412 E. 87th St.
Chicago, IL 60619
312/487-7700

Chicago Citizen
412 E. 87th St.
Chicago, IL 60619
312/489-7700

Chicago Crusader
6429 S. Martin Luther
King Jr. Dr.
Chicago, IL 60637
312/752-2500

Chicago Daily Defender
2400 S. Michigan Ave.
Chicago, IL 60616
312/225-2400

Chicago Independent Bulletin
2037 W. 95th St.
Chicago, IL 60616
312/225-2400

Chicago New Metro News
501 E. 32nd St., #501
Chicago, IL 60616
312/791-0880

Chicago Shoreland News
11740 S. Elizabeth
Chicago, IL 60643
312/568-7091

Chicago South Shore Scene
PO Box 49007
Chicago, IL 60649
312/363-0441

Chicago South Standard News
615 S. Halsted St.
Chicago Heights, IL 60411
312/755-5021

Chicago Weekend
412 E. 87th St.
Chicago, IL 60619
312/487-7700

Chicago Westside Journal
16618 S. Hermitage
Markham, IL 60426
708/333-2210

Decatur Voice
625 E. Wood St.
Decatur, IL 62523-1152
217/423-2231

Muslim Journal
910 W. Van Buren
Chicago, IL 60607
312/243-7600

Nightmoves
105 W. Madison St., #1100
Chicago, IL 60602
312/346-7765

Observer
6040 S. Harper St.
Chicago, IL 60637
312/288-5840

South End Citizen
412 E. 87th St.
Chicago, IL 60619
312/487-7700

South Suburban Citizen
412 E. 87th St.
Chicago, IL 60619
312/487-7700

South Suburban Standard
615 S. Halsted St.
Chicago Heights, IL 60411
312/755-5021

Tri-City Journal
8 S. Michigan Ave., #1111
Chicago, IL 60603
312/346-8123

INDIANA

American
2268 Broadway
Gary, IN 46407
219/883-4903

Frost Illustrated
3121 S. Calhoun St.
Fort Wayne, IN 46807-1901
219/745-0552

Gary Info
PO Box M-587
Gary, IN 46401-0587
219/882-5591

Gary New Crusader
1549 Broadway
Gary, IN 46407
219/885-4359

Indiana Herald
2170 N. Illinois St.
Indianapolis, IN 46202
317/923-8291

Indianapolis Recorder
PO Box 18267
Indianapolis, IN 46218
317/924-5143

Muncie Times
1304 N. Broadway
Muncie, IN 47303
317/741-0037

IOWA

New Iowa Bystander
PO Box 65640
West Des Moines, IA 50265
515/278-8736

KANSAS

Republican
PO Box 389
Paola, KS 66071
913/294-2311

Western Spirit
PO Box 389
Paola, KS 66071
913/294-2311

KENTUCKY

Louisville American Baptist
1715 Chestnut St.
Louisville, KY 40203
502/587-8714

Louisville Defender
PO Box 2557
Louisville, KY 40210
502/772-2591

Suspension Press
PO Box 2064
Covington, KY 41012
606/431-6786

LOUISIANA

Alexandria News Weekly
PO Box 608
Alexandria, LA 71301
318/443-7664

Baton Rouge Community Leader
1010 North Blvd.
Baton Rouge, LA 70802
504/343-0544

Baton Rouge Weekly Press
1384 Swan St.
Baton Rouge, LA 70807
504/775-2002

Louisiana Weekly
1001 Howard Ave., #2600
New Orleans, LA 70113
504/524-5563

Monroe Dispatch
PO Box 4823
Monroe, LA 71211
318/387-3001

New Orleans Black Data
PO Box 51933
New Orleans, LA 70151
504/522-1418

Shreveport Sun
PO Box 38357
Shreveport, LA 71133
318/631-6222

MARYLAND

Afro-American
628 N. Eutaw St.
Baltimore, MD 21201
301/728-8200

MASSACHUSETTS

Bay State Banner
925 Washington St.
Dorchester, MA 02124
617/288-4900

Boston Greater News
PO Box 497
Roxbury, MA 02119-0004
617/445-7063

MICHIGAN

Blazer News
PO Box 806
Jackson, MI 49204
517/787-0450

Ecorse Telegram
4122 10th St.
Ecorse, MI 48229
313/928-2955

Grand Rapid Times
2061 Eastern Ave. SW
Grand Rapids, MI 49501
616/245-8737

Michigan Chronicle
479 Ledyard St.
Detroit, MI 48201
313/963-5522

Michigan Citizen
12541 2nd St.
Highland Park, MI 48203
313/869-0033

Michigan Sentinel
27350 Southfield Rd., #127
Lathrup Village, MI 48076
313/559-1010

MINNESOTA

Minneapolis Spokesman
3744 4th Ave. S
Minneapolis, MN 55409
612/827-4021

St. Paul Recorder
590 Endicott Ave.
St. Paul, MN 55407
612/827-4021

Twin Cities Courier
84 S. 6th St., #501
Minneapolis, MN 55402
612/332-3211

MISSISSIPPI

Jackson Advocate
PO Box 3708
Jackson, MS 39207
601/948-4122

Mississippi Enterprise
PO Box 3313
Jackson, MS 39207
601/371-3878

Mississippi Memo Digest
PO Box 5782
Meridian, MS 39301
601/693-2372

MISSOURI

Call
PO Box 410477
Kansas City, MO 64141
816/842-3804

East St. Louis Monitor
1501 State St.
East St. Louis, MO 62205
618/271-0468

Evening Whirl
PO Box 5088
Nagel Station
St. Louis, MO 63115

Kansas City Globe
PO Box 090410
Kansas City, MO 64109
816/531-5253

St. Louis American
4144 Lindell Blvd.
St. Louis, MO 63108
314/533-8000

St. Louis Argus
4595 Martin Luther King Jr. Dr.
St. Louis, MO 63113
314/531-1323

St. Louis Crusader
4371 Finney Ave.
St. Louis, MO 63113
314/531-5860

St. Louis Metro Sentinel
2900 N. Market St.
St. Louis, MO 63106
314/531-2101

NEBRASKA

Omaha Star
2216 N. 24th St.
Omaha, NE 68110
402/346-4041

NEVADA

Las Vegas Sentinel-Voice
1201 S. Eastern Ave.
Las Vegas, NV 89104
702/383-4030

NEW JERSEY

Afro-American
429 Central Ave.
Newark, NJ 07108
201/672-9102

New Jersey Greater News
1188 Raymond Blvd., #178
Newark, NJ 07102
201/643-3364

NEW YORK

Afro-American Times
1360 Fulton St.
Brooklyn, NY 11216
718/636-9500

Amsterdam News
2340 Frederick Douglass Blvd.
New York, NY 10027
212/932-7400

Black American
310 Lenox Ave., #304
New York, NY 10027
212/564-5110

Brooklyn New York Recorder
86 Bainbridge St.
Brooklyn, NY 11233
718/493-4616

Buffalo Challenger
1303 Fillmore Ave.
Buffalo, NY 14211
716/897-0442

Buffalo Criterion
623–625 William St.
Buffalo, NY 14206
716/882-9570

Buffalo Fine Print News
806 Fillmore Ave.
Buffalo, NY 14212
716/855-3810

Caribbean Life
1733 Sheepshead Bay Blvd.
Brooklyn, NY 11235
718/769-4400

City Sun
GPO 560
Brooklyn, NY 11202
718/624-5959

Communicade
67 Elba St.
Rochester, NY 14615
716/235-6695

Hudson Valley Black Press
PO Box 2160
Newburgh, NY 12550
914/562-1313

Impartial
PO Box 98
Syracuse, NY 13205
315/635-6318

Militant
410 West St.
New York, NY 10014
212/243-6392

New York Beacon
15 E. 40th St., #402
New York, NY 10016
212/213-8585

New York Carib News
15 W. 39th St.
New York, NY 10018
212/944-1991

New York Daily Challenge
1360 Fulton St.
Brooklyn, NY 11216
718/636-9500

New York Source
594 Broadway, #510
New York, NY 10012
212/274-0464

New York Voice
75-43 Parsons Blvd.
Flushing, NY 11366
718/591-6600

Westchester County Press
PO Box 152
White Plains, NY 10602
914/684-0006

NORTH CAROLINA

Carolina Peacemaker
PO Box 20853
Greensboro, NC 27420
919/274-6210

Carolina Times
PO Box 3825
Durham, NC 27702
919/682-2913

Carolinian
PO Box 25308
Raleigh, NC 27601
919/834-5558

Charlotte Post
1531 Camden Rd.
Charlotte, NC 28203
704/376-0496

Charlotte Star of Zion
401 E. 2nd St.
Charlotte, NC 28231
704/377-4329

Fayetteville Black Times
PO Box 863
Fayetteville, NC 28302
919/484-4840

Iredell County News
PO Box 407
Statesville, NC 28677
919/873-1054

Metro Times Reporter
PO Box 1935
Goldsboro, NC 27533
919/734-0302

Public Post
122 Elwood Ave.
Raeford, NC 28376
919/875-8938

Wilmington Journal
PO Box 1618
Wilmington, NC 28402
919/762-5502

Winston-Salem Chronicle
617 N. Liberty St.
Winston-Salem, NC 27102
919/722-8624

OHIO

Akron Reporter
PO Box 2042
Akron, OH 4309
216/773-4196

Buckeye Review
626 Belmont Ave.
Youngstown, OH 44502
216/743-2250

Call & Post
PO Box 6237
Cleveland, OH 44106
216/791-7600

Cincinnati Herald
836 Lincoln Ave.
Cincinnati, OH 45206
513/221-5440

Toledo Journal
PO Box 2536
Toledo, OH 43616
419/472-4521

OKLAHOMA

Black Chronicle
PO Box 17498
Oklahoma City, OK 73136
405/424-4695

Oklahoma Eagle
PO Box 3267
Tulsa, OK 74101
918/582-7124

OREGON

Portland Observer
PO Box 3137
Portland, OR 97208
503/288-0033

The Skanner
PO Box 5455
Portland, OR 97228-5455
503/278-3562

PENNSYLVANIA

New Pittsburgh Courier
315 E. Carson St.
Pittsburgh, PA 15219
412/481-8302

Nite Scene
2951 N. 22nd St.
Philadelphia, PA 19132
215/229-8253

Philadelphia New Observer
1930 Chestnut St., #900
Philadelphia, PA 19103
215/665-8400

Philadelphia Tribune
522 S. 16th St.
Philadelphia, PA 19146
215/893-4050

SOUTH CAROLINA

Charleston Black Times
1310 Harden St.
Columbia, SC 29204
803/799-5252

Charleston Chronicle
PO Box 2548
Charleston, SC 29403
803/723-2785

Coastal Times
2106 Mount Pleasant St., #1
Charleston, SC 29403
803/723-5318

Columbia Black News
PO Box 11128
Columbia, SC 29211-1128
803/799-5252

Florence Black Sun
1310 Harden St.
Columbia, SC 29204
803/799-5252

Greenville Black Star
1310 Harden St.
Columbia, SC 29204
803/799-5252

Orangeburg Black Star Voice
1310 Harden St.
Columbia, SC 29204
803/799-5252

Rock Hills Black View
1310 Harden St.
Columbia, SC 29204
803/799-5252

Sumter Black Post
PO Box 11128
Columbia, SC 29211
803/799-5252

View South News
PO Box 1849
Orangeburg, SC 29116
803/531-1662

TENNESSEE

Christian Recorder
PO Drawer 24730
Nashville, TN 37202-4730
615/256-8548

Memphis Silver Star News
3144 Park Ave.
Memphis, TN 38111
901/452-8828

Memphis Tri-State Defender
124 E. Calhoun Ave.
Memphis, TN 38101
901/523-1818

TEXAS

Dallas Examiner
424 Centre St.
Dallas, TX 75208
214/948-9175

Dallas Post Tribune
2726 S. Beckley St.
Dallas, TX 75224
214/946-7678

Dallas Weekly
3101 Martin Luther King Jr. Blvd.
Dallas, TX 75215
214/428-8958

Houston Defender
PO Box 8005
Houston, TX 77288
713/663-7716

Houston Forward Times
PO Box 8346
Houston, TX 77004
713/526-4727

Houston Informer
PO Box 3086
Houston, TX 77253
713/527-8261

Houston Sun
1520 Isabella St.
Houston, TX 77004
713/524-4474

San Antonio Register
PO Box 1598
San Antonio, TX 78296
210/222-1721

Southwest Digest
902 E. 28th St.
Lubbock, TX 79404
806/762-3612

Texas Times
PO Box 1228
Fort Worth, TX 76101
817/926-4666

Villager
1223-A Rosewood Ct.
Austin, TX 78702
512/476-0082

Waco Messenger
PO Box 2087
Waco, TX 76703
817/799-6911

VIRGINIA

New Journal and Guide
362 Campostella Rd.
Norfolk, VA 23523
804/543-6531

Richmond Afro-American & Planet
214 E. Clay St.
Richmond, VA 23219
804/649-8478

Tribune
PO Box 6021
Roanoke, VA 24017
703/343-0326

WASHINGTON

Facts
PO Box 22015
Seattle, WA 98122
206/324-0552

Northwest Dispatch
PO Box 5637
Tacoma, WA 98405
206/272-7587

Seattle Medium
2600 S. Jackson Ave.
Seattle, WA 98144
206/323-3070

Tacoma True Citizen
2600 S. Jackson St.
Tacoma, WA 98144
206/627-1103

WEST VIRGINIA

West Virginia Beacon Digest
PO Box 981
Charleston, WV 25324
304-342-4600

WISCONSIN

Beloit Chronicle
PO Box 133
Beloit, WI 53511
608/364-0166

Milwaukee Community Journal
3612 N. Martin Luther King Dr.
Milwaukee, WI 53212
414/265-5300

Milwaukee Courier
2431 W. Hopkins St.
Milwaukee, WI 53206
414/449-4860

Milwaukee Star
2431 W. Hopkins St.
Milwaukee, WI 53206
414/449-4867

Milwaukee Times
2216 N. Martin Luther King Dr.
Milwaukee, WI 53212
414/263-5088

MEDIA ORGANIZATIONS

Black Awareness in Television
13217 Livernois Ave.
Detroit, MI 48238
313/931-3427

Black Religious Broadcasters
2416 Orcutt Ave.
Newport News, VA 23607
804/380-6118

Capital Press Club
PO Box 19403
Washington, DC 20036
301/933-3863

Minorities in Cable and New Technologies
1900 E. 78th St.
Chicago, IL 60617
312/721-7500

National Alliance of Third World Journalists
PO Box 43208
Washington, DC 20010
202/462-8197

National Association of Black Journalists
PO Box 4222
Reston, VA 22091
703/648-1270

National Association of Black Owned Broadcasters Inc.
1730 M St., #412
Washington, DC 20036
202/463-8970

National Association of Media Women Inc.
123-16 126th Ave.
Laurelton, NY 11413
718/712-4544

National Association of Minority Media Executives
1401 Concord Point La.
Reston, VA 22901-1307
703/709-5245

National Black Media Coalition
38 New York Ave. NE
Washington, DC 20002
202/387-8155

National Black Programming Consortium Inc.
929 Harrison Ave., #104
Columbus, OH 43215
614/299-5355

National Conference of Editorial Writers
6223 Executive Blvd.
Rockville, MD 20852
301/984-3015

National Newspaper Publishers Association
3200 23rd St. NW
Washington, DC 20045
202/588-8764

National TV Art Association
2100 N.E. 52nd St.
Oklahoma City, OK 73711
405/427-5461

Young Black Programmer's Coalition
PO Box 11243
Jackson, MS 39213
601/634-5775

ARTS AND ENTERTAINMENT

MUSIC

THE PERFORMERS

Aaliyah
c/o Jive Records
137–139 W. 25 St.
New York, NY 10001
R&B singer

Abrams, Colonel
c/o Mic Mac Records
166 5th Ave.
New York, NY 10010
R&B singer

Abbott, Gregory
PO Box 68
Bergenfield, NJ 07621-0068
R&B singer

Above the Law
c/o Ruthless/Relativity Records
2052 Manhattan Pl.
Torrance, CA 90501
Rap group

Adams, Oleta
c/o Fontana Records
825 8th Ave.
New York, NY 10019
R&B singer

Adams, Yolanda
PO Box 1125
Shreveport, LA 71163
Gospel singer

A.D.O.R.
c/o Untouchables Entertainment
1560 Broadway, #407
New York, NY 10036
R&B singing group

Adoration-N-Prayze
PO Box 501584
Indianapolis, IN 46250
Gospel choir

The Afros
c/o Rush Communications
298 Elizabeth St.
New York, NY 10012
Rap group

After 7
c/o Virgin Records
9247 Alden Dr.
Beverly Hills, CA 90210
R&B singing group

Akinyele
10900 Wilshire Blvd., #91230
Los Angeles, CA 90024
Rap group

Albright, Gerald
10100 Santa Monica Blvd., #1600
Los Angeles, CA 90024
Musician

The Alkaholiks
c/o RCA Records
1133 Avenue of the Americas
New York, NY 10309
Rap group

All 4 One
c/o Atlantic Records
75 Rockefeller Plaza
New York, NY 10019
R&B singing group

Almighty RSOP
c/o The Flava Unit
155 Morgan St.
Jersey City, NJ 07302
Rap artist

Alston, Gerald
c/o Scotti Brothers
2114 Pico Blvd.
Santa Monica, CA 90405
R&B singer

Anderson, Ernestine
c/o Warner Brothers Records
3300 Warner Blvd.
Burbank, CA 91510
Jazz singer

Angelic Voices of Faith
c/o CGI/Light Records
1416 N. LaBrea Ave.
Hollywood, CA 90028
Gospel group

Angie and Debbie
PO Box 28450
Santa Ana, CA 90028
R&B singing group

Annointed
c/o Word Records
3319 W. End
Nashville, TN 37203
Gospel group

Another Bad Creation
c/o Motown Records
6255 Sunset Blvd., #1700
Los Angeles, CA 90028
Hip-hop group

Antoinette
c/o Next Plateau Records
1650 Broadway
New York, NY 10019
Rapper

Apache
c/o The Flava Unit
155 Morgan St.
Jersey City, NJ 07302
Rapper

Apache Indian
c/o Island Records
400 Lafayette St.
New York, NY 10003
Rapper

Apollonia
9000 Sunset Blvd., #1200
Los Angeles, CA 90069
Singer, actor

Armstrong, Vanessa Bell
c/o Jive Records
137-139 W. 25th St.
New York, NY 10001
Gospel singer

Arnold, David
c/o Grant House
309 Wood St.
Burlington, NJ 08016
Opera singer

Arrested Development
c/o Chrysalis Records
1290 Avenue of the Americas
New York, NY 10104
Rap group

Arroyo, Marina
c/o Thea Dispeker
59 E. 54th St.
New York, NY 10022
Opera singer

Ashford and Simpson
254 W. 72nd St., #1A
New York, NY 10023
Singers, producers

Assault and Battery
c/o Attitude Records
2071 Elmerson St., #16
Jacksonville, FL 32207
Rap group

Austin, Dallas
c/o Rowdy Records
75 Marietta Ave., 3rd Floor
Atlanta, GA 30303
*Producer, record company
   executive*

Austin, Dennis
3319 W. End
Nashville, TN 37203
Gospel singer

Austin, Patti
10100 Santa Monica Blvd., #1600
Los Angeles, CA 90067
Pop singer

Avant, Clarence
c/o Motown Records
6255 Sunset Blvd.
Los Angeles, CA 90028
Record company executive

B Angie B
c/o Bust It! Management
39510 Paseo Padre Pkwy., #250
Fremont, CA 94538
R&B singer

B.B.O.T.I.
c/o A & M Records
1416 N. La Brea Ave.
Los Angeles, CA 90028
Rap group

B.O.U.
c/o Atch Records and Productions
Fondren St., #380
Houston, TX 77096-4502
Rap group

B Tribe
75 Rockefeller Plaza
New York, NY 10019
Rap group

Baby Wayne
c/o Big Beat Records
19 W. 21st St.
New York, NY 10010
Reggae singer

Babyface
c/o La'Face Records
PO Box 921
Atlanta, GA 30092
*Singer, producer, record company
   executive*

Bad Brains
c/o Columbia Records
550 Madison Ave.
New York, NY 10022
Rock group

Bailey, Phillip
28405 Sand Canyon Rd., #A
Canyon Country, CA 91351
Pop singer

Baker, Anita
c/o BNB
9545 Wilshire Blvd.
Beverly Hills, CA 90212
R&B singer

Bala Men
c/o Atlantic Records
75 Rockefeller Plaza
New York, NY 10019
Reggae singers

Banks, Ant
c/o Jive Records
137-139 W. 25th St.
New York, NY 10001
Reggae singer

Banks, Jeff
c/o Savoy Records
1123 Broadway, #507
New York, NY 10010
Gospel singer

Bar-Kays
c/o Philadelphia International
309 S. Broad St.
Philadelphia, PA 19107
Soul singing group

Barnes, F. C.
881 Memorial Dr.
Atlanta, GA 30316
Gospel singer

Battle, Kathleen
c/o Herbert Breslin Agency
119 W. 57th St.
New York, NY 10019
Opera singer

Baxter, Blake
c/o RCA Records
1133 Avenue of the Americas
New York, NY 10036
Musician

Baylor, Helen
3319 W. End
Nashville, TN 37203
Gospel singer

Beatnuts
c/o Relativity Records
187-07 Henderson Ave.
Hollis, NY 11423
Rap group

Belafonte, Harry
c/o Triad Artists
10100 Santa Monica Blvd.
Los Angeles, CA 90067
Singer, actor, director

Bell Biv Devoe
c/o Hiram Hicks
413 S. Broad St.
Philadelphia, PA 19147
Hip-hop group

Belle, Regina
c/o Worldwide
641 Lexington Ave.
New York, NY 10022
R&B singer

Benson, George
519 Next Day Hill Dr.
Englewood, NJ 07631
R&B singer, musician

Berry, Chuck
c/o Berry Park
Buckner Rd.
Wentzville, MO 63385
Singer

Big Bub
c/o Motown Records
6255 Sunset Blvd., #1700
Los Angeles, CA 90028
R&B singer

Big Scoob and the Booty Bandits
c/o Cold Chillin' Records
1995 Broadway, 18th Floor
New York, NY 10023
Rap group

Bigga Sistas
c/o The Flava Unit
155 Morgan St.
Jersey City, NJ 07302
Rap group

Bitches With Problems
c/o Rush Communications
298 Elizabeth St.
New York, NY 10012
Rap group

Bivins, Michael
c/o Motown Records
6255 Sunset Blvd., 17th Floor
Los Angeles, CA 90028
*Artist, producer, manager, record
   company executive*

Biz Markie
c/o Cold Chillin' Records
1995 Broadway, 18th Floor
New York, NY 10023
Rapper

Bizarre Inc.
c/o Columbia Records
550 Madison Ave.
New York, NY 10022
Rap group

Blackgirl
c/o RCA Records
1133 Avenue of the Americas
New York, NY 10036
R&B singing group

Black Moon
209 Wieland Ave.
Staten Island, NY 10309
Rap group

Black Sheep
c/o Mercury Records
825 8th Ave.
New York, NY 10019
Rap group

Black Street
c/o L.O.R. Entertainment
349 S. Port Circle, #110
Virginia Beach, VA 23452
R&B singing group

Blakeley, Art
c/o Bridge
106 Fort Green Pl.
Brooklyn, NY 11217
Jazz musician

Blakk Media
c/o Atch Records
Fondren, #380
Houston, TX 77096-4502
Rapper

Blu, Peggi
PO Box 279
Hopkins, MN 55343
Singer

Bodyguard
c/o Jive Records
137-139 W. 25th St.
New York, NY 10001
Rap group

Bofill, Angela
c/o Jive Records
137-139 W. 25th St.
New York, NY 10001
R&B singer

Booker, Chuckii
9229 Sunset Blvd.
Los Angeles, CA 90069
Singer, producer, musician

Born Jamericans
c/o Delicious Vinyl
6607 Sunset Blvd.
Los Angeles, CA 90028
Reggae group

Boss
c/o Rush Communications
298 Elizabeth St.
New York, NY 10012
Rap artist

Boston, Tony
c/o Deco/Warlock Records
19 W. 21st St.
New York, NY 10010
R&B singer

The Boys
c/o Motown Records
6255 Sunset Blvd., #1700
Los Angeles, CA 90028
Singing group, producers

Boys Choir of Harlem
127 W. 127th St.
New York, NY 10027
Youth choir

Boys II Men
c/o Motown Records
6255 Sunset Blvd., #1700
Los Angeles, CA 90028
R&B group

Brand Nubian
c/o Atlantic Records
75 Rockefeller Plaza
New York, NY 10019
Rap group

Braxton, Toni
c/o La'Face Records
3350 Peachtree St., #1500
Atlanta, GA 30326
R&B singer

The Braxtons
c/o La'Face Records
3350 Peachtree St., #1500
Atlanta, GA 30326
R&B singing group

Brinkley, Derrick
3310 W. End Ave.
Nashville, TN 37203
Gospel singer

Brooklyn Assault Team
c/o The Flava Unit
155 Morgan St.
Jersey City, NJ 07032
Rap group

Brown, Bobby
18653 Ventura Blvd., #707
Tarzana, CA 91356
*Singer, producer, record company
   executive*

Brown, James
1217 W. Medical Park Dr.
Augusta, GA 30909
"Godfather of Soul," singer

**Bruce Parham and the Outreach
   Choir of Philadelphia**
21 Bala Cynwyd
Bala Cynwyd, PA 19004
Choir

Bryson, Peabo
c/o Columbia Records
550 Madison Ave.
New York, NY 10022
R&B singer

Buju Banton
c/o Mercury Records
825 8th Ave.
New York, NY 10019
Reggae singer

Bumbry, Grace
c/o Columbia Artists Management
165 W. 57th St.
New York, NY 10019
Opera singer

Busboys
8833 Sunset Blvd., PH West
Los Angeles, CA 90069
Go-go group

Butler, Jerry
c/o ECI
200 Inwood Dr.
Wheeling, IL 60090
Soul singer

By All Means
c/o Island Records
400 Lafayette St.
New York, NY 10012
Rap group

Byrd, Chris
c/o Tyscot Records
3532 N. Keystone
Indianapolis, IN 46218
Gospel singer

Byron, Don
c/o Columbia Records
550 Madison Ave.
New York, NY 10022
Classical and jazz musician

Caesar, Shirley
PO Box 3336
Durham, NC 27702
"Queen of Gospel," singer,
*   minister, politician*

Campbell, Lucretia
c/o PepperCo Records
324 Elm St., #204A
Monroe, CT 06468
Gospel singer

Campbell, Luther
c/o Luke Records
8400 N.E. 2nd Ave.
Liberty City, FL 33138
Rapper, producer, and entrepreneur

Campbell, Tevin
c/o Qwest Records
3300 Warner Blvd.
Burbank, CA 91510
R&B singer

Capitol Tax
c/o MCA Records
70 Universal Plaza
Universal City, CA 91608
Rap group

Cara, Irene
8033 Sunset Blvd., #735
Los Angeles, CA 90046-2427
Pop singer, actor

Carey, Mariah
c/o Columbia Records
550 Madison Ave.
New York, NY 10022
Singer

Carrington, Terri
c/o Bill Darlington
9034 Sunset, #205
Los Angeles, CA 90069
Musician

Carroll, Dina
1416 N. La Brea Ave.
Los Angeles, CA 90028
Singer

Carter, Betty
Be-Car Productions
117 St. Felix St.
Brooklyn, NY 11217
Jazz singer

Casual
c/o Jive Records
137-139 W. 25th St.
New York, NY 10001
Rapper

C.E.B.
c/o Ruffhouse/Columbia
550 Madison Ave.
New York, NY 10022
Rap group

Chaka Demus and the Pliers
c/o Island Records
400 Lafayette St.
New York, NY 10003
Reggae group

Chapman, Tracy
c/o Lookout
506 Santa Monica Blvd.
Santa Monica, CA 90401
Singer

Charles, Ray
4863 Southridge Ave.
Los Angeles, CA 90008
Singer

Charles, Suzette
c/o RCA Records
1133 Avenue of the Americas
New York, NY 10036
Singer, former Miss America

Cherry, Nenah
PO Box 1622
London, NW10 5TF
England
Hip-hop artist

Chic
250 W. 57th St., #330
New York, NY 10107
Singing group

Chicago Mass Choir Featuring Minister Dennis Cole
9959 S. Winston St.
Chicago, IL 60643
Gospel choir

Chill Rob G
c/o Wild Pitch Records
231 W. 29th St.
New York, NY 10001
Rapper

Chilly Tee
c/o MCA Records
70 Universal Plaza
Universal City, CA 91608
Rapper

Christensen, Maria
75 Rockefeller Plaza
New York, NY 10019
Singer

Chubby Checker
1650 Broadway, #1011
New York, NY 10019
Singer

Chunk
4400 Horner St., #63
Union City, CA 94587
Rapper

The Click
c/o Perspective Records
4330 Nicollet Ave.
Minneapolis, MN 55409
Singing group

Cliff, Jimmy
c/o Victor Chambers
41 Lady Musgrave Rd.
Kingston, Jamaica
Reggae artist

Clinton, George
3300 Warner Blvd.
Burbank, CA 91510
Funk singer

Coal, Steve
4815 Trousdale Dr., #418
Nashville, TN 37220
Gospel rapper

Cole, Natalie
19218 Wells Dr.
Tarzana, CA 91356

Fan Club:
PO Box 67991
Los Angeles, CA 90067
Singer

Coleman, George
63 E. 9th St.
New York, NY 10003
Saxophonist

Coley, Daryl
c/o Sparrow Communications
101 Winner Circle
Nashville, TN 37027
Gospel singer

Collins, Bootsy
414 E. Walnut St., #3920
Cincinnati, OH 25402
Singer

Coming of Age
c/o Zoo Entertainment
309 S. Broad St.
Philadelphia, PA 19107
R&B singing group

Common Sense
c/o Relativity Records
187-07 Henderson Ave.
Hollis, NY 11423
Rapper

Cool G Rap and Polo
c/o Cold Chillin' Records
1995 Broadway, 18th Floor
New York, NY 10023
Rap group

The Coup
c/o Wild Pitch Records
231 W. 29th St.
New York, NY 10001

Crawford, Randy
c/o Ken Fritz
648 N. Robertson Blvd.
Los Angeles, CA 90069
R&B singer

Crouch, Andre
5221 North O'Connor Blvd.,
  #1000
Irving, TX 75039
Gospel singer, songwriter, producer

Crouch, Sandra
c/o Eric McDaniel
PO Box 6963
FDR Station
New York, NY 10022
Gospel singer

Cultural Revolution
c/o New Deal Records
550 Madison Ave.
New York, NY 10022
Rap group

Cut Throat
c/o Jive Records
137-139 W. 25th St.
New York, NY 10001
Rap group

Cutty Ranks
740 Broadway
New York, NY 10003
Reggae artist

Cypress Hill
c/o Ruffhouse/Columbia
550 Madison Ave.
New York, NY 10022
Rap group

Da'Brat
c/o So So Def
2849 Piedmont Rd.
Atlanta, GA 30301
Rapper

Da Youngstas
c/o East West Records
75 Rockefeller Plaza
New York, NY 10019
Rap group

Dale, Clamma
PO Box 898
Ansonia Station
New York, NY 10023
Opera singer

Dan Willis and the Pentacostals
   of Chicago
c/o Tyscot Records
3532 N. Keystone
Indianapolis, IN 46218
Gospel choir

D'Arby, Terence Trent
PO Box 910L
London, NWI 9AQ
England
Singer

Das EFX
c/o Atlantic Records
75 Rockefeller Plaza
New York, NY 10019
Rap group

Davis, Billy, Jr.
c/o Sterling Winters Company
1900 Avenue of the Stars, #739
Los Angeles, CA 90067
Singer

Davis, Delissa
PO Box 252
Hollywood, CA 90078
Pop singer

Dawkins and Dawkins
c/o Benson Music Group
365 Great Circle Rd.
Nashville, TN 37228
Gospel duo

Dawson, Melvin
c/o Tyscot Records
3532 N. Keystone
Indianapolis, IN 46218
Gospel singer

Day, Morris
3580 Wilshire Blvd., #184
Los Angeles, CA 90010
Singer, actor

DC Talk
7106 Moores La., #200
Brentwood, TN 37027
Gospel rap group

De La Soul
c/o Tommy Boy Records
902 Broadway
New York, NY 10010
Rap group

Debarge, El
c/o Warner Bros.
3300 Warner Blvd.
Burbank, CA 91510
R&B singer

D.E.F.
c/o MCA Records
70 Universal Plaza
Universal City, CA 91608
Rap group

Del the Funky Homosapien
9229 Sunset Blvd.
Los Angeles, CA 90069
Rap artist

Derek B
c/o Profile Records
740 Broadway
New York, NY 10003
Rap artist

Detroit's Most Wanted
c/o Ichiban Records
PO Box 724677
Miami, Florida 31139-1677
Rap group

Diamond D
c/o Rush Communications
298 Elizabeth St.
New York, NY 10012
Rap artist

D-Influence
c/o East West Records
75 Rockefeller Plaza
New York, NY 10019
Rap group

Dis-N-Dat
c/o Epic Records
550 Madison Ave.
New York, NY 10022
Rap group

Digable Planet
London Terrace Station
PO Box 20116
New York, NY 10011
Rap group

Digital Underground
c/o Profile Records
740 Broadway
New York, NY 10003
Rap group

D.O.A.
c/o Profile Records
704 Broadway
New York, NY 10003
Rap group

The D.O.C.
c/o Relativity Records
2052 Manhattan Pl.
Torrance, CA 90501
R&B singing group

Dominion and Power
c/o PepperCo Records
324 Elm St., #204A
Monroe, CT 06468
Gospel singing group

Domino
c/o Rush Communications
298 Elizabeth St.
New York, NY 10012
Rap artist

Domino, Fats
5515 Marais St.
New Orleans, LA 70117
Singer

Dottie Peoples and the Lumzy Sisters
881 Memorial Dr.
Atlanta, GA 30316
Gospel singing group

Dougie E. Fresh
c/o Gee Street Records
14 E. 4th St.
New York, NY 10012
Rap artist

Downing, Will
c/o Mercury Records
825 8th Ave.
New York, NY 10019
Singer

Dr. Dre
10900 Wilshire, #91230
Los Angeles, CA 90024
Rapper, producer

The Drifters
c/o Alexas Productions
3365 W. Millerbergway St.
West Jordan, UT 84084
Soul group

DRS
c/o Capitol Records
550 Madison Ave.
New York, NY 10022
R&B singing group

Duice
c/o Bellmark Records
7060 Hollywood Blvd.
Hollywood, CA 90028
Rap group

Duke, George
6430 Sunset Blvd., #1500
Hollywood, CA 90028
Musician, producer

Earth, Wind and Fire
c/o Warner/Reprise Records
3300 Warner Blvd.
Burbank, CA 91510
Soul band

**East St. Louis Community
Performance Ensemble**
1200 N. 13th St.
East St. Louis, MO 62205
Choir

Eazy-E
c/o Ruthless/Relativity Records
2052 Manhattan Pl.
Torrance, CA 90501
Rapper, producer

Ellington, Lance
c/o Big Beat Records
19 W. 21st St.
New York, NY 10010
Musician

Emage
c/o Mercury Records
825 8th Ave.
New York, NY 10019
R&B singing group

En Vogue
PO Box 252
Hollywood, CA 90078
R&B singing group

England, Colin
c/o Motown Records
6255 Sunset Blvd., #1700
Los Angeles, CA 90028
Singer

Estes, Simon
165 W. 57th St.
New York, NY 10019
Opera singer

Eternal
75 Rockefeller Plaza
New York, NY 10019
Singing group

E.U.
c/o EMI/Manhattan Records
1370 Avenue of the Americas
New York, NY 10019
Go-go band

Fairfield Four
24 Music Square E
Nashville, TN 37203
Gospel singing group

Falana, Lola
10100 Santa Monica Blvd., #1600
Los Angeles, CA 90067
Singer, dancer, actor

Fat Joe
c/o Violator/Relativity Records
187-07 Henderson Ave.
Hollis, NY 11423
Rap artist

Father
c/o Steve Lucas Management
152 W. 57 St., 9th Fl.
New York, NY 10019
Rap artist

Ferrell, Jerome
c/o PepperCo Records
324 Elm St., #204A
Monroe, CT 06468
Gospel singer

A Few Good Men
c/o La'Face Records
3350 Peachtree, #1500
Atlanta, GA 30326
R&B singing group

5th Dimension
c/o Marc Gorgan
1022 N. Palm Ave.
Los Angeles, CA 90009
Singing group

Fischer, Lisa
c/o Sherry Ring Ginsberg
75 Rockefeller Plaza, 17th Floor
New York, NY 10019
Singer

Fitzgerald, Ella
c/o Norman Granz
451 N. Canon Dr.
Beverly Hills, CA 90210
Jazz vocalist

Five XI
c/o RCA Records
1133 Avenue of the Americas
New York, NY 10036
R&B singing group

Flack, Roberta
c/o Atlantic Records
75 Rockefeller Plaza
New York, NY 10019
Singer, songwriter

Flex
c/o MCA Records
70 Universal Plaza
Universal City, CA 91608
Reggae artist

Florida Mass Choir
PO Box 9287
Jackson, MS 39206
Gospel choir

Flunder, Yvette
c/o PepperCo Records
324 Elm St., #204A
Monroe, CT 06468
Gospel singer

Ford, Penny
c/o Columbia Records
550 Madison Ave.
New York, NY 10022
R&B singer

Four Play
c/o Warner Bros.
3300 Warner Blvd.
Burbank, CA 91510
Jazz quartet

Four Tops
6255 W. Sunset Blvd.
Los Angeles, CA 90028
R&B singing group

Frank Ski
c/o Big Beat
19 W. 21st St.
New York, NY 10010
Rapper

Franklin, Aretha
PO Box 12137
Birmingham, MI 48012
"Queen of Soul," singer

Franklin, Kirk
c/o Gospocentric Records
417 E. Regent St.
Inglewood, CA 90301
Gospel singer

Freddie Foxxx
c/o The Flava Unit
155 Morgan St.
Jersey City, NJ 07302
Rapper

Fu Schnickens
c/o Jive Records
137-139 W. 25th St.
New York, NY 10001
Rap group

Fugees
c/o Sony Music Group
550 Madison Ave.
New York, NY 10022
Rap group

Full Force
c/o Columbia Records
550 Madison Ave.
New York, NY 10022
R&B singing group, producers

Gable, Eric
c/o Epic Records
550 Madison Ave.
New York, NY 10022
R&B singer

Gaines, Rosie
c/o NPG Records
9401 Kiowa Trail
Chanhassen, MN 55317
R&B singer

Gales, Eric
c/o Atlantic Records
75 Rockefeller Plaza
New York, NY 10019
Musician

Gangstarr
c/o Empire Artist Management
154 Stanton St.
New York, NY 10002
Rap group

Garrett, Siedah
c/o William Morris Agency
151 El Camino Dr.
Beverly Hills, CA 90212
Pop singer

Garnett Silk
c/o Big Beat
19 W. 21st St.
New York, NY 10010
Reggae artist

Gideon
c/o Tyscot Records
3532 N. Keystone
Indianapolis, IN 46218
Gospel singing group

Gill, Johnny
c/o Clarence Avant
9229 Sunset Blvd., #813
Los Angeles, CA 90069
R&B singer

Gospel Music Workshop of America Los Angeles Chapter Choir
c/o PepperCo Records
324 Elm St., #204A
Monroe, CT 06468
Gospel choir

Gospel Music Workshop of America Men's Chorus
c/o PepperCo Records
324 Elm St., #204A
Monroe, CT 06468
Gospel choir

Grand Daddy I.U.
c/o Cold Chillin' Records
1995 Broadway, 18th Floor
New York, NY 10023
Rap artist

Grand Hank
1821 S. 58th St.
Philadelphia, PA 19143
Rap artist

Grant, Eddy
c/o RCA Records
1133 Avenue of the Americas
New York, NY 10036
Reggae artist

Green, Al
3319 W. End
Nashville, TN 37203
Gospel singer, minister

Grier, Rosey
11656 Montana St., #301
Los Angeles, CA 90049
Gospel singer, former football player

Grist, Reri
c/o Metropolitan Opera Association
Lincoln Center Plaza
New York, NY 10023
Opera singer

Guess
c/o Warner Bros
3300 Warner Blvd.
Burbank, CA 91510
R&B singing group

Guru
1290 Avenue of the Americas
New York, NY 10104
Rapper

H-Town Record
c/o Luke Records
8400 N.E. 2nd Ave.
Liberty City, FL 33138
R&B singing group

Hall, Aaron
c/o MCA Records
70 Universal Plaza
Universal City, CA 91608
Singer

Hall, Damian
c/o Silas Records
70 Universal Plaza
Universal City, CA 91608
Singer

Hammer
c/o Bust It! Management
39510 Paseo Padre Parkway, #250
Fremont, CA 94539
Rapper, producer, record company executive

Hampton, Lionel
1995 Broadway
New York, NY 10023
Musician

Hancock, Herbie
202 Riverside Dr.
New York, NY 10025
Musician

Handy, John
618 Baker St.
San Francisco, CA 94117
Saxophonist

Harvey, Dee
c/o Motown Records
6255 Sunset Blvd.
Los Angeles, CA 90028
Singer

Hawkins, Edwin
PO Box 656
Pomona, NY 10970
Gospel singer

Hawkins, Tramaine
101 Winners Circle
Nashville, TN 37027
Gospel singer

Hayes, Isaac
1962 Spectrum Circle, #700
Marietta, GA 30067
Singer

Heavy D
c/o Uptown Entertainment
729 7th Ave.
New York, NY 10019
Rapper

Hendricks, Barbara
c/o Columbia Artist Management
165 W. 57th St.
New York, NY 10019
Opera singer

Here and Now
c/o Third Stone/Atlantic Records
75 Rockefeller Plaza
New York, NY 10019
R&B singing group

Heron, Gil Scott
c/o TVT Records
23 E. 4th St.
New York, NY 10003
Singer

Hi-C
c/o Skanless
PO Box 3429
Alhambra, CA 91803
Rap group

Hi-Five
c/o Jive Records
137-139 W. 25th St.
New York, NY 10001
R&B singing group

Hoes With Attitude (H.W.A.)
c/o Ruthless/Relativity Records
2052 Manhattan Pl.
Torrance, CA 90501
Rap group

Hoodratz
c/o Epic Records
550 Madison Ave.
New York, NY 10022
Rapper

Hopkins, Linda
2055 N. Ivan St., #PH
Los Angeles, CA 90069
Gospel singer

Horne, Lena
1090 Vermont Ave. NW
Washington, DC 20005
Singer, actor

Houston, Thelma
4296 Mt. Vernon St.
Los Angeles, CA 90008
Singer

Houston, Whitney
c/o Triad Artists
10100 Santa Monica Blvd.
Los Angeles, CA 90067
Singer, actor

Howard, George
c/o GRP Records
550 Madison Ave.
New York, NY 10022
Musician

Howard, Miki
c/o Giant Records
1290 Avenue of the Americas
New York, NY 10104
R&B singer

Hubbard, Freddie
119 W. 57th St.
New York, NY 10019
Musician

Hyman, Phyllis
c/o Zoo Entertainment
309 S. Broad St.
Philadelphia, PA 19107
Singer

Ice Cube
c/o Gangsta Merchandise Co.
5959 Triumph SE
Los Angeles, CA 90040
Rap artist, actor

Ice T
6430 W. Sunset Blvd.
Los Angeles, CA 90028
Rapper

Indiana State Mass Choir
3532 N. Keystone
Indianapolis, IN 46218
Gospel choir

Ingram, James
867 Murfield Rd.
Los Angeles, CA 90005
R&B singer

Inner Circle
c/o Big Beat Records
19 W. 21st St.
New York, NY 10010
Reggae group

Intelligent Hoodlum
c/o A & M Records
1416 N. La Brea Ave.
Los Angeles, CA 90028
Rapper

Intro
c/o Untouchables Entertainment
1560 Broadway
New York, NY 10036
Singing group

Isley Brothers
446 Liberty Rd.
Inglewood, NJ 07631
R&B singing group

Jackson, Freddie
1750 N. Vine St.
Hollywood, CA 90028
R&B singer

Jackson, Isiah
c/o United Artists
3906 Sunbeam Dr.
Los Angeles, CA 90065
Orchestra conductor

Jackson, Jackie
4641 Havenhurst
Encino, CA 91316
R&B singer

Jackson, Janet
12546 The Vista
Los Angeles, CA 90049
Singer

Jackson, Jermaine
4641 Havenhurst
Encino, CA 91316
R&B singer

Jackson, Latoya
8560 Sunset Blvd.
Los Angeles, CA 90069
R&B singer

Jackson, Marlon
4100 Admiral Highway
Marina Del Rey, CA 90292
R&B singer

Jackson, Michael
Neverland Ranch
Los Olivos, CA 93441
Singer

Jackson, Paul
c/o Atlantic Records
75 Rockefeller Plaza
New York, NY 10019
Musician

Jackson, Randy
4641 Havenhurst
Encino, CA 91316
Singer

Jackson, Rebbie
4641 Havenhurst
Encino, CA 91316
R&B singer

Jackson, Tito
15255 Del Gado Dr.
Sherman Oaks, CA 91403
R&B singer

Jade
c/o Giant Records
1290 Avenue of the Americas
New York, NY 10104
R&B singing group

Jamal, Ahmad
PO Box 395
Ashley Falls, MA 01222
Jazz musician

James, Etta
642 W. Athens Blvd.
Los Angeles, CA 90061
Jazz singer

James, Freeman
c/o Artist Representation and
   Management
792 29th Ave. SE
Minneapolis, MN 55414
R&B singer

James, Rick
8116 Mulholland Terr.
Los Angeles, CA 90046
Singer

Jarreau, Al
c/o Patrick Rains
9034 Sunset Blvd., #250
Los Angeles, CA 90069
Jazz singer

Jazzy Jeff and the Fresh Prince
c/o Jive Records
137-139 W. 25th St.
New York, NY 10001
Rap group

Jodeci
c/o Uptown Records
729 7th Ave.
New York, NY 10019
R&B singing group

Joe
c/o Mercury Records
825 8th Ave.
New York, NY 10019
R&B singer

Johnny P
c/o Relativity Records
187-07 Henderson Ave.
Hollis, NY 11423
R&B singer

Johnson, Troy
c/o Word Records
3319 W. End
Nashville, TN 37203
Gospel singer

Joi
c/o Rowdy Records
75 Marietta Ave., 3rd Floor
Atlanta, GA 30303
R&B singer

Jones, Grace
c/o Island Records
400 Lafayette St.
New York, NY 10003
Singer, actor

Jones, London
c/o MCA Records
70 Universal Plaza
Universal City, CA 91608
R&B singer

Jones, Quincy
PO Box 48249
Los Angeles, CA 90048
Musician, producer

K-7
c/o Tommy Boy Records
902 Broadway
New York, NY 10010
Rapper

Kane, Big Daddy
c/o MCA Records
70 Universal Plaza
Universal City, CA 91608
Rapper

Kee, John P.
c/o Tyscot Records
2532 N. Keystone
Indianapolis, IN 46218
Gospel singer

Keith, Tribett and the Elements of Faith Choir
c/o PepperCo Records
324 Elm Street, #204A
Monroe, CT 06468
Gospel choir

Kelly, R.
c/o Jive Records
137-139 W. 25th St.
New York, NY 10001
R&B singer, musician

Key West
c/o Big Beat Records
19 W. 21st St.
New York, NY 10010
Reggae group

Khan, Chaka
c/o Triad Artists
10100 Santa Monica Blvd.
Los Angeles, CA 90067
R&B singer

Kid N' Play
902 Broadway
New York, NY 10019
Rap group

Kilo
c/o Ichiban Records
PO Box 724677
Miami, FL 31139-1677
Rap group

The King and I
c/o Rowdy Records
75 Marietta Ave., 3rd Floor
Atlanta, GA 30303
Rap group

King, B. B.
c/o Sidney A. Sedenberg
1414 Avenue of the Americas
New York, NY 10019
Blues musician, singer

Kinnector
c/o Tyscot Records
3532 N. Keystone
Indianapolis, IN 46218
Christian rap group

Kitt, Eartha
1524 LaBaig Ave.
Los Angeles, CA 90028
Singer, actor

Knight, Gladys
c/o Shakeji Inc.
3221 La Mirada Ave.
Las Vegas, NV 89120-3011
Soul singer

Kokane
c/o Ruthless/Relativity Records
2052 Manhattan Pl.
Torrance, CA 90501
Rapper

Kraig Mack
1325 5th Ave., 3rd Floor
New York, NY 10029
Rapper

Kravitz, Lenny
450 Broome St.
New York, NY 10013
Rock singer

Kriss Kross
1422 W. Peachtree St. NW
Atlanta, GA 30309
Rap group

KRS-1
c/o Jive Records
137-139 W. 25th St.
New York, NY 10001
Rapper

Krush
c/o Perspective Records
4330 Nicollet Ave.
Minneapolis, MN 55409
R&B singing group

KY
c/o 3rd and Lex Management
902 Broadway, 13th Floor
New York, NY 10010
Rap group

LaBelle, Patti
8730 Sunset Blvd.
Los Angeles, CA 90069
R&B singer, actor

Laine, Cleo
c/o Sonoma-Hope Inc.
PO Box 282
Hope, NJ 07844-0282
Singer

Latee
c/o The Flava Unit
155 Morgan St.
Jersey City, NJ 07302
Rap artist

Laurence Thompson and the Music City Mass Choir
1203 16th Ave.
Nashville, TN 37212
Gospel choir

Le Shaun
c/o Tommy Boy Records
902 Broadway
New York, NY 10010
Rap artist

Leaders of the New School
c/o Rush Communications
298 Elizabeth St.
New York, NY 10012
Rap group

Legacy of Sounds
c/o RCA
1133 Avenue of the Americas
New York, NY 10036
R&B singing group

The Legion
c/o Mercury Records
825 8th Ave.
New York, NY 10019
Rappers

Levert
110-112 Lantoga Rd.
Wayne, PA 19087
R&B singing group

Levert, Gerald
c/o East West Records
74 Rockefeller Plaza
New York, NY 10010
Soul singer

Lewis, Ramsey
180 N. LaSall St., #2200
Chicago, IL 60601-1538
Musician

Lincoln, Abby
c/o Verve Records
825 8th Ave.
New York, NY 10019
Singer

Lisa Lisa
747 10th Ave.
New York, NY 10019
Pop singer

Little Richard
c/o Bud Hole Inc.
8383 Wilshire Blvd., #900
Beverly Hills, CA 90211
Rock singer

L.L. Cool J
c/o Rush Communications
298 Elizabeth St.
New York, NY 10012
Rap artist, actor

Lo-Key
c/o Perspective Records
4330 Nicollet Ave.
Minneapolis, MN 55409
R&B group

Lords of the Underground
c/o Pendulum Records
1290 Avenue of the Americas
New York, NY 10019
Rap group

Lorenz, Trey
c/o Columbia Records
550 Madison Ave.
New York, NY 10022
Pop singer

Love, Darlene
PO Box 762
Nanuet, NY 10954
Pop singer

Lucas, Tammy
c/o L.O.R. Entertainment
349 S. Port Circle, #110
Virginia Beach, VA 23452
R&B singer

Mac Arthur
c/o La'Face Records
3350 Peachtree, #1500
Atlanta, GA 30326
R&B singer

Mad Flavor
6430 W. Sunset Blvd.
Los Angeles, CA 90028
Rap group

Mad Kap
209 Wieland Ave.
Staten Island, NY 10309
Rap artist

Madame Star
c/o Cold Chillin' Records
1995 Broadway, 18th Floor
New York, NY 10023
Rapper

Mahoghany Blue
c/o MCA Records
70 Universal Plaza
Universal City, CA 91608
R&B singing group

Main Source
c/o Wild Pitch Records
231 W. 29th St.
New York, NY 10001
Rap group

Malaika
c/o A & M Records
PO Box 118
Hollywood, CA 90078
R&B singer

Malloy, Donald
c/o CGI/Light
PO Box 851
Irvington, NJ 70711
Gospel singer

The Manhattans
c/o Worldwide Entertainment
641 Lexington Ave.
New York, NY 10022
Soul singing group

Mario
c/o Greg Aliferis Management
PO Box 11841
Ft. Lauderdale, FL 33339-1841
Rap artist

Marley Marl
c/o Cold Chillin' Records
1995 Broadway, 18th Floor
New York, NY 10023
DJ, producer

Marsalis, Branford
PO Box 55398
Washington, DC 20040
Musician

Marsalis, Wynton
327 E. 18th St.
New York, NY 10003
Musician

Masta Ace
75 Rockefeller Plaza
New York, NY 10019
Rap artist

Mathis, Johnny
2500 W. Olive Ave., #750
Burbank, CA 91505
Singer

Matthews, Denise (Vanity)
c/o William Morris Agency
151 El Camino Dr.
Beverly Hills, CA 90212
Singer, actor

Mayall, John
c/o Jive Records
137-139 W. 25th St.
New York, NY 10001
Musician

Maze Featuring Frankie Beverly
c/o Sony Music Group
550 Madison Ave.
New York, NY 10022
Soul group

MC Chance
c/o L.O.R. Entertainment
349 S. Port Circle, #110
Virginia Beach, VA 23452
Rap artist

MC Choice
PO Box 701156
Houston, TX 77270
Rap artist

MC Knowledge
c/o L.O.R. Entertainment
349 S. Port Circle, #110
Virginia Beach, VA 23452
Rap artist

MC Lyte
PO Box 004-537
Staten Island, NY 10304-0010
Rap artist

MC Ren
c/o Relativity Records
2052 Manhattan Pl.
Torrance, CA 90501
Rap artist

MC Rod
PO Box 724677
Miami, FL 31139-1677
Rap artist

MC Shan
c/o Cold Chillin' Records
1995 Broadway, 18th Floor
New York, NY 10023
Rap artist

McCoo, Marilyn
c/o William Morris Agency
151 El Camino Dr.
Beverly Hills, CA 90212
Pop singer

McFerren, Bobby
600 W. 58th St., #9188
New York, NY 10019
Jazz musician, singer

McGhee, Jacci
c/o Elektra Records
75 Rockefeller Plaza
New York, NY 10019
R&B singer

McKnight, Brian
c/o Mercury Records
825 8th Ave.
New York, NY 10019
Singer

McWilliams, Bridget
Virgin Records
9247 Alden Dr.
Beverly Hills, CA 90210
R&B singing group

Mello K
6253 Hollywood Blvd., #915
Hollywood, CA 90028
Rap artist

Mel-low
c/o Rush Communications
298 Elizabeth St.
New York, NY 10012
Rap artist

Melvin, Harold
PO Box 82
Great Neck, NY 11021
Soul singer

Men at Large
c/o East West Records
75 Rockefeller Plaza
New York, NY 10019
R&B singing group

Menageri
c/o Sony Music Corp.
550 Madison Ave.
New York, NY 10022
R&B singing group

Method Man
c/o Rush Communications
298 Elizabeth St.
New York, NY 10012
Rap artist

The Mighty Clouds of Joy
3319 W. End
Nashville, TN 37203
Gospel group

Miller, Douglas
c/o CGI/Light Records
PO Box 77093
Greensboro, NC 27417
Gospel singer

Miller, Shirley
c/o PepperCo Records
324 Elm St., #204A
Monroe, CT 06468
Gospel singer

Mint Condition
c/o Perspective Records
4330 Nicollet Ave.
Minneapolis, MN 55409
R&B singing group

Mississippi Children's Choir
c/o Blackberry Records
PO Box 11279
Jackson, MS 39213
Gospel choir

Mississippi Mass Choir
c/o Blackberry Records
PO Box 9287
Jackson, MS 39206
Gospel choir

Mkeba, Miriam
14011 Ventura Blvd., #200-B
Sherman Oaks, CA 91423
Singer

Mobb Deep
c/o New World Management
David Moore and Lance Rieves
2355 Justine Terr.
Lithia Springs, GA 30057
Rap group

Moby
9229 Sunset Blvd.
Los Angeles, CA 90069
Rap group

M.O.G.
4400 Horner St., #63
Union City, CA 94587
Rap group

Monica
c/o Rowdy Records
75 Marietta Ave., 3rd Floor
Atlanta, GA 30303
R&B singer

Monie Love
c/o Warner Bros.
3300 Warner Blvd.
Burbank, CA 91510
Rapper

Moore, Chante
c/o Silas Records
70 Universal Plaza
Universal City, CA 91608
R&B singer

Moore, James
c/o Blackberry Records
PO Box 9287
Jackson, MS 39206
Gospel singer

Moore, Melba
200 Central Park South, #8R
New York, NY 10019
Singer, actor

Moore, Tina
c/o Scotti Bros.
2114 Pico Blvd.
Santa Monica, CA 90405
R&B singer

Morales, David
c/o Mercury Records
825 8th Ave.
New York, NY 10019
Producer

Moten, Wendy
1290 Avenue of the Americas
New York, NY 10104
Pop singer

Mr. Mystic
c/o THG Music
New York, NY 10019
Rapper

Ms. Kilo
c/o Jive Records
137-139 W. 25th St.
New York, NY 10001
Rapper

**Murphy Pace III and the Voices
  of Power**
c/o Blackberry Records
PO Box 818
Summit, MS 39666
Choir

Najee
1290 Avenue of the Americas
New York, NY 10104
Jazz musician

Nas
c/o Columbia Records
550 Madison Ave.
New York, NY 10022
Rapper

Naughty By Nature
c/o The Flava Unit
155 Morgan St.
Jersey City, NJ 07302
Rap group

Ndege Ocello, Me'Shell
c/o Maverick Records
3300 Warner Blvd.
Burbank, CA 91510
Singer

**Neal, Willie, and the Gospel
  Keynotes**
c/o Blackberry Records
PO Box 9287
Jackson, MS 39206
Gospel quartet

Nefertiti
c/o Mercury Records
825 8th Ave.
New York, NY 10019
Rap artist

Nelson, Shara
c/o Chrysalis/ERG Records
9255 Sunset Blvd.
Los Angeles, CA 90069
R&B singer

Neptune
c/o L.O.R. Entertainment
349 S. Port Circle, #110
Virginia Beach, VA 23452
R&B singing group

Neville, Aaron
PO Box 24752
New Orleans, LA 70184
Pop singer

The Neville Brothers
PO Box 24752
New Orleans, LA 70184
Country group

New Edition
PO Box 604
San Francisco, CA 94101
R&B singing group

New Kingdom
Gee Street Records
14 E. 4th St.
New York, NY 10012
Rap group

New 2 Live Crew
c/o Luke Records
8400 N.E. 2nd Ave.
Liberty City, FL 33138
Rap group

Nice and Smooth
c/o Rush Communications
298 Elizabeth St.
New York, NY 10012
Rap group

Nikki D
c/o The Flava Unit
155 Morgan St.
Jersey City, NJ 07302
Rapper

Nikki Kixx
c/o Scotti Bros.
2114 Pico Blvd.
Santa Monica, CA 90405
Rap artist

95 South
Wrap/Ichiban Records
PO Box 724677
Miami, FL 31139-1677
Rap group

NKRU
c/o RCA Records
1133 Avenue of the Americas
New York, NY 10036
R&B singing group

Norman, Jessye
c/o Shaw
1900 Broadway
New York, NY 10023
Opera singer

Norwood, Dorothy
c/o Blackberry Records
PO Box 9287
Jackson, MS 39206
Gospel singer

N-Tyce
c/o Wild Pitch Records
231 W. 29th St.
New York, NY 10001
R&B singing group

Nut 'N Nice
c/o Jive Records
137-139 W. 25th St.
New York, NY 10001

O'Bryan
PO Box 483066
Los Angeles, CA 90048
Singer

Ocean, Billy
c/o Jive Records
137-139 W. 25th St.
New York, NY 10001
Singer

O'Jays
c/o EMI Records
1290 Avenue of the Americas
New York, NY 10104
Soul singing group

One II 3
c/o EMI Records
1290 Avenue of the Americas
New York, NY 10104
R&B singing group

One of the Girls
c/o East West Records
75 Rockefeller Plaza
New York, NY 10019
R&B singing group

O'Neal, Alexander
101 S. Rainbow, #28
PO Box 213
Las Vegas, NV 89128
R&B singer

Onyx
c/o Rush Communications
298 Elizabeth St.
New York, NY 10012
Rap group

Original Koncept
c/o Rush Communications
298 Elizabeth St.
New York, NY 10012
Rap group

Osborne, Jeffrey
c/o Jack Nelson
5800 Valley Oak Dr.
Los Angeles, CA 90068
Soul singer

**Oscar Hayes and the Abundant
Life Fellowship Chorale**
c/o Tyscot Records
3532 N. Keystone
Indianapolis, IN 46218
Gospel choir

Outkast
c/o La'Face Records
3350 Peachtree, #1500
Atlanta, GA 30326
Rap group

Owens, Jimmy
c/o Jay-Oh Music Co.
236 Park Avenue South
New York, NY 10003
Musician

Paris, Mica
c/o The Garfield Group
325 Lafayette St.
New York, NY 10012
Singer

**Paul Morton and His Greater St.
Stephens Mass Choir**
c/o Blackberry Records
PO Box 818
Summit, MS 39666
Gospel choir

Payne, Freda
10160 Cielo Dr.
Beverly Hills, CA 90210
Singer

Peaches and Herb
18034 Ventura Blvd, #18
Encino, CA 91316
R&B singing group

Pearson, Carlton
24 Music Sq. E
Nashville, TN 37203
Gospel singer

Pebbles
c/o Pebbtone Records
3340 Peachtree Rd. NE, #420
Atlanta, GA 30326
Pop singer

Pendergrass, Teddy
c/o Teddy Bear Entertainment
35 Rockhill Rd.
Bala Cynwyd, PA 19004
R&B singer

Penniston, Cece
c/o Perspective Records
4330 Nicollet Ave.
Minneapolis, MN 55409
R&B singer

The Pharcyde
c/o Delicious Vinyl Records
6607 Sunset Blvd.
Los Angeles, CA 90028
Rap group

Phat Twins
c/o Rowdy Records
75 Marietta Ave., 3rd Floor
Atlanta, GA 30303
Rap group

Pickett, Wilson
200 W. 57th St., #907
New York, NY 10019
Singer

Pilgrim Jubilees
c/o Blackberry Records
PO Box 9287
Jackson, MS 39206
Gospel quartet group

The Platters
PO Box 39
Las Vegas, NV 89101
Singing group

PM Dawn
c/o Gee Street Records
14 E. 4th St.
New York, NY 10012
Rap group

Point of View (POV)
c/o Giant Records
1290 Avenue of the Americas
New York, NY 10104

Pointer Sisters
10100 Santa Monica Blvd., 16th
   Floor
Los Angeles, CA 90067
R&B singing group

Poison Clan
c/o Luke Records
8400 N.E. 2nd Ave.
Liberty, FL 33138
Rap group

Poor Righteous Teachers
c/o Profile Records
740 Broadway
New York, NY 10003
Rap group

Portrait
c/o Columbia Records
550 Madison Ave.
New York, NY 10022
R&B singing group

Positive K
301 125th St., 3rd Floor
New York, NY 10027
Rap artist

Powell, Hubert
c/o PepperCo Records
324 Elm St., #204A
Monroe, CT 06468
Gospel singer

Preston, Billy
5221 North O'Connor Blvd.,
   #1000
Irving, TX 75039
R&B singer

Price, Leontyne
c/o Columbia Artists
 Management Inc.
165 W. 57th St.
New York, NY 10019
Opera singer

Pride, Charlie
3198 Royal La., #209
Dallas, TX 75229
Country singer

Priest, Maxi
c/o Columbia Records
550 Madison Ave.
New York, NY 10022
Reggae artist

**Prince (The artist formerly
 known as)**
9401 Kiowa Trail
Chanhasson, MN 55317
Singer, musician, producer

Professor X
c/o Mercury Records
825 8th Ave.
New York, NY 10019
Rap artist

Public Enemy
c/o Rush Communications
298 Elizabeth St.
New York, NY 10012
Rapper

Pudgie the Phat Bastard
1290 Avenue of the Americas
New York, NY 10104
Rapper

Q
c/o Bad Boy Entertainment
1325 5th Ave.
New York, NY 10029
Singer

Queen Latifah
c/o The Flava Unit
155 Morgan St.
Jersey City, NJ 07302
Rapper, actor

R.A. Posse
c/o La'Face Records
3350 Peachtree, #1500
Atlanta, GA 30326
Rap group

Raheem the Dream
c/o Bellmark Records
7060 Hollywood Blvd., 10th Fl.
Hollywood, CA 90028
Rap artist

Rakim
c/o MCA Records
70 Universal Plaza
Universal City, CA 91608
Rap artist

Rawls, Lou
9200 Sunset Blvd., #823
Los Angeles, CA 90069
Soul singer

Real Seduction
c/o Atlantic Records
1416 N. La Brea Ave.
Los Angeles, CA 90028
R&B singing group

Redd, Jeff
c/o Giant Records
1290 Avenue of the Americas
New York, NY 10104
R&B singer

The Reddings
1995 Broadway
New York, NY 10023
R&B singers

Reed, Eric
9255 Sunset Blvd.
Los Angeles, CA 90028
R&B singer

Reeves, Diane
c/o William Morris Agency
1350 Avenue of the Americas
New York, NY 10019
R&B singer

Reeves, Martha
168 Orchid Dr.
Pearl River, NY 10965
Soul singer

Richards, Deleon
c/o Word Records
3319 W. End
Nashville, TN 37203
Gospel singer

RIFF
c/o Giant Records
1290 Avenue of the Americas
New York, NY 10104
R&B singing group

Riley, Cheryl "Pepsi"
c/o Reprise/Warner Bros. Records
3300 Warner Blvd.
Burbank, CA 91510
R&B singer

Ritchie, Lionel
5750 Wilshire Blvd., #590
Los Angeles, CA 90036
Pop singer

Rivers, Johnny
3141 Coldwater Canyon La.
Beverly Hills, CA 90210
Singer

R.J.'s Latest Arrival
c/o ICM
40 W. 57th St.
New York, NY 10019
R&B singing group

Roach, Max
c/o Willard Alexander Inc.
101 Park Ave.
New York, NY 10178
Musician

Rob and Ray
1325 5th Ave.
New York, NY 10029
R&B singing group

Rob Base and E-Z Rock
c/o General Talent
1700 Broadway
New York, NY 10019
Rap group

Robin S.
c/o Big Beat Records
19 W. 21st St.
New York, NY 10010
House singer

Robinson, Cleophus
c/o Blackberry Records
PO Box 9287
Jackson, MS 39206
Gospel singer

Robinson, Smokey
c/o Michael Roshkind
6255 Sunset Blvd., 18th Floor
Los Angeles, CA 90028
Soul singer

Rogers, Kenton
c/o Blackberry Records
PO Box 818
Summit, MS 39666
Gospel singer

Rollins, Sonny
310 Greenwich St.
New York, NY 10013
Musician

Ross, Diana
PO Box 11059
Glenville Station
Greenwich, CT 06831
Pop singer

Run DMC
c/o Rush Communications
298 Elizabeth St.
New York, NY 10012
Rap group

RuPaul
c/o Tommy Boy Records
902 Broadway
New York, NY 10010
House singer

Rushen, Patricia
c/o Moultrie Entertainment
4950 Wilshire Blvd.
Los Angeles, CA 90010
Musician, singer

Russell, Brenda
1290 Avenue of the Americas
New York, NY 10104

Saints In Praise
c/o Sparrow Communications
101 Winners Circle
Nashville, TN 37027
Gospel choir

Salt N' Pepa
c/o Next Plateau Records
1650 Broadway
New York, NY 10019
Rap group

Sample This
c/o Atlantic Records
Rockefeller Plaza
New York, NY 10019
Rap group

Savage, Chantay
c/o RCA Records
1133 Avenue of the Americas
New York, NY 10019
R&B singer

Scott, Eddie
1290 Avenue of the Americas
New York, NY 10104
Singer, musician

Seal
c/o Sire/Warner Bros.
3300 Warner Blvd.
Burbank, CA 91510
Pop singer

Seant
440 Horner St., #63
Union City, CA 94587
R&B singer

Sease, Marvin
c/o Jive Records
137-139 W. 25th St.
New York, NY 10001
R&B singer

Se-Kou
c/o L.O.R. Entertainment
349 S. Port Circle, #110
Virginia Beach, VA 23452
R&B singer

Sermon, Erick
c/o Rush Communications
298 Elizabeth St.
New York, NY 10012
Rapper

7A3
c/o Geffen Records
9130 Sunset Blvd.
Los Angeles, CA 90069

Shabba Ranks
c/o Columbia Records
550 Madison Ave.
New York, NY 10022
Reggae artist

Shaggy
c/o Virgin Records
9247 Alden Dr.
Beverly Hills, CA 90210
Reggae artist

Shai
c/o Gasoline Alley/MCA Records
70 Universal Plaza
Universal City, CA 91608
R&B singing group

Shanice
8455 Fountain Ave., #530
Los Angeles, CA 90069
Singer

Shante (Roxanne)
c/o Cold Chillin' Records
1995 Broadway, 18th Floor
New York, NY 10023
Rapper

Shawn Best and Nutta Butta
c/o L.O.R. Entertainment
349 S. Port Circle
Virginia Beach, VA 23452
Rapper

Shazzy
c/o Warner Brothers Records
75 Rockefeller Plaza
New York, NY 10019
Reggae artist

Short, Bobby
c/o Betty Lee Hunt Association
444 E. 57th St.
New York, NY 10022
Singer

Side F-X
Greg Aliferis Management
PO Box 11841
Ft. Lauderdale, FL 33339-1841
Rapper

Silk
9229 Sunset Blvd.
Los Angeles, CA 90069
R&B singing group

Simone, Nina
c/o Elektra Entertainment
75 Rockefeller Plaza
New York, NY 10019
Soul singer

Sister Nancy
c/o Big Beat Records
19 W. 21st St.
New York, NY 10010
Reggae artist

Sister Souljah
c/o Rush Communications
298 Elizabeth St.
New York, NY 10012
Rapper

Slick Rick
c/o Rush Communications
298 Elizabeth St.
New York, NY 10012
Rapper

Smallwood, Richard
c/o Sparrow Communications
101 Winners Circle
Nashville, TN 37027
Gospel singer

Smooth
c/o Jive Records
137-139 W. 25th St.
New York, NY 10001
Rapper

Snoop Doggy Dog and the Dog Pound
c/o Death Row Records
10900 Wilshire Blvd., #91230
Los Angeles, CA 90024
Rap group

Souls of Mischief
c/o Jive Records
137-139 W. 25th St.
New York, NY 10001
Rap group

Spectrum
c/o Jive Records
137-139 W. 25th St.
New York, NY 10001
Rapper

Spencer, J.
c/o MoJazz Records
9255 Sunset Blvd.
Los Angeles, CA 90028
Jazz musician

Spenser, Tracy
c/o Columbia Records
1801 Century Park W
Los Angeles, CA 90067
R&B singer

Spice 1
c/o Jive Records
137-139 W. 25th St.
New York, NY 10001
Rapper

Spinners
65 W. 50th St., #6C
New York, NY 10019
Soul singing group

Spirit in Praise
21 Bala Cynwyd
Bala Cynwyd, PA 19004
Gospel choir

Staples, Mavis
c/o NPG Records
9401 Kiowa Trail
Chanhassen, MN 55317
Soul singer

Steele, Jvetta
c/o Columbia Records
550 Madison Ave.
New York, NY 10019
R&B singer

Stephens, Richie
c/o Motown Records
9255 Sunset Blvd., #1700
Los Angeles, CA 90028
R&B singer

Stone Coal
4815 Trousdale Dr., #418
Nashville, TN 37220
Gospel rapper

Stone, Sly
6255 Sunset Blvd., #200
Los Angeles, CA 90028
Soul singer

Street Military
c/o Wild Pitch Records
231 W. 29th St.
New York, NY 10001
Rap group

Summer, Donna
c/o Geffen/Warner Bros.
3300 Warner Blvd.
Burbank, CA 91510
Singer

Supercat
c/o Columbia Records
550 Madison Ave.
New York, NY 10022
Reggae artist

Sure, Al B.
c/o Warner Brothers Records
75 Rockefeller Plaza
New York, NY 10019
R&B singer, producer

Surrender
c/o Tyscot Records
3532 N. Keystone
Indianapolis, IN 46218
Gospel group

Sweet Honey in the Rock
c/o Doubleday
1540 Broadway
New York, NY 10036
Singing group

Sweet Sable
c/o Scotti Bros.
2114 Pico Blvd.
Santa Monica, CA 90405
R&B singer

Sybil
c/o Next Plateau Records
1650 Broadway
New York, NY 10019
House singer

Tag Team
c/o Bellmark Records
7060 Hollywood Blvd.
Hollywood, CA 90028
Rap group

Take 6
24 Music Square E.
Nashville, TN 37203
Gospel group

Tam Rock
c/o Biv 10 Records
6255 Sunset Blvd., #1700
Los Angeles, CA 90028
Rapper

Tashan
c/o Rush Communications
298 Elizabeth St.
New York, NY 10012
R&B singer

Tavares
c/o Brain Panella
3820 Castlerock Rd.
Malibu, CA 90265
Soul singing group

Taylor, Billy
555 W. 57th St.
New York, NY 10019
R&B singer

Taylor, Lisa
9255 Sunset Blvd.
Los Angeles, CA 90028
R&B singer

T.C.F. Crew
c/o Cold Chillin' Records
1995 Broadway, 18th Floor
New York, NY 10023

The Temptations
c/o Star Direction
605 N. Oakhurst Dr.
Beverly Hills, CA 90210
Soul singing group

Teri and Monica
c/o Columbia Records
550 Madison Ave.
New York, NY 10022
R&B singing group

Terror Fabulous
c/o Atlantic Records
75 Rockefeller Plaza
New York, NY 10019
Reggae artist

Terry, Ruby
c/o Blackberry Records
PO Box 9287
Jackson, MS 39206
Gospel singer

Terry, Tony
c/o Epic Records
550 Madison Ave.
New York, NY 10022
R&B singer

Third World
10100 Santa Monica Blvd., #1600
Los Angeles, CA 90067
Reggae group

Threat
c/o DaBomb/Mercury Records
825 8th Ave.
New York, NY 10019
Rap group

Tiger
c/o Rush Communications
298 Elizabeth St.
New York, NY 10012
Reggae artist

Tim Dog
c/o Uptown Entertainment
729 7th Ave.
New York, NY 10019
Rapper, record executive

Tischner, Denise
c/o Tyscot Records
3532 N. Keystone
Indianapolis, IN 46218
Gospel singer

TLC
c/o La'Face Records
3350 Peachtree, #1500
Atlanta, GA 30326
R&B singing group

To Be Continued
c/o East West Records
75 Rockefeller Plaza
New York, NY 10019
R&B singing group

Tone Lōc
6525 Sunset Blvd., 2nd Floor
Los Angeles, CA 90028
Rapper, actor

Tony Rebel
c/o Columbia Records
550 Madison Ave.
New York, NY 10022
Reggae artist

Tony! Toni! Toné!
c/o Wing/Mercury Records
810 7th Ave.
New York, NY 10019
Soul singing group

Too Short
c/o Jive Records
137-139 W. 25th St.
New York, NY 10001
Rapper

Total
c/o Bad Boy Entertainment
1325 5th Ave., 3rd Floor
New York, NY 10029
R&B singer

Totally Committed
c/o CGI Records
610 N. Fairbanks St.
Chicago, IL 60611
Gospel group

Townsell, Lidell
c/o Mercury Records
825 8th Ave.
New York, NY 10019
R&B singer

Tresvant, Ralph
c/o MCA Records
70 Universal Plaza
Universal City, CA 91608
R&B singer

A Tribe Called Qwest
c/o Jive Records
137-139 W. 25th St.
New York, NY 10001
Rap group

Trinity Temple Full Gospel Mass Choir
c/o Tyscot Records
3532 N. Keystone
Indianapolis, IN 46218
Gospel choir

Troop
c/o ICM
40 W. 57th St.
New York, NY 10019
R&B singing group

True Victory
c/o Tyscot Records
3532 N. Keystone
Indianapolis, IN 46218
Choir

Truth Ministries Youth Mass Choir
c/o TM Records
PO Box 501584
Indianapolis, IN 46250
Gospel choir

Turner, Ike
1800 N. Highland Ave., #411
Hollywood, CA 90028
Singer, musician

Turner, Tina
c/o Roger Davies
3575 Cahuenga Blvd.
West Los Angeles, CA 90068
Rock singer

12 Gauge
c/o Scotti Bros.
2114 Pico Blvd.
Santa Monica, CA 90405
Rap artist

II D Extreme
c/o MCA Records
70 Universal Plaza
Universal City, CA 91608
R&B singing group

2 Pac
10900 Wilshire, #91230
Los Angeles, CA 90024
Rap artist, actor

UGK's
c/o Jive Records
137-139 W. 25th St.
New York, NY 10001
Rap group

UMC's
c/o Wild Pitch Records
232 W. 29th St.
New York, NY 10001
Rap group

U-Mynd
c/o Luke Records
8400 N.E. 2nd Ave.
Liberty City, FL 33138
R&B singing group

Universal Nubian Voices (UNV)
c/o Maverick Records
3300 Warner Blvd.
Burbank, CA 91510
R&B singing group

Ultra Magnetic MC's
c/o Wild Pitch Records
231 W. 29th St.
New York, NY 10001
Rap group

Usher, Raymond
c/o La'Face Records
3350 Peachtree, #1500
Atlanta, GA 30326
R&B singer

Vandross, Luther
1414 Seabright Dr.
Beverly Hills, CA 90210
R&B singer

Verrett, Shirley
c/o Basil Horsfield Artist
   International Management
5 Regents Park Rd.
London, NW 1
England

Vertical Hold
A & M Records
1416 N. La Brea Ave.
Los Angeles, CA 90028
R&B singing group

Voices
c/o Zoo Entertainment
309 S. Broad St.
Philadelphia, PA 19107
R&B singing group

Walden, Narada Michael
PO Box 690
San Francisco, CA 94101
Musician, producer

Walker, Chris
1290 Avenue of the Americas
New York, NY 10104
R&B singer

Walker, Junior
c/o Autry DeWitt, Jr.
141 Dunbar Ave.
Fords, NJ 08863
Soul singer

Warfield, Justin
c/o Qwest Records
3300 Warner Blvd.
Burbank, CA 91510
Rap artist

Warwick, Dionne
9200 Sunset Blvd., #420
Los Angeles, CA 90069
Pop singer

Wash, Martha
c/o Columbia Records
550 Madison Ave.
New York, NY 10022
House singer

Washington, Grover, Jr.
c/o Zane Management
1515 Market St.
Philadelphia, PA 19102
Musician

Washington, Keith
c/o Qwest Records
3300 Warner Blvd.
Burbank, CA 91510
R&B singer

Waters, Muddy
c/o Cameron Organization
320 S. Waiola Ave.
La Grange, IL 60525
Blues musician

Watford, Michael
c/o Atlantic Records
75 Rockefeller Plaza
New York, NY 10019
Musician

Watley, Jody
8439 Sunset Blvd., #103
Los Angeles, CA 90069
Pop singer

Wells, Junior
c/o American Famous
816 W. Evergreen
Chicago, IL 60622
Soul singer

Wells, Mary
1680 N. Vine St., #214
Hollywood, CA 90028
Singer

**West Angeles Church of God In
    Christ's (COGICS)**
c/o Sparrow Communications
101 Winners Circle
Nashville, TN 37027
Gospel choir

West Coast Regional Mass Choir
c/o PepperCo Records
324 Elm St., #204A
Monroe, CT 06468
Gospel choir

Wheeler, Caron
c/o Giant Records
1290 Avenue of the Americas
New York, NY 10104
Singer

Whispers
9229 Sunset Blvd., #414
Los Angeles, CA 90069
Soul singing group

White, Barry
2434 Main St., #202
Santa Monica, CA 90405
Soul singer

White, Karyn
c/o Warner Brothers
3300 Warner Blvd.
Burbank, CA 91510
Pop singer

White, Maurice
4803 W. Verdugo Ave.
Burbank, CA 91505
Musician, singer

The Whooliganz
c/o Tommy Boy Records
902 Broadway
New York, NY 10010
Rap group

Wiggins, Alan, T. D.
c/o PepperCo Records
324 Elm St., #204A
Monroe, CT 06468
Gospel singer

Wilde, Eugene
PO Box 11981
Philadelphia, PA 19145
R&B singer

Williams Brothers
c/o Blackberry Records
PO Box 818
Summit, MS 39666
Gospel quartet group

Williams, Christopher
c/o Giant Records
1290 Avenue of the Americas
New York, NY 10104
Soul singer

Williams, Deniece
c/o Alive Entertainment
8271 Melrose Ave.
Los Angles, CA 90046
R&B and gospel singer

Williams, Joe
c/o John Levy
5455 Wilshire Blvd.
Los Angeles, CA 90036
Blues musician

Williams, Melvin
c/o Blackberry Records
PO Box 818
Summit, MS 39666
Gospel singer

Williams, Tene
c/o Pendulum Records
1290 Avenue of the Americas
New York, NY 10104
R&B singer

Williams, Vanessa
c/o Hervey and Co.
9034 Sunset Blvd., #1107
Los Angeles, CA 90069
Singer, former Miss America

Williams, Vesta
5301 Mullen Ave.
Los Angeles, CA 90027
R&B singer

Williams, Wendy O.
PO Box 837
New York, NY 10013
Pop singer

Wilson, Mary
1601 E. Flamingo Rd.
Las Vegas, NV 89110
Pop singer

Wilson, Nancy
5455 Wilshire Blvd., #1606
Los Angeles, CA 90039
Jazz singer

Winan, Bebe and Cece
c/o Capitol Records
550 Madison Ave.
New York, NY 10022
Inspirational singing group

Winan, Vicki
c/o CGI/Light Records
610 N. Fairbanks St.
Chicago, IL 60611
Gospel singer

The Winans
24 Music Square E
Nashville, TN 37203
Gospel group

Winbush, Angela
446 Liberty Rd.
Englewood, NJ 07631
R&B singer, musician, producer

Witherspoon, Jimmie
c/o Abby Hoffer Enterprises
223½ E. 48th St.
New York, NY 10017
Musician

Witness
c/o CGI/Light Records
610 N. Fairbanks St.
Chicago, IL 60611
Gospel singing group

Womack and Womack
1174 Longwood Ave.
Los Angeles, CA 90019
R&B singing group

Wonder, Stevie
4616 Magnolia Blvd.
Burbank, CA 91505
Singer, musician

Wreckx-N-Effect
c/o L.O.R. Entertainment
349 S. Port Circle, #110
Virginia Beach, VA 23452
Rap group

Wright, Timothy
c/o Savoy Records
611 Broadway, #428
New York, NY 10012
Gospel singer

Wu-Tang Clan
c/o RCA Records
1133 Avenue of the Americas
New York, NY 10036
Rap group

Xcellence
4390B Parliament Place
Lanham, MD 20706
R&B singing group

Xscape
c/o So So Def
2849 Piedmont Rd.
Atlanta, GA 30301
R&B singing group

YG'Z
c/o Warner Brothers Records
3300 Warner Blvd.
Burbank, CA 91510
Rap group

Yo Yo
c/o East West Records
75 Rockefeller Plaza
New York, NY 10019
Rapper

Young MC
c/o Capitol Records
9229 Sunset Blvd., #319
Los Angeles, CA 90069
Rapper

Y-Z
c/o Cold Chillin' Records
1995 Broadway, 18th Floor
New York, NY 10023

Zapp and Roger
c/o Reprise/Warner Brothers
3300 Warner Blvd.
Burbank, CA 91510
Funk group

Zhane
c/o The Flava Unit
155 Morgan St.
Jersey City, NJ 07302
R&B singing group

Zhigge
c/o Mercury Records
810 7th Ave.
New York, NY 10019
Rap group

RECORD COMPANIES AND LABELS

Bad Boy Entertainment
1325 5th Ave.
New York, NY 10029

Bellmark/Life
7060 Hollywood Blvd., #1700
Hollywood, CA 90028

Biv 10 Records
c/o Motown Records
6255 Sunset Blvd., 17th Floor
Los Angeles, CA 90028

Blackberry Records
PO Box 818
Summit, MS 39666

Bust It!
39510 Paseo Padre Pkwy., #250
Fremont, CA 94538

Chaos/Def Jam/Rush Associated Labels
c/o Rush Communications
298 Elizabeth St.
New York, NY 10012

Cold Chillin' Records
1995 Broadway, 18th Floor
New York, NY 10023

Comptown Records
c/o MCA Records
70 Universal Plaza
Universal City, CA 91608

Death Row Records
10900 Wilshire Blvd., #91230
Los Angeles, CA 90024

Flava Unit Records
155 Morgan St.
Jersey City, NJ 07302

Harlem Pride Recordings
PO Box 1710
New York, NY 10026

Illtown Records
c/o Motown Records
9255 Sunset Blvd., #1700
Los Angeles, CA 90028

Jab Records
PO Box 5638
Capitol Heights, MD 20791-5638

Kia Records
9229 Sunset Blvd.
Los Angeles, CA 90069

La'Face Records
3350 Peachtree, #1500
Atlanta, GA 30326

L.O.R. Records
349 S. Port Circle, #110
Virginia Beach, VA 23452

Luke Records
8400 N.E. 2nd Ave.
Liberty, FL 33138

MJJ Records
2100 Colorado Ave.
Santa Monica, CA 90404

NPG (New Power Generation)
9401 Kiowa Trail
Chanhassen, MN 55317

One Love Records
c/o Mercury Records
825 8th Ave.
New York, NY 10019

PepperCo Records
324 Elm St., #204A
Monroe, CT 06468

Perspective
4330 Nicollet Ave.
Minneapolis, MN 55409

Philadelphia International
309 S. Broad St.
Philadelphia, PA 19107

Qwest Records
7250 Beverly Blvd.
Los Angeles, CA 90036

Rap-a-lot Records
PO Box 701156
Houston, TX 77270

Rowdy Records
75 Marietta Ave., 3rd Floor
Atlanta, GA 30303

Rude Boy Records
594 Broadway
New York, NY 10012

Ruthless Records
c/o Relativity Records
2052 Manhattan Pl.
Torrance, CA 90501

Silas Records
c/o MCA Records
70 Universal Plaza
Universal City, CA 91608

So So Def
2848 Piedmont Rd.
Atlanta, GA 30301
404/233-1370

Sweet Rain Records
21 Bala Cynwyd St.
Bala Cynwyd, PA 19004

Triple B Records
18653 Ventura Blvd., #707
Tarzana, CA 91356

Truth Ministries (TM)
PO Box 501584
Indianapolis, IN 46250

Tyscot Records
3532 N. Keystone
Indianapolis, IN 46218

Umoja Records
PO Box 724677
Atlanta, GA 30311

Untouchables Entertainment
1560 Broadway
New York, NY 10036

Uptown Records
729 7th Ave.
New York, NY 10019

Vintertainment Records
PO Box 1002
Bronx, NY 10466

ORGANIZATIONS

**African Heritage Center for
    African Music**
4018 Minnesota Ave. NE
Washington, DC 20019
202/399-5252

Bessie Smith Society
c/o Prof. Michal Roth
Franklin and Marshall College
Lancaster, PA 17604
717/291-3915

Black Arts Music Society
PO Box 3214
Jackson, MS 39207
601/354-1049

Black Music Association
1500 Locust St.
Philadelphia, PA 19102

**Black Music Hall of Fame and
    Foundation**
755 Carondelet St.
New Orleans, LA 70130
504/565-7591

Black Rock (Music) Coalition
PO Box 1054
Cooper Station
New York, NY 10276
213/713-5097

Center for Black Music Research
Columbia College
623 S. Wabash St., #623
Chicago, IL 60606-1996
312/663-1600

**Charlie Parker Memorial
    Foundation**
c/o Academy of the Arts
4605 The Paseo
Kansas City, MO 64110
816/924-2200

**Community Music Center of
    Houston**
5613 Alameda
Houston, TX 77004
713/472-5731

International Association of African American Music
Box 382
Gladwyne, PA 19035
215/664-1677

International Rap Music Alliance
309 5th Ave., #482
Brooklyn, NY 11215

International Rhythm and Blues Association
PO Box 16215
Chicago, IL 60616
312/326-5270

Motown Museum and Historical Foundation
2648 W. Grand Blvd.
Detroit, MI 48208
313/867-0991

National Association of Negro Musicians
PO Box S-011
237 E. 115th St.
Chicago, IL 60628
312/779-1325

National Black Music Caucus
Music Educators' National Conference
c/o Dr. Willis Patterson
University of Michigan
Ann Arbor, MI 48109
313/764-0586

Rhythm and Blues Foundation
14th St. and Constitution Ave. NW, #4603
Washington, DC 20560

Rhythm and Blues Rock and Roll Society Inc.
PO Box 1949
New Haven, CT 06510
203/924-1079

Society of Black Composers
1365 St. Nicholas Ave., #3J
New York, NY 10033
212/923-4950

Talking Drums
400 Plaza Middlesex
Middleton, CT 06457
203/347-4304

360 Degrees Black
235 W. 48th St.
New York, NY 10036
212/664-0360

Wiregrass Sacred Harp Singers
Route 6, PO Box 187
Ozark, AL 36360
205/774-6617

DANCE

THE PERFORMERS, CHOREOGRAPHERS, AND TEACHERS

Dove, Ulysses
238 E. 85th St.
New York, NY 10128
Choreographer, teacher, dancer

Dunham, Katherine
10th St.
East St. Louis, IL
Dancer, choreographer

Fagan, Garth
State University at Brockport College
Hartwell Hall
Brockport, NY 14420
Dancer, choreographer

Hines, Gregory
9830 Wilshire Blvd.
Beverly Hills, CA 90212
Dancer, actor

Jamison, Judith
211 W. 61st St., 3rd Floor
New York, NY 10023
*Dancer, choreographer, dance
administrator*

Jones, Bill T.
c/o Sheldon Solfer Management
130 W. 56th St.
New York, NY 10019
Dancer

Miller, Bebe
54 W. 21st St., #502
New York, NY 10010
Dancer, choreographer

Nicholas, Fayard
23388 Mulholland Dr.
Woodland Hills, CA 91364
Dancer

Primus, Pearl
c/o Dance Magazine
503 W. 33rd St.
New York, NY 10101
Dancer, choreographer

COMPANIES AND ORGANIZATIONS

African American Dance Co.
394 5th Ave.
San Francisco, CA 94118
415/386-2832

African American Dance Ensemble
Royal Center for the Arts
120 Morris St.
Durham, NC 27701
919/560-2727

African Cultural Art Forum
237 S. 60th St.
Philadelphia, PA 19139
215/476-0680

African Heritage Dancers and Drummers Inc.
4018 Minnesota Avenue NE
Washington, DC 20019
202/399-5252

Afro-One Dance, Drama and Drum Theater
Park Plaza Mall, Rt. 130 S.
Willingsboro Plaza, NJ 08046
609/871-8340

Andrew Caho African Drummers and Dancers
PO Box 15282
Washington, DC 20003
202/889-0350

Black Experience Ensemble
5 Homestead Ave.
Albany, NY 12203
518/482-6683

Black Repertoire Dance Troupe
ASUC Davis Campus
Davis, CA 95616
916/752-1011

Chicago City Theater Company
Joel Hall Dancers
3340 N. Clark St.
Chicago, IL 60657
312/880-1002

Dance Theater of Harlem
466 W. 152nd St.
New York, NY 10031
212/690-2800

Ezibu Muntu African Dance Co.
PO Box 137
Richmond, VA 23201
804/643-1213

Gateway Dance Theater
1225 Stephenson Way
Des Moines, IA 50314
515/282-8696

Harambee Dance Ensemble
3026 5th Ave.
Oakland, CA 94605
510/532-8558

Harlem Dance Foundation
144 W. 121st St.
New York, NY 10027
212/662-2057

Hedzoleh African Dance Troupe
2333 Carling Dr.
Madison, WI 53711
608/294-9769

Ko-Thi Dance Company
PO Box 1093
Milwaukee, WI 53201
414/933-7007

Ladji Camara African Music Dance Ensemble
1706 Davidson Ave., #513
Bronx, NY 10453
212/716-4711

Oakland Ensemble Theater
1428 Alice St.
Oakland, CA 94612
510/763-7774

Pashami Dancers
PO Box 874
East Lansing, MI 48823
517/351-5282

Tuskegee Dance Theater
Department of Cultural Affairs
City of Tuskegee
214 N. Main St.
Tuskegee, AL 36083
205/724-2131

Umoja Dance Club
35 Havey Ave.
Charleston, SC 29405
803/744-5834

TELEVISION, FILM, AND THEATER

THE PERFORMERS

Ajaye, Franklin
c/o Tinsel Townsend
10202 W. Washington Blvd.
Lean Bldg., #100
Culver City, CA 90232
Comedian, writer

Alexander, Erika
c/o Warner Bros. Television
4000 Warner Blvd.
Burbank, CA 91522
Actor

Alexander, Terry
c/o ABC-TV
157 Columbus Ave.
New York, NY 10023
Actor

Ali, Tatiyana
c/o Quincy Jones Productions
3800 Barham Blvd., #503
Los Angeles, CA 90068
Actor

Allen, Debbie
955 S. Carillo Dr., #200
Los Angeles, CA 90048
*Director, actor, choreographer,
dancer, singer*

Allen, Jonelle
c/o The Agency
10351 Santa Monica Blvd., #211
Los Angeles, CA 90025
Actor

Amos, John
431 W. 162nd St.
New York, NY 10032
Actor

Arnold, Tichina
c/o HBO Independent Productions
2049 Century Park E., #4100
Los Angeles, CA 90067-3215
Actor, singer

Avery, James
c/o Quincy Jones Productions
3800 Barham Blvd., #503
Los Angeles, CA 90068
Actor

Baker, Shaun
c/o Michael Jacobs Productions/
   Touchtone Television
500 S. Buena Vista St.
Animation Building, #2A
Burbank, CA 91521
Actor

Bassett, Angela
c/o Ambrosio Mortimer
165 W. 46th St., #1214
New York, NY 10036
Actor

Belafonte, Gina
7083 Hollywood Blvd.
Los Angeles, CA 90028
Actor

Belafonte, Shari
3546 Longridge Ave.
Sherman Oaks, CA 91423
Actor

Bell-Calloway, Vanessa
c/o Fred Amsel and Associates
6310 San Vicente Blvd., #407
Los Angeles, CA 90048
Actor

Bellamy, Bill
c/o MTV
1515 Broadway
New York, NY 10019
TV show host, comedian

Berry, Halle
9255 Sunset Blvd., #515
Los Angeles, CA 90069
Actor

Bethea, Ellen
c/o ABC-TV
157 Columbus Ave.
New York, NY 10023
Actor

Beyer, Troy
c/o William Morris Agency
151 El Camino Dr.
Beverly Hills, CA 90212
Actor

Bledsoe, Tempestt
8230 Beverly Blvd., #23
Los Angeles, CA 90048
Actor

Bonet, Lisa
c/o William Morris Agency
151 El Camino Dr.
Beverly Hills, CA 90212
Actor

Bridges, Todd
7550 Zombar Ave., #1
Van Nuys, CA 91406
Actor

Brooks, Richard
10100 Santa Monica Blvd., 16th
  Floor
Los Angeles, CA 90067
Actor

Brown, Georg Stanford
3130 Benedict Canyon Dr.
Beverly Hills, CA 90210
Actor

Brown, Olivia
c/o Light Co.
901 Bringham
Los Angeles, CA 90049
Actor

Browne, Roscoe Lee
c/o Georgia Gilly 8721
9225 Sunset Blvd., #103
Los Angeles, CA 90069
Actor

Burton, LeVar
c/o Delores Robinson
  Management
7319 Beverly Blvd., #7
Los Angeles, CA 90036
Actor, children's show host

Campbell, Tisha
c/o Jane Frazier
Michelle Marx Inc.
8756 Holloway Dr.
Los Angeles, CA 90069
Actor, singer

Carey, Julius
4024 Radford Ave.
Studio City, CA 91604
Actor

Carroll, Diahann
PO Box 2999
Beverly Hills, CA 90213
Actor

Carroll, Rocky
c/o HBO Independent Productions
2049 Century Park, #4100
Los Angeles, CA 90067
Actor

Carson, T. C.
4000 Warner Blvd.
Burbank, CA 91522
Actor

Carter, Christopher
c/o Jeff Franklin Productions
300 S. Lorimar
Bldg. 140, #103
Burbank, CA 90068
Actor

Carter, Nell
c/o Jeff Franklin Productions
300 S. Lorimar
Bldg. 140, #103
Burbank, CA 90068
Actor, singer

Carter, Sherry
c/o Black Entertainment
  Television
1700 N. Moore St., #2200
Rosslyn, VA 22209
Television show host

Carter, T. K.
c/o David and Goliath
  Productions/Touchtone
  Television
500 S. Buena Vista
Burbank, CA 91505
Actor

Cash, Rosalind
c/o Kackie Veglie
Actor's Equity
165 W. 46th St.
New York, NY 10036
Actor

Chestnutt, Morris
10351 Santa Monica Blvd., #211
Los Angeles, CA 90025
Actor

Chong, Rae Dawn
PO Box 181
Bearsville, NY 12409
Actor

Christian, Spencer
c/o ABC-TV
7 W. 66th St.
New York, NY 10023
Weatherman

Christian, William
c/o ABC-TV
320 W. 66th St.
New York, NY 10023
Actor

Clayton, Xerona
c/o TBS Inc.
1 CNN Center
PO Box 105366
Atlanta, GA 30348-5366
Broadcasting executive

Coleman, Gary
c/o Victor Perillo Talent Agency
9229 Sunset Blvd.
Los Angeles, CA 90069
Actor

Coles, Kim
c/o Warner Bros. Television
4000 Warner Blvd.
Burbank, CA 91522
Actor, comedian

Cooke, LaCrystal
c/o Katie Face Production/
  Columbia Television
10202 W. Washington
Lean Building, #100
Culver City, CA 90232
Actor

Cornelius, Don
9255 Sunset Blvd., #420
Los Angeles, CA 90069
Music show host

Cosby, Bill
PO Box 808
Greenfield, MA 01301
Comedian, actor

Covan, Deforest
c/o Lil Cumber Agency
6515 Sunset Blvd., #300A
Los Angeles, CA 90028
Actor

Crable, Deborah
c/o Ebony/Jet Showcase
820 S. Michigan Ave.
Chicago, IL 60605
Talk show host

Curry, Mark
c/o Jeff Franklin Productions
300 S. Lorimar Bldg. 140, #103
Los Angeles, CA 91522
Comedian, actor

David, Keith
c/o Joshua Silver
MSI Entertainment Inc.
10866 Wilshire Blvd., #1000
Los Angeles CA 90026
Actor

Davidson, Tommy
c/o Twentieth Television
10201 W. Pico Blvd.
Los Angeles, CA 90035
Actor, comedian

Davis, Clifton
c/o International Famous Agency
1301 Avenue of the Americas
New York, NY 10019
Actor, minister

Davis, Erin
c/o David and Goliath
  Productions/Touchtone
  Television
500 S. Buena Vista St.
Burbank, CA 91505
Actor

Davis, Ossie
44 Cortland Ave.
New Rochelle, NY 10801
Actor, writer, director

Day, Morris
c/o Warner Bros. Records
3300 Warner Blvd.
Burbank, CA 91510
Actor, singer

Deanda, Peter
3721 Weslin Ave.
Sherman Oaks, CA 91403
Actor

Dee, Ruby
44 Cortland Ave.
New Rochelle, NY 10801

Derricks, Clevant
c/o Castle Rock Entertainment
335 N. Maple Dr., #135
Beverly Hills, CA 90210
Actor

DeShields, Andre
256 W. 21st St.
New York, NY 10011
Broadway actor

Doctor Dre
c/o MTV
1515 Broadway
New York, NY 10019
Television show host

Doug E. Doug
c/o Michael Jacobs/Touchtone
  Television
500 S. Buena Vista St.
Animation Building, #2A
Burbank, CA 91521
Actor, comedian

Douglass, Suzanne
c/o William Blaylock
Cathay Circle
213 Stanley Dr.
Beverly Hills, CA 90211
Actor

Doyle, Yunoka
c/o Michael Jacobs Production/
  Touchtone Television
South Buena Vista
Animation Building, #2A
Burbank, CA 91521
Actor

DuBois, Janet
405 West Ivy St., #204
Glendale, CA 91204
Actor

Duncan, Robert
4130 16th St. NW
Washington, DC 20011
Actor

Dutton, Charles
c/o HBO Independent Productions
2049 Century Park E, #4100
Los Angeles, CA 90067
Actor

Esposito, Giancarlo
c/o Touchtone Television
500 S. Buena Vista St.
Burbank, CA 91521
Actor

Fab Five Freddy
c/o MTV
1515 Broadway
New York, NY 10019
Television show host, hip-hop
   personality

Ferrell, Tyra
c/o STE Representation
9301 Wilshire Blvd., #312
Beverly Hills, CA 90210
Actor

Fields, Kim
c/o Warner Bros. Television
4000 Warner Blvd.
Burbank, CA 91522
Actor

Fishbourne, Laurence
c/o Michelle Marx Inc.
8756 Holloway Dr.
Los Angeles, CA 90069
Actor

Flex
c/o Michael Jacobs Productions/
   Touchtone Television
500 S. Buena Vista St.
Animation Building, #2A
Burbank, CA 91521
Actor, comedian

Ford, Tommy
c/o HBO Independent Productions
2049 Century Park E, #400
Los Angeles, CA 90067
Actor

Foxx, Jamie
c/o Twentieth Television
10201 W. Pico Blvd.
Los Angeles, CA 90035
Actor, comedian

Francis, Elliot
c/o Johnson Publishing Company
820 S. Michigan Ave.
Chicago, IL 60605
TV show host

Franklin, Don
100 Universal City Plaza
Bungalo 477
Universal City, CA 91608-1085
Actor

Freeman, Al, Jr.
Howard University College of
   Fine Arts
Washington, DC 20059
Actor

Freeman, Morgan
c/o Jeff Hunter
Triad Artists
888 7th Ave., #1610
New York, NY 10036
Actor, director

Gibbs, Marla
c/o Marla Gibbs Enterprises
4310 Degman Blvd.
Los Angeles, CA 90028
Actor

Gilliard, Larry, Jr.
10202 W. Washington Blvd.
Lean Bldg., #100
Culver City, CA 90232
Actor

Gimpel, Erica
888 7th Ave., #201
New York, NY 10019
Actor

Givens, Robin
8818 Thrasher Ave.
Los Angeles, CA 90069
Actor

Glass, Ron
c/o Lawrence Kubik
PO Box 4669
Los Angeles, CA 90046
Actor

Glover, Danny
3900 W. Alameda Ave., #1700
Burbank, CA 91505
Actor

Goldberg, Whoopi
c/o Whoop Inc.
5555 Melrose Ave.
Wilder Building, #114
Hollywood, CA 90038
Actor, comedian

Gooding, Cuba, Jr.
10100 Santa Monica Blvd., #200
Los Angeles, CA 90067
Actor

Gordan, Carl
2049 Century Park E, #4100
Los Angeles, CA 90067
Actor

Gossett, Louis, Jr.
11601 Wilshire Blvd., 21st Floor
Los Angeles, CA 90025
Actor

Grier, David Alan
PO Box 741226
Los Angeles, CA 90004
Actor, comedian

Grier, Pam
c/o Agency for Performing Arts
9000 Sunset Blvd.
Los Angeles, CA 90069
Actor

Guillame, Robert
c/o Peters Entertainment
    Productions Inc.
1438 N. Gower
Los Angeles, CA 90028
Actor

Guy, Jasmine
c/o Columbia Records/Sony Music
550 Madison Ave.
New York, NY 10022
Actor, singer

Hairston, Jester
5047 Valley Ridge Ave.
Los Angeles, CA 90043
Actor

Hall, Arsenio
Arsenio Hall Communications
5555 Melrose Ave.
Hollywood, CA 90038
*Actor, former television show host,
    comedian*

Hardison, Kadeem
324 N. Brighton St.
Burbank, CA 91506
Actor

Harewood, Dorian
6399 Wilshire Blvd., #PH1
Los Angeles, CA 90048
Actor

Harper, Ken
c/o Emmanuel Azenburg
165 W. 6th St., #914
New York, NY 10036
Producer, actor

Hart, Thomas A., Jr.
1221 11th St. NW
Washington, DC 20001
Director, producer

Harvey, Steve
c/o Showtime at the Apollo
253 W. 125th St.
New York, NY 10027
Comedian, television show host

Haysbert, Dennis
c/o Gore/Fields Talent
10100 Santa Monica Blvd., #700
Los Angeles, CA 90067
Actor

Headley, Shari
c/o ABC-TV
320 W. 66th St.
New York, NY 10023
Actor

Hemphill, Shirley
539 Trona Ave.
West Covina, CA 91790
Actor

Hemsley, Sherman
8033 Sunset Blvd., #193
Los Angeles, CA 90046
Actor

Henton, John
c/o Warner Bros. Television
4000 Warner Blvd.
Burbank, CA 91522
Actor, comedian

Holder, Geoffrey
275 W. 92nd St.
New York, NY 10025
Actor

Hollar, Lloyd
551 Hudson St.
New York, NY 10014
Actor

Hooks, Robert
145 N. Valley St.
Burbank, CA 91505
Actor, director

Horseford, Anna Maria
PO Box 29765
Los Angeles, CA 90029
Actor

Hubert-Whitten, Janet
c/o Michael Slessinger
8730 Sunset Blvd., #22
Los Angeles, CA 90069
Actor

Hudson, Ernie
c/o Monique Moss
8730 Sunset Blvd., 6th Floor
Los Angeles, CA 90069
Actor

Hughley, D. L.
c/o Black Entertainment
   Television
1700 N. Moore St., #2200
Rosslyn, VA 22209
Television show host, comedian

Hyman, Earle
c/o Manhattan Towers
484 W. 43rd St., #33-E
New York, NY 10036
Actor

Iman
c/o Elite Modelling Agency
111 E. 22nd St.
New York, NY 10010
Model, actor

Irlanda, Pablo
c/o Katie Face Productions/
   Columbia Television
10202 W. Washington
Lean Building, #100
Culver City, CA 90232
Actor

Jackee
8649 Metx Place
Los Angeles, CA
Actor

Jackson, Stoney
1602 N. Fuller Ave., #102
Los Angeles, CA 90046
Actor

Jefferson, Brendan
c/o Castle Rock Entertainment
335 N. Maple Dr., #135
Beverly Hills, CA 90210-3867
Actor

Jeffries, Adam
c/o Castle Rock Entertainment
335 N. Maple Dr., #135
Beverly Hills, CA 90210-3867
Actor

Johnson, Anna Marie
2606 Ivan Hill Terrace
Los Angeles, CA 90026
Actor, comedian

Johnson, Belma
c/o Black Entertainment
   Television
1700 N. Moore St., #2200
Rosslyn, VA 22209
Television show host

Johnson, Beverly
c/o Prima Modelling Agency
933 N. LaBrea
Los Angeles, CA 90038
Model, actor

Jones, Bobby
c/o Black Entertainment
   Television
1700 N. Moore St., #2200
Rosslyn, VA 22209
Television show host, gospel singer

Jones, James Earl
PO Box 55337
Sherman Oaks, CA 91413
Actor

Jones, Renee
3000 W. Alameda Ave.
Burbank, CA 91523
Actor

Joyce, Ella
c/o HBO Independent Productions
2049 Century Park E, #4100
Los Angeles, CA 90067
Actor

Julien, Isaac
c/o Miramax Film Corps
375 Greenwich St.
New York, NY 10013
Actor

Kelly, Paula
c/o Smith-Stevens
   Representations
434 N. Rodeo Dr.
Beverly Hills, CA 90210
Actor

Kennedy, Leon Isaac
PO Box 361039
Los Angeles, CA 90036
Actor

Kennedy-Overton, Jayne
1223 Wilshire,Blvd., #141
Santa Monica, CA 90403
Actor, former model

Keymah, T'Keyah Crystal
c/o Twentieth Television
10201 W. Pico Blvd.
Los Angeles, CA 90035
Actor, comedian

King, Yolanda
3870 Crenshaw Blvd., #10-704
Los Angeles, CA 90008
Actor, producer, director

Knight-Pulliam, Keshia
PO Box 866
Teaneck, NJ 07666
Actor

Laneuville, Eric
c/o Iris Burton
1450 Belfast
Los Angeles, CA 90069
Actor

Lange, Ted
c/o Arnold Soloway Associates
118 S. Beverly Dr.
Beverly Hills, CA 90212
Actor

Lawson, Richard
c/o ABC-TV
320 W. 66th St.
New York, NY 10023
Actor

LeBeauf, Sabrina
133 St. Nichols Ave.
Englewood, NJ 07632
Actor

Lee, Joie
c/o Forty Acres and a Mule
   Filmworks
124 DeKalb Ave.
Brooklyn, NY 11217
Actor

LeNoire, Rosetta
c/o Bickley-Warren/Miller-Boyett
1020 W. Washington Blvd.
Culver City, CA 90232
Actor

Lewis, Dawnn
9229 Sunset Blvd., #607
Los Angeles, CA 90069
Actor

Lewis, Emmanuel
c/o Monica Stuart Schuller Talent
276 5th Ave., #1001
New York, NY 10001
Actor

Lewis, Thyme
c/o Corday Productions Inc.
3000 W. Alameda Ave.
Burbank, CA 91523
Actor

Long, Nia
c/o D'Arcy, Massius, Benton &
   Bowles Inc.
222 E. 44th St.
New York, NY 10017
Actor

Lover, Ed
c/o MTV
1515 Broadway
New York, NY 10019
Television show host

MacLachlan, Janet
c/o Global Business Management
9601 Wilshire Blvd.
Beverly Hills, CA 90210
Actor

Major, Clarence
1312 Toyon Pl.
Davis, CA 95616
Actor

Marcell, John
c/o Quincy Jones Productions
3800 Barham Blvd., #503
Los Angeles, CA 90068
Actor

Marshall, Amelia
c/o D'Arcy, Massius, Benton &
   Bowles Inc.
222 E. 44th St.
New York, NY 10017
Actor

Marshall, Donald
c/o Abraham Ruballiff Lawrence
8075 W. 3rd St., #303
Los Angeles, CA 90048
Actor

McClure, Bryton
c/o Miller-Boyett Productions
1020 W. Washington Blvd.
Culver City, CA 90232
Actor

McCoo, Harold
c/o Black Entertainment
    Television
1700 N. Moore St., #2200
Rosslyn, VA 22209
Television anchor

McDaniel, James
c/o Steven Bocho Productions
10201 W. Pico Blvd.
Los Angeles, CA 90035
Actor

McEachin, James
PO Box 5166
Sherman Oaks, CA 91403
Actor

McGee, Vonetta
9744 Wilshire Blvd.
Beverly Hills, CA 90212
Actor

McKee, Lonette
8 St. Felix St.
Brooklyn, NY 11217
Actor, singer

McNair, Barbara
c/o Moss Agency Ltd.
113 N. San Vincente Blvd.
Beverly Hills, CA 90211
Actor

McQueen, Butterfly
31 Hamilton Terr.
New York, NY 10031
Actor

Mitchell, Daryl "Chill"
c/o Witt-Thomas Productions
3000 W. Alameda Ave.
Burbank, CA 91523
Actor

Montgomery, Barbara
6565 Sunset Blvd., #525
Los Angeles, CA 90028
Actor

Morgan, Debbie
c/o ABC-TV
320 W. 66th St.
New York, NY 10023
Actor

Morris, Garrett
c/o Abrams Artists
9200 Sunset Blvd., #625
Los Angeles, CA 90069
Actor

Morris, Greg
8721 Sunset Blvd., #205
Los Angeles, CA 90069
Actor

Morton, Joe
105 E. 19th St.
New York, NY 10003
Actor, director

Moseley, Roger
c/o Aimee Entertainment
14241 Ventura Blvd.
Sherman Oaks, CA 91423
Actor

Mr. T
395 Green Bay Rd.
Lake Forest, IL 60045
Actor

Murphy, Eddie
c/o Eddy Murphy Productions
5555 Melrose Ave.
Los Angeles, CA 90038
Actor, comedian, producer

Nichols, Nichelle
c/o Ar-Way Productions
22647 Ventura Blvd., #121
Woodland Hills, CA 91364
Actor

Norman, Cleandre
c/o Katie Face Productions/
    Columbia Television
10202 W. Washington Blvd.
Lean Building, #100
Culver City, CA 90232
Actor

Norwood, Brandy
c/o Castle Rock Entertainment
335 N. Maple Dr., #135
Beverly Hills, CA 90210-3867
Actor

Norwood, Willie
c/o David and Goliath
    Productions/Touchtone
    Television
500 S. Buena Vista St.
Burbank, CA 91521
Actor

O'Neal, Ron
c/o Gores Fields Agency
10100 Santa Monica Blvd., #700
Los Angeles, CA 90067
Actor

Parks, Gordon
c/o Paramount Pictures
860 United Nations Plaza
New York, NY 10017
Photographer, director, writer

Parsons, Karen
c/o Quincy Jones Productions
3800 Barham Blvd., #503
Los Angeles, CA 90068
Actor

Payne, Allen
c/o William Morris Agency
151 El Camino Ave.
Beverly Hills, CA 90212
Actor

Payne, Carl
c/o HBO Independent Productions
2049 Century Park, #400
Los Angeles, CA 90067
Actor

Payton-France, Jo Marie
c/o Miller-Boyett Productions
10202 W. Washington Blvd.
Culver City, CA 90232
Actor

Perry, Felton
c/o Lori DeWaal
The Garrett Company
6922 Hollywood Blvd.
Los Angeles, CA 90028
Actor

Peters, Brock
1968 W. Adams Blvd.
Los Angeles, CA 90018
Actor

Pettiford, Valerie
c/o ABC-TV
157 Columbus Ave.
New York, NY 10023
Actor

Pinkett, Jada
c/o William Morris Agency
151 El Camino Dr.
Beverly Hills, CA 90212
Actor

Pitkins, Tonya
c/o ABC-TV
320 W. 66th St.
New York, NY 10023
Actor, singer

Poitier, Sidney
9350 Wilshire Blvd.
Beverly Hills, CA 90212
Actor, director

Prince DuJour
c/o Black Entertainment
   Television
1700 N. Moore St.
Rosslyn, VA 22209
Television show host

Pryor, Richard
8899 Beverly Blvd.
Los Angeles, CA 90048
Comedian, actor

Purdee, Nathan
c/o ABC-TV
157 Columbus Ave.
New York, NY 10023
Actor

Ralph, Sheryl Lee
c/o Katie Face Productions/
   Columbia Television
10202 W. Washington
Lean Building, #100
Culver City, CA 90232
Actor, singer

Rashad, Phylicia
c/o Artist Agency Inc.
10000 Santa Monica Blvd., #305
Los Angeles, CA 90067
Actor

Raven-Simone
c/o MCA Records
70 Universal Plaza
Universal City, CA 91608
Actor, singer

Redd-Forest, Veronica
3400 Riverside Dr.
Burbank, CA 91505
Actor

Reese, Della
c/o William Morris Agency
151 El Camino Dr.
Beverly Hills, CA 90212
Actor

Reid, Tim
16030 Ventura Blvd., #380
Encino, CA 91436
Actor, producer

Reynolds, James
3000 Alameda Ave.
Burbank, CA 91523
Actor

Ribero, Alphonso
c/o Quincy Jones Productions
3800 Barham Blvd., #503
Los Angeles, CA 90068
Actor, dancer, singer

Richmond, Deon
c/o Miller-Boyett Productions
10202 W. Washington Blvd.
Culver City, CA 90404
Actor

Rippy, Rodney Allen
c/o Dorothy Day Otis Agency
6430 Sunset Blvd.
Los Angeles, CA 90028
Actor

Robinson, Charlie
c/o Shukovsky-English
   Entertainment
4024 Radford Ave.
Studio City, CA 91604
Actor

Robinson, Holly
c/o Delores Robinson
  Management
899 Beverly Blvd.
Los Angeles, CA 90048
Actor

Rock, Chris
c/o Twentieth Television
10201 W. Pico Blvd.
Los Angeles, CA 90035
Actor, comedian

Rodgers, Ingrid
c/o ABC-TV
77 W. 66th St.
New York, NY 10023
Actor

Roker, Roxie
3518 W. Cahuenga Blvd., #304
Los Angeles, CA 90068
Actor

Rolle, Esther
c/o Triad Artists Inc.
10100 Santa Monica Blvd.
Los Angeles, CA 90067
Actor

Rollins, Howard
10100 Santa Monica Blvd.,
  16th Floor
Los Angeles, CA 90067
Actor

Roundtree, Richard
c/o Agency Performing Arts Inc.
9000 Sunset Blvd.
Los Angeles, CA 90069
Actor

Rowell, Victoria
c/o Bell Dramatic Serial Co.
7800 Beverly Blvd.
Los Angeles, CA 90036
Actor

Russell, Kimberly
11617 Laurelwood Dr.
Studio City, CA 91604
Actor

Russell, Nipsey
353 W. 57th St.
New York, NY 10019
Actor, comedian

St. Jacques, Raymond
c/o William Morris Agency
151 El Camino Dr.
Beverly Hills, CA 90212
Actor

St. John, Christopher
c/o Bell Dramatic Serial Co.
3400 Riverside Dr.
Burbank, CA 91505
Actor

Sanders, Henry
c/o CBS-TV
51 W. 52nd St.
New York, NY 10019
Actor

Sanford, Isabel
9157 Sunset Blvd., #200
Los Angeles, CA 90069
Actor

Santana, Merlin
Miller-Boyett Productions
10202 W. Washington Blvd.
Culver City, CA 90232
Actor

Scott, Larry B.
c/o Harris and Goldberg
1999 Avenue of the Stars, #2850
Los Angeles, CA 90067
Actor

Segar, Leslie
c/o Black Entertainment
  Television
1700 N. Moore St., #2200
Rosslyn, VA 22209
*Dancer, choreographer, and TV
  show host*

Sharp, Monti
c/o CBS-TV
51 W. 52nd St.
New York, NY 10017
Actor

Shaw, Stan
c/o Henderson Hogan Agency
247 S. Beverly Dr.
Beverly Hills, CA 90212
Actor

Sinbad
20061 Merriday St.
Chatsworth, CA 91311
Actor, comedian

Sinclair, Madge
1999 N. Sycamore Ave.
Hollywood, CA 90068
Actor

Smith, Will
c/o Quincy Jones Productions
3800 Barham Blvd., #503
Los Angeles, CA 90068
Actor, rapper

Snipes, Wesley
9830 Wilshire Blvd.
Beverly Hills, CA 90212
Actor

Spears, Aries
5555 Melrose Ave.
Los Angeles, CA 90038
Actor

Spencer, Donielle
c/o Katie Face Productions/
  Columbia Television
10202 W. Washington Blvd.
Lean Building, #100
Culver City, CA 90232
Actor

Taylor, Meschach
9150 Wilshire Blvd., #205
Beverly Hills, CA 90212
Actor

Thomas, Michelle
c/o Miller-Boyett Productions
10202 W. Washington Blvd.
Culver City, CA 90232
Actor

Thomas, Phillip Michael
c/o Miami Way Theatre
12615 W. Dixie Highway
North Miami, FL 33161
Actor

Todd-1
c/o MTV
1515 Broadway
New York, NY 10019
Television show host, comedian

Todd, Beverly
4888 Valley Ridge
Los Angeles, CA 90043
Actor

Tolbert, Berlinda
c/o 20th Century Artists
13273 Ventura Blvd.
Studio City, CA 91604
Actor

Tunie, Tamara
10201 W. Pico Blvd.
Los Angeles, CA 90035
Actor

Tyra (Banks)
c/o Quincy Jones Productions
3800 Barham Blvd., #503
Los Angeles, CA 90068
Actor, model

Tyson, Cicely
315 W. 70th St.
New York, NY 10023
Actor

Uggams, Leslie
400 S. Beverly Dr.
Beverly Hills, CA 90212
Actor

Underwood, Blair
7148 Woodrow Wilson Dr.
Los Angeles, CA 90046
Actor

Van Peebles, Mario
c/o William Morris Agency
151 El Camino Dr.
Beverly Hills, CA 90212
Actor, director

Van Peebles, Melvin
850 7th Ave., #1203
New York, New York 10019
Director, actor

Vel Johnson, Reginald
9229 Sunset Blvd., #607
Los Angeles, CA 90069
Actor

Vereen, Ben
c/o William Morris Agency
1350 Avenue of the Americas
New York, NY 10019
Actor, dancer, singer

Vidale, Thea
c/o Castle Rock Entertainment
335 N. Maple Dr., #135
Beverly Hills, CA 90210
Actor, comedian

Walker, Arnetia
1438 N. Gower
Hollywood, CA 90028
Actor

Walker, Jimmy
c/o General Management Corp.
9000 Sunset Blvd., #400
Los Angeles, CA 90069
Actor, comedian

Walker, Sullivan
c/o Michael Jacobs Productions
500 S. Buena Vista St.
Animation Building, #2A
Burbank, CA 91521
Actor

Ward, Douglass Turner
222 Ell St.
New York, NY 10003
Playwright, actor

Warfield, Marsha
PO Box 691713
Los Angeles, CA 90069
Actor, comedian

Warner, Malcolm Jamal
c/o Warner Management
1301 Colony
Hartsdale, NY 10530
Actor, director

Warren, Michael
c/o Sandy Bressler and Associates
1560 Ventura Blvd., #1730
Encino, CA 91436
Actor, producer

Washington, Denzel
c/o Public Relations
955 S. Carrillo Dr., #200
Los Angeles, CA 90048
Actor

Watkins, Velma
881 Memorial Dr.
Atlanta, GA 30316
Actor

Watts, Franklin
387 Park Ave. South
New York, NY 10016
Actor

Wayans, Damon
10201 W. Pico Blvd.
TRA 732, 12
Los Angeles, CA 90035
Actor, comedian

Wayans, Keenen Ivory
PO Box 900
Beverly Hills, CA 90213
Actor, director, producer, comedian

Wayans, Kim
5746 Sunset Blvd.
Hollywood, CA 90028
Actor, comedian

Wayans, Shawn
5746 Sunset Blvd.
Hollywood, CA 90028
Actor

Weathers, Carl
17452 Sunset Blvd.
Pacific Palisades, CA 90212
Actor

Weaver, Jason
c/o Castle Rock Entertainment
335 N. Maple Dr., #135
Beverly Hills, CA 90210
Actor

Whitaker, Forest
c/o David Eideberg,
9301 Wilshire Blvd., #312
Beverly Hills, CA 90212
Actor, director

White, Jaleel
1450 Belfast Dr.
Los Angeles, CA 90069
Actor

Whitfield, Dondre
c/o ABC-TV
320 W. 66th St.
New York, NY 10023
Actor

Williams, Billy Dee
605 N. Oakhurst Dr.
Beverly Hills, CA 90210
Actor

Williams, Hal
c/o David and Goliath
   Productions/Columbia
   Television
500 S. Buena Vista
Burbank, CA 91505
Actor

Williams, Tonya Lee
c/o ABC-TV
157 Columbus Ave.
New York, NY 10023
Actor

Williams, Vanessa
c/o William Morris Agency
151 El Camino Dr.
Beverly Hills, CA 90212
*Actor (not the former Miss
   America!)*

Williams, Vince
c/o D'Arcy, Massius, Benton &
   Bowles Inc.
222 E. 44th St.
New York, NY 10017
Actor

Wilmore, Marc
10201 W. Pico Blvd.
Los Angeles, CA 90035
Actor, comedian

Wilson, Demond
c/o Demond Wilson Ministries
PO Box 30730
Laguna Hills, CA 92654
Actor, minister

Wilson, Flip
21970 Pacific Coast Highway
Malibu, CA 90265
Actor, comedian

Wilson, Marquise
c/o Jeff Franklin Productions
300 S. Lorimar, Bldg. #140
Burbank, CA 91522
Actor

Winfield, Paul
c/o Dale C. Olson and Associates
292 S. La Cienega Blvd.,
   Penthouse Suite
Beverly Hills, CA 90211
Actor

Woodard, Alfre
9301 Wilshire Blvd., #312
Beverly Hills, CA 90210
Actor

**PRODUCERS, DIRECTORS, AND
EXECUTIVES**

Allen, Flo
3400 Riverside Dr., #755
Burbank, CA 91505

Ashurst-Watson, Carmen
c/o Rush Communications
298 Elizabeth St.
New York, NY 10013

Campanella, Roy, Jr.
2049 Century Park, #4100
Los Angeles, CA 90067

Cannon, Reuben
1640 S. Sepulveda Blvd.,
   4th Floor
Los Angeles, CA 90025

Carew, Topper (Colin)
PO Box 93697
Los Angeles, CA 90023

Dash, Julie
2439 Aiduna Dr., #C
Atlanta, GA 30329

dePasse, Suzanne
6255 W. Sunset Blvd.
Los Angeles, CA 90028

Duke, Bill
PO Box 609
Pacific Palisades, CA 90272

Goode, Fritz
6922 Hollywood Blvd., #401
Hollywood, CA 90028

Greene, Dennis
c/o Columbia Studios
10202 W. Washington St.
Culver City, CA 90232

Hankerson, Barry
23460 Hatteras St.
Woodland Hills, CA 91367

Hawkins
30 E. Huron St., #5304
Chicago, IL 60611

Higgensen, Vy
SuperVision Productions
26 W. 71st St.
New York, NY 10023

Hooks, Kevin
2240 Anvil La.
Hillcrest, MD 20031

Hudlin, Reginald
375 Greenwich St., 6th Floor
New York, NY 10013

Hudlin, Warrington
375 Greenwich St., 6th Floor
New York, NY 10013

Hughes, Albert
c/o William Morris Agency
151 El Camino Dr.
Beverly Hills, CA 90212

Hughes, Allen
c/o William Morris Agency
151 El Camino Dr.
Beverly Hills, CA 90212

Lane, Charles
c/o William Morris Agency
151 El Camino Dr.
Beverly Hills, CA 90212

Lawson, Jennifer
1320 Braddock Pl.
Alexandria, VA 22314

Lee, Spike
c/o 40 Acres and a Mule
  Filmworks
124 DeKalb Ave.
Brooklyn, NY 11217

Martin, Darnell
201 E. 12th St., #504
New York, NY 10003

Martin, Lionel
c/o Classic Concepts
444 W. 35th St.
New York, NY 10001

McDaniels, Ralph
c/o Classic Concepts
444 W. 35th St.
New York, NY 10001

Muse, Melvin J.
3600 Wilshire Blvd., #832
Los Angeles, CA 90010

Parkes, Gordon
c/o Doubleday
1540 Broadway
New York, NY 10036

Rich, Matty
c/o William Morris Agency
151 El Camino Dr.
Beverly Hills, CA 90212

Ross, Monty
8 St. Felix St.
Brooklyn, NY 11217

Scultz, Michael
Crystalite Productions
PO Box 1940
Santa Monica, CA 90406

Singleton, John
c/o Bradford W. Smith
Creative Arts Agency Inc.
188 Century Park E, #1400
Los Angeles, CA 90067

Townsend, Robert
8033 Sunset Blvd., #890
Los Angeles, CA 90069

PRODUCTION COMPANIES AND MANAGEMENT FIRMS

Arsenio Hall Communications
5555 Melrose Ave.
Hollywood, CA 90038
213/956-5688

Bethann Management
3 N. Moore St.
New York, NY 10013
212/925-2153

Bil-Mar Productions
4311 Wilshire Blvd., #314
Los Angeles, CA 90010
213/930-1907

Blackbird Productions
3518 Cahuenga Blvd. W., #316
Los Angeles, CA 90068
213/850-9947

Block and Chip Inc.
353 W. 56th St., #10F
New York, NY 10019
212/489-6570

Carrie Productions
3900 West Alameda Ave., #1700
Burbank, CA 91505
818/972-1747

Classic Concepts
444 W. 35th St.
New York, NY 10001
212/268-3849

Communications Bridge Institute
1968 W. Adams Blvd.
Los Angeles, CA 90018
213/766-9815

Don Cornelius Productions
9255 Sunset Blvd.
Los Angeles, CA 90069
213/858-8232

Drop Squad Pictures
594 Broadway, #405
New York, NY 10012
212/925-9308

DS Productions Inc.
1579F Monroe Drive, #337
Atlanta, GA 30324
404/876-6186

Eddie Murphy Productions Inc.
5555 Melrose, Demille, #200
Hollywood, CA 90038
213/956-4545

Enleyetening Concepts Inc.
1223 Wilshire Blvd., #141
Santa Monica, CA 90403
213/821-4677

**Forty Acres and a Mule
Filmworks Inc.**
124 DeKalb Ave.
Brooklyn, NY 11217
718/624-3703

Future Agency
4311 Wilshire Blvd., #314
Los Angeles, CA 90010
310/338-9602

Gordy dePasse Productions
6255 Sunset Blvd.
Los Angeles, CA 90028-7497
213/965-2580

Harambee Productions
PO Box 25578
Newark, NJ 07101
201/642-0132

Harpo Productions
110 N. Carpenter St.
Chicago, IL 60607
312/633-0808

Hudlin Brothers
375 Greenwich St.
New York, NY 10013
212/941-4004

Ivory Way Productions
5746 Sunset Blvd.
Los Angeles, CA 90028

Juice
3600 Wilshire Blvd., #832
Los Angeles, CA 90010
213/384-9811

Lenox-Greene Films
Columbia Studios
10202 W. Washington Blvd.
Culver City, CA 90232
213/280-8239

Logo Entertainment
11601 Wilshire Blvd., 21st Floor
Los Angeles, CA 90025

Longridge
1520 Ventura Blvd., #800
Sherman Oaks, CA 91403
818/783-6251

Masai Films
6922 Hollywood Blvd., #401
Hollywood, CA 90028
213/466-5451

Mecca Motion Picture Company
2980 Cobb Pkwy., #19218
Atlanta, GA 30339
404/808-7139

Midwest Group Inc.
23460 Hatteras Ave.
Woodland Hills, CA 91367
818/704-5568

Mundy Lane Productions
3400 Riverside Dr., #755
Burbank, CA 91505
818/972-8771

900 Frame
10 E. 46th St., #3C
New York, NY 10017
212/661-6599

On the Potomac Productions Inc.
1221 11th St. NW
Washington, DC 20001
202/898-0899

Paradise Group Video Products
1737 S. Michigan Ave.
Chicago, IL 60616
312/427-4011

Quiet Fury Video
PO Box 349
Petersburg, VA 23803

Reuben Cannon Productions
1640 S. Sepulveda Blvd., 4th
  Floor
Los Angeles, CA 90025
213/575-1257

Studio II Productions
2025 74th Ave.
Philadelphia, PA 19138
215/548-5894

Tinsel Townsend
8033 Sunset Blvd., #890
Los Angeles, CA 90046
213/962-2240

Tribune Central City Productions
1 E. Erie St., #540
Chicago, IL 60611
312/664-5900

Underdog Films
1396 S. Orange Dr.
Los Angeles, CA 90019
213/936-3111

United Image Entertainment
990 San Vincente Blvd., #310
Beverly Hills, CA 90212
213/274-7253

Warner Management
130 The Colony
Hartsdale, NY 10530
914/683-8525

Whoop Inc.
5555 Melrose Ave.
Wilder Building, #114
Hollywood, CA 90038
213/956-5673

Yaga Productions
PO Box 609
Pacific Palisades, CA 90272
213/454-3643

Yeah Inc.
353 W. 56th St., #10F
New York, NY 10019
212/489-6570

FILM ORGANIZATIONS

Black American Cinema Society
3617 Montclair St.
Los Angeles, CA 90018
213/737-3585

Black Filmmaker Foundation
Tribeca Film Center
375 Greenwich St.
New York, NY 10013
212/941-3944

Black Filmmakers Hall of Fame
405 14th St., #515
Oakland, CA 94612
510/465-0804

Black Stuntmen's Association
8949 W. 24th St.
Los Angeles, CA 90034
213/870-9020

PLAYWRIGHTS, DIRECTORS, AND EXECUTIVES

Carroll, Vinnette
431 N.E. 5th Ave.
Ft. Lauderdale, FL 33301

Franklin, J. E.
2900 Van Ness St. NW
Washington, DC 20008

Fuller, Charles
c/o William Morris Agency
1350 Avenue of the Americas
New York, NY 10036

Graham, Charles E.
c/o Bobbs-Merrill Co.
4300 W. 62nd St.
Indianapolis, IN 46268

Merchant, Darryl
90 E. Huron St., #5304
Chicago, IL 60611

Shange, Ntozake
c/o Alan Walker Program
599 W. Hartsdale Ave.
White Plains, NY 10607

Shrine, Ted
c/o Prairie View A&M University
Prairie View, TX 77446

Ward, Douglas Turner
222 E. 11th St.
New York, NY 10003

Williams, Kimmika
c/o Writer in Residence
Bushfire Theatre
52nd and Locust St.
Philadelphia, PA 19139

Williams, Lee R.
c/o Chasman and Associates
6725 Sunset Blvd., #506
Hollywood, CA 90028

Wilson, August
c/o Joanie Phillippi
553 11th Ave. S
Minneapolis, MN 55417

Wolfe, George C.
c/o Joseph Papp Theatre
425 Lafayette St.
New York, NY 10003

THEATERS AND THEATRICAL COMPANIES

African American Drama Company of California
394 5th Ave.
San Francisco, CA 94118
415/386-2832

Afro-American Studio Theater
17138 Hickory
Detroit, MI 48205
313/527-0277

Alonzo Players
317 Clermont Ave.
Brooklyn, NY 11205
718/622-5062

Apollo Foundation Theater
253 125th St.
New York, NY 10027
212/222-0992

Avante Theater Co.
Manheim and Pulaski St.
Philadelphia, PA 19144
215/848-9099

Billie Holiday Theater
1368 Fulton St.
Brooklyn, NY 11216
718/636-0919

Black American Cinema Society
3617 Montclair Street
Los Angeles, CA 90018
213/737-3585

Black Experience Ensemble
5 Homestead Ave.
Albany, NY 12203
518/482-6683

Black Experimental Theater
47 McKeever Pl., #6H
Brooklyn, NY 11225
718/735-4290

Black N' Blue
PO Box 6709
Portland, OR 97228-6709

Black Repertory Group
3201 Adeline St.
Berkeley, CA 94703
510/652-2120

Black Spectrum Theater Co.
119 Roy Wilkins Park
Jamaica, NY 11434
718/723-1800

Black Theater Alliance of Chicago
7558 S. Chicago Ave.
Chicago, IL 60619
312/288-5100

Black Theater Troupe
333 E. Portland St.
Phoenix, AZ 85004
602/258-8128

Black Theatre Network
Fisher Bldg. Station
PO Box 11502
Detroit, MI 48211
714/880-5892

Chicago City Theater Company
Joel Hall Dancers
3340 N. Clark Street
Chicago, IL 60657
312/880-1002

Crossroads Theater Co.
320 Memorial Pkwy.
New Brunswick, NJ 08901
201/249-5561

Eden Theatrical Workshop
1570 Gilpin St.
Denver, CO 80218
303/321-2320

Emmy Gifford Children's Theater
3504 Center St.
Omaha, NE 68105
402/345-4849

**Harmonie Park Playhouse and
Actor's Lab**
279 E. Grand River
Detroit, MI 48226
313/965-2480

**Henry Street Settlement New
Federal Theater**
Arts for Living Center
466 Grand St.
New York, NY 10002
212/598-0400

Jomandi Productions
1444 Maysen St. SE
Atlanta, GA 30324
404/876-6346

Jubilee Players
3114 E. Rosedale
Fort Worth, TX 76105
817/926-8017

Just Us Theater
187 Edgewood Ave. SE
Atlanta, GA 30303
404/876-2350

**Marla Gibbs Crossroads National
Education Arts and Theatre**
4310 Degnan Blvd.
Los Angeles, CA 90008
213/291-7321

**McCree Theater and Performing
Arts Center**
115 E. Pierson Rd.
Flint, MI 48505
313/785-3475

National Black Theatre
9 E. 125th St.
New York, NY 10035
212/427-5615

Negro Ensemble Co.
165 W. 46th St.
New York, NY 10036
212/575-5860

New Freedom Theater
1346 N. Broad St.
Philadelphia, PA 19121
215/765-2793

New Muse Community of Brooklyn
1530 Bedford Ave.
Brooklyn, NY 11216
718/774-2900

**North Carolina Black Repertory
Company**
610 Coliseum Dr.
Winston-Salem, NC 27106
919/723-7907

Oakland Ensemble Theater
1428 Alice St.
Oakland, CA 94612
510/763-7774

Odadaa!
2809 Boswell Ave.
Alexandria, VA 22306
703/768-4839

Passmart: A Theatre Company
PO Box 8582
Portland, OR 97207
503/284-4455

Pin Points Traveling Theater
4353 DuBois Pl. SE
Washington, DC 20019
202/582-0002

Rites and Reason
Brown University
PO Box 1148
Providence, RI 02912
401/863-3558

St. Louis Black Repertory Co.
2240 St. Louis Ave.
St. Louis, MO 63106
314/231-3706

Sojourner Truth Players
PO Box 17209
Fort Worth, TX 76102
817/332-2504

Theater North
PO Box 6255
Tulsa, OK 74148
918/587-8937

Ujima Youth Theater
4417 Redick Ave.
Omaha, NE 68112
402/455-0910

THEATRICAL ORGANIZATIONS

African American Women on Tour
PO Box 15819
San Diego, CA 92175
619/560-2770

Alliance of Black Community Theaters
3936 Magazine St.
New Orleans, LA 70115
504/897-0411

Audience Development Committee
PO Box 30
Manhattanville Station
New York, NY 10027
212/368-6906

AUTHORS AND PUBLISHERS

WRITERS

Alers, Rochelle
c/o Pinnacle Books
475 Park Ave. S
New York, NY 10016

Ali, Shahrazad
2019 S. 7th St.
Philadelphia, PA 19148
Author, publisher

Allen, Samuel W.
145 Cliff Ave.
Winthrop, MA 02152
Poet

Andrew, Raymond
c/o Susan Anne Protter
110 W. 40th St., #1408
New York, NY 10018
Children's book author

Angelou, Maya
3240 Valley Rd.
Winston-Salem, NC 27106
*Author, poet, screenwriter,
   director, educator*

Ansa, Tina McElroy
c/o Harcourt Brace & Company
525 "B" St., Suite 1900
San Diego, CA 92101
Novelist

Asante, Molefi Kete
707 Medary Ave.
Philadelphia, PA 19126
Author, educator

Atkins, Russell
6005 Grand Ave.
Cleveland, OH 44104
Author

Austin, Doris Jean
448 State St.
Brooklyn, NY 11217
Novelist

Bambera, Toni Cade
5720 Wissahickon Ave.
Philadelphia, PA 19144
Short fiction author

Baraka, Amiri
c/o Sterling Lord Literary Agency
1 Madison Ave., 2nd Floor
New York, NY 10010
Poet, author

117

Barrax, Gerald
808 Cooper Rd.
Raleigh, NC 27610
Author

Bell-Mathis, Sharon
c/o Curtis Brown Ltd.
10 Astor Pl.
New York, NY 10003
Young adult author

Birtha, Becky
5116 Cedar Ave.
Philadelphia, PA 19143
Author

Bogus, Diane
PO Box 137
San Francisco, CA 94114
Poet

Boyd, Julia A.
c/o Dutton Publishers
375 Hudson St.
New York, NY 10014
Author

Bradley, David
c/o Wendy Weil
232 Madison Ave.
New York, NY 10016
Author

Briscoe, Connie
c/o HarperCollins
10 E. 53rd St.
New York, NY 10022
Author

Brooks, Gwendolyn
The Contemporary Forum
2528A W. Jerome St.
Chicago, IL 60640
Poet, author

Brown, Claude
c/o New American Library
375 Hudson St.
New York, NY 10014
Author

Brown, Les
Les Brown Unlimited, Inc.
2180 Penobscot Bldg.
Detroit, MI 48226
*Author, motivational speaker,
    former talk show host*

Brown, Sterling
1222 Kearney St. NE
Washington, DC 20017
Poet, author

Butler, Octavia
c/o Freelance Writers Group
PO Box 6604
Los Angeles, CA 90055
Science fiction novelist

Campbell, Bebe Moore
c/o Janklow & Nesbit Associates
598 Madison Ave.
New York, NY 10036
Novelist, journalist

Chambers, Ruth
PO Box 2991
Sacramento, CA 95812
Author

Cleage, Pearl
c/o The Cleage Group
Evergreen Plaza, #326
Southfield, MI 48076
Author

Clifton, Lucille
Distinguished Professor of
    Humanities
St. Mary's College of Maryland
St. Mary's City, MD 20686
Children's book author

Coleman, Wanda
PO Box 29154
Los Angeles, CA 90029
Author

Cooper, J. California
c/o Doubleday
1540 Broadway
New York, NY 10036
Author

Copage, Eric
c/o William Morrow & Co.
1350 Avenue of the Americas
New York, NY 10019
Author

Corbin, Steven
4358 Melbourne Ave.
Los Angeles, CA 90027
Author

Danner, Margaret
626 E. 102nd Pl.
Chicago, IL 60628
Poet

Davis, George
Department of English
Rutgers University
New Brunswick, NJ 08903
Author

Davis, Dr. Larry E.
c/o Noble Press
213 Institute Pl., #508
Chicago, IL 60610
Author

Delaney, A. Elizabeth
c/o Kodansha Publishers
114 5th Ave.
New York, NY 10011
Author

Delaney, Samuel
University of Massachusetts
South College Building
Amherst, MA 01003
Science fiction author

Delaney, Sara
c/o Kodansha Publishers
114 5th Ave.
New York, NY 10011
Author

Demby, William
PO Box 363
Sag Harbor, NY 11963
Author

De Veaux, Alexis
135 Eastern Parkway, #8K
Brooklyn, NY 11238
Author

Diallo
2855 Tremont Pl.
Denver, CO 80205
Poet

Dixon, Melvin
English Department
Queens College
65-30 Kissena Blvd.
Flushing, NY 11367
Author

do Nascimento, Abidias
7822 S. Dobson Ave.
Chicago, IL 60619
Author, poet

Dove, Rita
University of Virginia
Department of English
Wilson Hall
Charlottesville, VA 22903
Poet

Evans, Mari
PO Box 483
Indianapolis, IN 46206
Author

Fair, Ronald
c/o Herbert Fair
201 W. 92nd St.
Chicago, IL 60620
Author

Flournoy, Valerie
505 Arch St.
Palmyra, NJ 08065
Author

Fortson, Elinora
5208 N. Broad St.
Philadelphia, PA 19141
Poet

Gaines, Ernest
932 Divisadero St.
San Francisco, CA 94115
Novelist

Garnett, Ruth
7822 S. Dobson Ave.
Chicago, IL 60619
Author

Gilmore, Brian
7822 S. Dobson Ave.
Chicago, IL 60619
Poet

Giovanni, Nikki
c/o William Morrow and
   Company
1350 Avenue of the Americas
New York, NY 10019
Poet

Graham, Lorenz Bell
1400 Niagara Ave.
Claremont, CA 91711
Children's author

Greenlee, Sam
6123 Eberhart, #2
Chicago, IL 60637
Children's book author

Guy, Rosa
c/o Ellen Levine Literary Agency
432 Park Ave. South
New York, NY 10016
Author

Hall, Bennett
c/o William Morris Agency Inc.
1350 Avenue of the Americas
New York, NY 10019
Author

Holland-Anderson, Mignon
7822 S. Dobson Ave.
Chicago, IL 60619
Author

Hull, Gloria T.
University of Delaware
Department of English
Newark, DE 19716
Author

Hunt, Terry
c/o Odyssey Books
9501 Monroe St.
Silver Spring, MD 20910
Romance author

Hunter, Kristin
English Department
University of Pennsylvania
119 Bennett, #D1
Philadelphia, PA 19104
Author, educator

Jenkins, Frank Shockley
PO Box 36012
Los Angeles, CA 90036
Poet

Johnson, Charles
Department of English
GN-30
University of Washington
Seattle, WA 08195
Novelist

Jones, Edward
American Ethnic Studies
    Department
University of Washington
3931 Brooklyn Ave. NE
Seattle, WA 90195
Author, educator

Jordan, June
English Department
SUNY Stony Brook
Stony Brook, NY 11794
Novelist

Jordan, Shirley M.
Department of English
Hampton University
Hampton, VA 23668
Author

Kelley, William Melvin
c/o The Wisdom Shop
PO Box 2658
New York, NY 10027
Author

Kenan, Randall G.
Sarah Lawrence College
Bronxville, NY 10708
Author, educator

Kent, Sandra
c/o Zebra Books
475 Park Ave. South
New York, NY 10016
Romance novelist

Kimbro, Dennis
3806 Brandeis Court
Decatur, GA 30034
Author, educator

Kimbrough, Marjorie L.
4340 Pompay Dr. SW
Atlanta, GA 30331
Author

Kincaid, Jamaica
c/o Farrar, Straus and Giroux
19 Union Square W
New York, NY 10003
Author

King, Anita
10 E. 138 St., #8E
New York, NY 10037
Author

Knight, Etheridge
3323 W. 33 Pl., #4
Indianapolis, IN 46222
Novelist

Lane, Pinkie Gordan
2738 77th Ave.
Baton Rouge, LA 70807
Poet, anthologist

Lester, Julius
PO Box 333
N. Amherst, MA 01059-0333
Novelist

Lewis, James
EIC/NE2 Babcock Pl.
West Orange, NJ 07052
Author

Madgett, Naomi L.
16886 Inverness St.
Detroit, MI 48221
Poet, professor, publisher, editor

Madhubuti, Haki R.
(Formerly known as Don Lee)
PO Box 730
Chicago, IL 60619
Author, poet, publisher

Mahiri, Jabari
7822 S. Dobson Ave.
Chicago, IL 60619
Children's book author

Major, Clarence
Professor of English
University of California at Davis
Davis, CA 95616
Author, educator

Majozo, Estella C.
7822 S. Dobson Ave.
Chicago, IL 60619
Children's book author

Marshall, Paule
407 Central Park West, #4C
New York, NY 10025
Novelist

Mathabane, Mark
c/o Kevin McShane
Fifi Oscard Agency
24 W. 40th St.
New York, NY 10018
Author, lecturer

McCluskey, John A.
35270 Roxbury Circle
Bloomington, IN 47401
Author

McKnight, Reginald
Department of English
Carnegie-Mellon University
Baker Hall
Pittsburgh, PA 15213
Author, educator

McLaughlin, Andrea
Professor of Humanities
Medgar-Evers College
1650 Bedford Ave.
Brooklyn, NY 11225
Poet, educator

McMillan, Terry
c/o Molly Friedrich
Aaron Priest Literary Agency
122 E. 42nd St., #3902
New York, NY 10168
Novelist

McPhearson, James
Professor of English
University of Iowa
430 English/Philosophy Bldg.
Iowa City, IA 52240
Author, educator

Merriweather, Louise
c/o Bikouta
392 Central Park West, #1C
New York, NY 10025
Author

Millard, Gregory
7822 S. Dobson Ave.
Chicago, IL 60619
Author

Miller, Ethelbert E.
Howard University
PO Box 746
Washington, DC 20059
Author, educator

Miller, Jeanne-Marie A.
Professor of English
Howard University
2400 6th St. NW
Washington, DC 20059
Author, educator

Miller, Ronald
15865 Montevista St.
Detroit, MI 48238
Author

Morrison, Toni
c/o Janklow & Nesbit Associates
598 Madison Ave.
New York, NY 10022
Novelist, educator

Moseley, Walter
c/o W. W. Norton and Co.
500 5th Ave.
New York, NY 10110
Mystery novelist

Murphy, Beatrice M.
3645 Barra Ave., #200
Titusville, FL 32780
Poet, author, editor

Murray, Albert
42 W. 137th St.
New York, NY 10037
Author

Mwadilifu, Mwalimu Imara
(also known as Dr. E. Curtis
  Alexander)
PO Box 15004
Chesapeake, VA 23320
Author, educator, publisher

Myers, Walter Dean
2543 Kennedy Blvd.
Jersey City, NJ 07304
Young adult author

Naylor, Gloria
c/o Houghton Mifflin
215 Park Ave. South
New York, NY 10017
Novelist

Okantan, Mwatabu
319 Indiana St., 2nd Floor
Union, NJ 07083
Poet

Patterson, Lindsay
c/o Denise Stinson
8120 E. Jefferson Ave. #6H
Detroit, MI 48214
Author

Perkins, Useni
7822 S. Dobson Ave.
Chicago, IL 60619
Children's book author

Perry, Elaine
c/o Farrar, Straus & Giroux, Inc.
19 Union Squre W
New York, NY 10003
Novelist

Pharr, Robert
c/o Doubleday
1540 Broadway
New York, NY 10036
Novelist

Plump, Sterling
1401 E. 55th St., #816-N
Chicago, IL 60615
Poet

Randall, Dudley
12651 Old Mill Pl.
Detroit, MI 48238
Poet

Redding, Jay
Department of English
Cornell University
Ithaca, NY 14853
Essayist, critic

Redmond, Eugene
3700 Kings Way, #2
Sacramento, CA 95821
Poet

Reed, Ishmael
1446 6th St., #D
Berkeley, CA 94710
Novelist

Sanchez, Sonia
Temple University
English Department
Philadelphia, PA 19122
Poet, educator

Sanders, Dori
c/o Algonquin Books of Chapel
  Hill
PO Box 2225
Chapel Hill, NC 27515
Author, farmer

Santiago, Roberto
PO Box 6617
New York, NY 10128
Author

Scott, John Sherman
Ethnic Studies and Resident
  Writer
Bowling Green State University
Shatel Hall
Bowling Green, OH 43402

Sharp, Saundra
PO Box 75796
Sanford Station
Los Angeles, CA 90075
Author

Shockley, Ann
1809 Morena St., #G-4
Nashville, TN 37208
Novelist

Simms, Darrell
PO Box 5729
Beaverton, OR 97006
Author

Sinclair, April
c/o Hyperion
114 5th Ave.
New York, NY 10011
Novelist

Smith, Barbara
PO Box 908
Latham, NY 12110
Author

Snoe, Eboni
c/o Zebra Books
475 Park Ave. South
New York, NY 10016
Romance novelist

Somé, Malidoma Patrice
c/o Jeremy P. Tarcher, Inc.
5858 Wilshire Blvd.
Los Angeles, CA 90036
Author, Dagara shaman

Southerland, Ellease
Department of English
Pace University
1 Pace Plaza
New York, NY 10038
Author, educator

Southern, Eileen
115-05 179th St.
St. Albans, NY 11434
Author

Soyinka, Wole
c/o Brandt and Brandt Literary
  Agency
1501 Broadway
New York, NY 10036
Author

Spellman, A. B.
c/o Morehouse College
223 Chestnut St. SW
Atlanta, GA 30314
Poet

Steptoe, John
840 Monroe St.
Brooklyn, NY 11221
Children's book author

Thomas, Joyce Carol
c/o Mitch Douglas
ICM
40 W. 57th St.
New York, NY 10019

Thurman, Ralph Cheo
7822 S. Dobson Ave.
Chicago, IL 60619
Author

Van Dyke, Henry
40 Waterside Plaza
New York, NY 10010
Novelist

Vanzant, Iyanla
c/o Simon & Schuster
1230 Avenue of the Americas
New York, NY 10020
Author, Yoruba priestess

Walker, Alice
c/o Julian Bach
Wendy Weil Agency, Inc.
232 Madison Ave., #1300
New York, NY 10016
Novelist

Walker, Margaret
Department of English
State College of Mississippi
Jackson, MS 39217
Author, educator

Waniek, Marilyn N.
English Department, #U-25
University of Connecticut
Storrs, CT 06268
Novelist, educator

Welburn, Ron
PO Box 692
Guilderland, NY 12084
Novelist

Wesley, Richard Errol
PO Box 43091
Upper Montclair, NJ 07043
Author

Wideman, John Edgar
Department of English
University of Massachusetts at
    Amherst Campus
Barlett Hall
Amherst, MA 01003
Author, educator

Wilkinson, Brenda
c/o Board of Global Ministries
5 Riverside Dr.
New York, NY 10115
Young-adult book author

Williams, John Alfred
Department of English
Rutgers University of Newark
360 Martin Luther King Jr. Blvd.
Newark, NJ 07102
Author, educator

Williams, Sherley Anne
Department of Literature
University of California
La Jolla, CA 92093
Novelist, educator

Williams, Walter E.
Economics Department
George Mason University
4400 University Dr.
Fairfax, VA 22030
Author

Wilson-Harris, Crystal
c/o Odyssey Books
9501 Monroe St.
Silver Spring, MD 20910
Romance novelist

Wolcott, Derek
Department of English
Boston University
236 Bay State Rd.
Boston, MA 02215

Woods, Alfred
7822 S. Dobson Ave.
Chicago, IL 60619
Author

Wright, Charles S.
138 6th Ave.
Brooklyn, NY 11217
Author

Wright, Sarah
c/o Roberta Pryor Inc.
24 W. 55th St.
New York, NY 10019
Novelist

Young, Albert James
514 Bryant St.
Palo Alto, CA 94301
Author

LITERARY AGENTS

Brown, Marie
Marie Brown Associates
625 Broadway
New York, NY 10012
212/533-5534

Childs, Faith
Faith Childs Literary Agency
275 W. 96th St.
New York, NY 10025
212/662-1232

Cohen, Rob
c/o Richard Curtis Literary
   Agency
17 E. 74 St.
New York, NY 10021

Connor, Marilyn
The Connor Agency
640 W. 153rd St.
New York, NY 10031
212/491-5233

Jordan, Lawrence
Lawrence Jordan Literary Agency
250 W. 57th St. #1527
New York, NY 10107
212/690-2748

Stinson, Denise
Stinson Literary Agency
8120 E. Jefferson Ave. #6H
Detroit, MI 48214
313/331-6504

WRITING AND PUBLISHING ORGANIZATIONS

African American Writer's Guild
PO Box 43874
Columbia Heights Station
Washington, DC 20010
202/722-2760

African Literature Association
Cornell University
Africana Studies and Research
310 Triphammer Rd.
Ithaca, NY 14850
607/255-0534

**American Black Writer's
   Association**
PO Box 10548
Marina Del Ray, CA 90295
213/822-5195

Black Women in Publishing Inc.
PO Box 6275
FDR Station
New York, NY 10150
212/772-5951

International Black Writers and Artists
PO Box 43576
Los Angeles, CA 90043
213/964-3721

International Black Writers Conference
PO Box 1030
Chicago, IL 60690
312/924-3818

Pan-African Booksellers, Authors and Publishers Association
51 Court St.
White Plains, NY 10603

Union of Writers of the African Peoples
University of Colorado at Boulder
Campus PO Box 339
Boulder, CO 80309-0039
303/492-7852

LITERARY CULTURE CENTERS

Afrikan Poetry Theater
176-03 Jamaica Ave.
Jamaica, NY 11423
718/523-3312

Black Periodical Literature Project
77 Dunster St.
Cambridge, MA 02138
617/496-7404

Center for Southern Folklore Archives
1216 Peabody Ave.
PO Box 40105
Memphis, TN 38104
901/726-4205

Ashley Publishing Company Inc.
4600 W. Commercial Blvd.
Fort Lauderdale, FL 33319
305/739-2221

Bayside To-Go
401 Biscayne Blvd., #P107
Miami, FL 33132
305/374-5935

Black Classic Press
PO Box 13414
Baltimore, MD 21203

Black Registry Publishing Company
1223 Rosewood Ave.
Austin, TX 78702
512/476-0082

Blind Beggar Press/Lamplight Editions
PO Box 437
Bronx, NY 10467
914/683-6792

Broadside Press
PO Box 04257
Detroit, MI 48207
313/934-1231

BOOK PUBLISHERS, EDITORS, AND INDUSTRY PROFESSIONALS

Afram Publishing
PO Box 2262
Philadelphia, PA 19101
609/871-6992

Africa Fund Publishing
198 Broadway, 4th Floor
New York, NY 10038
212/962-1210

Africa World Press
PO Box 1892
Trenton, NJ 08607
609/771-1666

Africana Publishing
30 Irving Pl.
New York, NY 10003
212/254-4100

Afro-Am Publishing Company Inc.
407 E. 25th St., #600
Chicago, IL 60616
312/791-1611

Amistad
1271 Avenue of the Americas
New York, NY 10020

Center for Afro-American Studies Publications
405 Hilgard Ave.
Los Angeles, CA 90024-1545
310/825-3528

Charhill Publishers
4468 San Francisco Ave.
PO Box 150124
St. Louis, MO 63115
314/382-4998

Civilized Publications
2023 S. 7th St.
Philadelphia, PA 19148
215/339-0449

Creative Press Works
PO Box 280556
Memphis, TN 38168-0556
901/382-8246

Disa Press
PO Box 9284
Wilmington, DE 19809
302/475-4509

Ducksworth, Marilyn
Executive Director, Publicity
G. P. Putnam's Sons
200 Madison Ave.
New York, NY 10016
212/951-8400

Duncan and Duncan Publishers
2809 Pulaski Highway
Edge Wood, MD 21040
410/538-5759

ECA Associates
PO Box 15004
Chesapeake, VA 23328-5004
800/547-5542

El-Hajj Malik Shabazz Press
455 Par Rd. NW
Washington, DC 20010
202/726-3559

Escher Publications
PO Box 1196
Waynesboro, VA 22980
703/942-2171

For Our Children
Department E
217 E. 85th St., #184
New York, NY 10028

Grinnell Fine Art Collections
800 Riverside Dr., #5E
New York, NY 10032
212/927-7941

Gumbs and Thomas Publishers
142 W. 72nd St., #9
New York, NY 10023

Howard University Press
1240 Randolph St. NE
Washington, DC 20008
202/806-4935

Juju Publishing Company Inc.
1310 Harden St.
Columbia, SC 22902
803/799-5252

Just Us Books
301 Main St., #2224
Orange, NJ 07050
201/672-7701

Kawaida Publications
2560 W. 54th St.
Los Angeles, CA 90043

Kitchen Table: Women of Color Press
PO Box 908
Latham, NY 12101
518/434-2057

Leading Edge Publishing Co.
16094 Meadow Oak Dr.
St. Louis, MO 63114
314/532-2234

Lotus Press
PO Box 21607
Detroit, MI 48221
313/861-1280

Love Child Publishing
6565 Sunset Blvd., #318
North Hollywood, CA 91601
213/960-5490

MacDonald, Errol
Pantheon Books
201 E. 50th St.
New York, NY 10022
212/572-2564

The Majority Press
PO Box 538
Dover, MA 02030
508/655-5636

Marcus Garvey Publishing Company
1 World Trade Center, #8817
New York, NY 10048

Marlock Publishing Company
PO Box 160
Columbia, MD 21045

Middle Passage Press
5517 Seacrest Dr.
Los Angeles, CA 90043
213/298-0266

The Noble Press, Inc.
213 Institute Pl., #508
Chicago, IL 60610
312/642-1168

One World
Ballantine Books
201 E. 50th St.
New York, NY 10022
212/940-7742

Path Press
53 W. Jackson Blvd., #724
Chicago, IL 60604
312/663-0167

R & M Publishing Company
PO Box 1276
Holly Hill, SC 29059
804/732-4094

Red Sea Press
15 Industry St.
Trenton, NJ 08638
609/771-1666

Renaissance Publications
1515 5th Ave.
Pittsburgh, PA 15219
412/391-9208

Sabayat Publication Inc.
PO Box 648-98
Chicago, IL 60664-0898
312/667-2227

Sage Women's Educational Press
PO Box 42741
Atlanta, GA 30311
404/223-8383

Struggler's Community Press
PO Box 9
Piney Woods, MS 39148
312/776-6400

Sundance Books
1520 N. Crescent Heights
Hollywood, CA 90046
213/654-2383

Sunlight Books
c/o Frank A. Woods
218 Wainberg Arcade
S. Prairie Street
Galesburg, IL 61401
309/342-6155

Syan Publications
PO Box 90168
Pasadena, CA 91103
818/791-9758

Techniplus Publishing Company
887 S. Lucerne Blvd., #4
Los Angeles, CA 90005
213/934-3001

Temple University Press
University Service Building
Broad and Oxford St.
Philadelphia, PA 19122
800/447-1656

Third Women Press
BH 849 Indiana University
Bloomington, IN 47405
812/335-5257

Third World Press
7524 S. Cottage Grove Ave.
Chicago, IL 60619
312/651-0700

Tree Holdings
7427 Dexter St.
Detroit, MI 48206
404/894-8284

Tucker Publications
5823 Queen Cove
Lisle, IL 60523

Urban Research Press Inc.
840 E. 87th St.
Chicago, IL 60619
312/994-7200

Vincom Inc.
PO Box 702400
Tulsa, OK 74170
918/254-1276

Wild Trees Press
PO Box 378
Navarro, CA 95463

Winston-Derek Publishers
1722 W. End Ave.
Nashville, TN 37203

Writers and Readers Publications
625 Broadway, 10th Floor
New York, NY 10012
212/982-3158

Yah Yah and Company
PO Box 55318
Trenton, NJ 08638
609/695-4244

BOOKSTORES

A & B Books
149 Lawrence St.
Brooklyn, NY 11201
718/596-3389

Abdul's Afrikan Arts
3958 Salem Ave.
Dayton, OH 45406
513/277-6010

About Black Children
4509 S. King Dr.
Chicago, IL 60653
312/285-4568

Adhiamobo Bookstore
703 Hooker St.
Jackson, MS 39204
601/948-5114

Adventures in Reading
1525 E. 53rd St., #901
Chicago, IL 60615
312/753-9313

Africa Books
515½ Northwood Rd.
West Palm Beach, FL 33407

Africa House
283 Lenox Ave.
New York, NY 10027

African American Book Centers
7524 S. Cottage Grove
Chicago, IL 60653
312/651-9101

African American Book Store
PO Box 851
Boston, MA 02120
617/445-9209

African American Bookstore
1801 E. 71st St.
Chicago, IL 60649
312/752-2275

African American Pride Gift Shop
1262 Estelle St.
Bossier City, LA 71112

African American Reflections
13086 Fairway Park
San Antonio, TX 78217
512/657-2376

African Artisan and Company
169 Baldwin Rd.
Hempstead, NY 11550
516/385-5642

African Bookshelf and Gift Shop
13240 Euclid Ave.
East Cleveland, OH 44112

African Caribbean Bookstore
8516 S. Throop
Chicago, IL 60620

African Connections
463 S. Bascom Ave.
San Jose, CA 95128
408/279-3342

African Culture
1356 W. North
Baltimore, MD 21217
410/728-0877

African Eye
2134 Wisconsin Ave. NW
Washington, DC 20007
202/625-2552

African Imprint Library Services
410 W. Falmouth Highway
PO Box 350
West Falmouth, VA 02574
508/540-5378

African Marketplace
2560 W. 54th St.
Los Angeles, CA 90043

Afro-Am Inc.
819 S. Wabash Ave., #610
Chicago, IL 60605
312/791-1611

Afro-American Book Distributor
2537 Prospect
Houston, TX 77004

Afro-American Book Source
70 Bookledge St.
Boston, MA 02121

Afrocentric Bookstore
234 S. Wabash Ave.
Chicago, IL 60604
312/939-1956

Afro-In Books N' Things
5575 N.W. 7th Ave.
Miami, FL 33127
305/756-6107

Akbar's Books and Things
8816 Manchester Rd., #117
St. Louis, MO 63144
314/962-0244

Alexander Book Company
50 2nd St.
San Francisco, CA 94105
415/495-2992

Alkebu Lan Arts
15734 W. Seven Mile Rd.
Detroit, MI 48235
313/836-8686

All African People's Books
PO Box 4036
Newark, NJ 07114

Alley Books
526 Pacific Ave., #2107
Atlantic City, NJ 08401
609/344-6754

Amatullah Books
22 Arthur St.
New Haven, CT 06519

Amen Ra & Isis Associates
260-2 W. 125th St.
New York, NY 10027
212/316-3680

Amistad Book Place
1413 Holman St.
Houston, TX 77004
713/528-3561

Anderson Bookstore
96-98 Chatsworth Ave.
Larchmont, NY 10538
914/834-6900

Aqua Books
275 Sequoyah View Dr.
Oakland, CA 94605
510/638-2857

Aquarian Bookshop
1302-42 W. Martin Luther King
 Jr. Blvd.
Los Angeles, CA 90037-1230
213/296-1633

Aradia Bookstore
116 W. Cottage St.
Flagstaff, AZ 86002
602/779-3817

Arawak Books
10011 Campus Way S
Largo, MD 20772

As Suq Booksellers
98 Smith St.
Brooklyn, NY 11201
718/596-0390

Asabi International Bookstore
4610 York Rd.
Baltimore, MD 21212
301/539-3270

Athena Book Shop
300 S. Kalamazoo Mall
Kalamazoo, MI 49007
616/342-4508

Authentic Book Distributors
PO Box 52916
Baton Rouge, LA 70892
504/356-0076

Awareness Books
1119 Fulton St.
Brooklyn, NY 11238

Awareness Community Bookstore
1150 Carroll St.
Brooklyn, NY 11225
718/774-3816

Baker Books
80 William St.
New Bedford, MA 02740
508/997-6700

Bantu Books
63 Westbank Express
Gretna, LA 70053
504/362-2688

Benjamin Books
LaGuardia Airport Main Terminal
Flushing, NY 11371
718/565-1119

Black and Latino Bookstore
23 N. Mentor Ave.
Pasadena, CA 91106
818/792-0117

Black Artist Cultural Center
241 N. Kalamazoo Mall
Kalamazoo, MI 49003-3505
616/349-1035

Black Book Connection
PO Box 706
Nutley, NJ 07710
201/667-5808

Black Books Plus Inc.
702 Amsterdam Ave.
New York, NY 10025
212/749-9632

Black Bookworm
605 E. Berry St., #114
Fort Worth, TX 76110
817/923-9661

Black Images Book Bazaar
230 Wynnewood Village
Dallas, TX 75224
214/943-0142

Black Images Book Co.
1322 Woodburn Trail
Dallas, TX 75231
214/375-1733

Black Market Bookstore
12006 St. Clair Ave.
Cleveland, OH 44108

Black Perspectives Book Bazaar
217 Page Bacon Rd., #8
Mary Esther, FL 32569

Blackberry
1611 S. Walter Reed Dr., #201
Arlington, VA 22204
703/486-2297

Blackbird Books
3130 E. Madison Ave.
Seattle, WA 98112
206/325-3793

Blackside Bookstore
1793 Coventry St.
Cleveland Heights, OH 44118
216/371-2207

Blessed Candles
19705 W. Seven Mile Rd.
Detroit, MI 43219
313/534-6480

Blue Door Bookstore
3823 5th Ave.
San Diego, CA 92103
619/298-8610

Book Feire
3818 N. 26th St.
Tacoma, WA 98406
206/759-4680

Book Gallery
1601 Willow Lawn Dr.
Richmond, VA 23230
804/673-9613

The Book Shelf
10390 Overland Rd.
Boise, ID 83709

The Book Store
263 Central Ave.
East Orange, NJ 07018
201/763-6221

Book World
499 Merrit Ave.
Nashville, TN 37203
615/254-8247

Bookfair
968 Farmington Ave.
West Hartford, CT 06107
203/523-7816

Bookland of Baton Rouge
3615 Perkins Rd.
Baton Rouge, LA 70808
504/343-9584

Bookpeople
7900 Edgewater Dr.
Oakland, CA 94621-2004
510/632-4700

Books and Things
1817 Chandler Rd.
Decatur, GA 30032
404/286-0748

Books Et Cetera
4145 South Tamiami Trail
Venice, FL 34293
813/493-2589

Books 'N Things
1040D Settlers Landing Rd.
Hampton, VA 23669
804/723-2696

Bookslinger
2402 University Ave., #507
St. Paul, MN 55114
612/649-0271

Borders Book Store
303 S. State St.
Ann Arbor, MI 48104
313/668-7652

Bridge's Bookstore
1480 Main St.
Rahway, NJ 07065
908/381-2040

Bronx Bookplace Inc.
2460 Grand Concourse
Bronx, NY 10458
212/295-7000

Buckeye Books and News
51 N. Pearl Alley
Columbus, OH 43201
614/464-0777

Caribcraft Gift and Novelty Shop
534 W. Church St.
Orlando, FL 32805
407/425-4439

Carolrhoda Books
241 First Ave. N
North Minneapolis, MN 55401
612/332-3344

Carol's Books and Things
5679 Freeport Blvd.
Sacramento, CA 95822
916/428-5611

Chatterton's Book Store
1818 Nuer St.
Los Angeles, CA 95822
213/664-3882

Children's Book Cart
6736 Brockton Ave.
Riverside, CA 92506
714/275-9860

Children's Books and Gift Market
375 Pharr Rd. NE
Atlanta, GA 30305
404/261-3442

Christ Universal Complex
11901 S. Ashland St.
Chicago, IL 60643
312/568-2282

Cody's Books Inc.
2454 Telegraph Ave.
Berkeley, CA 94704
510/845-7852

Cokesbury Bookstore
2730 Broad River Rd.
Columbia, SC 29210
803/798-3220

Collegiate Book Store
616 Harding Blvd.
Baton Rouge, LA 70807
504/775-2299

Community Book Center
1200 Ursulines St.
New Orleans, LA 70116
504/561-0036

Council Oaks Books
1428 S. St. Louis St.
Tulsa, OK 74120
918/587-6454

Crescent Imports and Publications
3066 Carpenter St.
Ypsilanti, MI 48197
313/665-3492

Cultural Expression
1008 State Ave.
Kansas City, KS 64319
913/321-4438

Cultural Learning Tree
1803 Dempster St.
Evanston, IL 60201
708/328-8409

Culturally Speaking
1601 E. 18th St.
Kansas City, MO 64108
816/842-8151

D. C. Tees
9124 51st Pl.
College Park, MD 20740
301/345-0168

Dare Books
33 Lafayette Ave.
Brooklyn, NY 11217
718/625-4651

Dawah Book Shop
47115 Crenshaw Blvd.
Los Angeles, CA 90043
213/299-0335

Detroit Books and Things
1605 W. Davidson St.
Detroit, MI 48238
313/883-3330

Doretha Afrikan American Books
5740-A Farrow Rd.
Columbia, SC 29204
803/754-3359

Dorr Worr Bookstore
107½ Hope St.
Providence, RI 02906
401/521-3230

**Dusable Museum Gift Shop/
   Bookstore**
740 E. 56th Pl.
Chicago, IL 60637
312/947-0600

Each One Teach One
1511 Livingston St.
Columbus, OH 43205
614/228-4319

Empire Baptist Bookstore
63 W. 125th St.
New York, NY 10027
212/289-7628

Empowerment Books
PO Box 2363
Merrifield, VA 22116
800/882-6651

Eso Won Books
900 N. LaBrea Ave.
Inglewood, CA 90302
310/674-6566

Fire Brand Books
141 The Commons
Ithaca, NY 14850
607/272-0000

First World Books
2801 Candler Rd.
Decatur, GA 30034
404/243-0343

First World Books
3600 Panola Rd.
Lithonian, GA 30038

**The Fountain of Life Record and
   Book Store**
515 W. 35th St.
Norfolk, VA 23608
804/461-2480

Freedom Found Books
5206 Harper St.
Chicago, IL 60615
312/288-2837

Genesis Books and Things
625 Chestnut St.
Camden, SC 29020
803/425-4873

Gordon's Bookstore
8 E. Baltimore St.
Baltimore, MD 21202
410/685-7313

Gospel Advocate Bookstore
207 Centre St.
Dallas, TX 75208
214/943-4466

Griot Booksellers
6500 Reistertown Rd.
Baltimore, MD 21215

Griot's Book Shelf
444 E. Belvedere Ave., #215
Baltimore, MD 21212
410/764-2908

Guild Books
2456 N. Lincoln Ave.
Chicago, IL 60614
312/525-3667

Hakim's Bookstore
842 Martin Luther King Jr.
  Dr. SW
Atlanta, GA 30314
404/221-0740

Hakim's Bookstore
210 S. 52nd St.
Philadelphia, PA 19139
215/474-9495

Hamilton Bookstore
209 9th St.
Augusta, GA 30901
404/722-1301

Haneef's Bookstore
530 Vandever Ave., #1
Wilmington, DE 19802-4241
302/656-4193

Happy Booker Inc.
Morris County Mall
Cedar Knolls, NJ 07927
201/539-4340

Harambee Books
1367 Fillmore St.
Buffalo, NY 14211
716/895-3010

Haslam's Book Store
2025 Central Ave.
St. Petersburg, FL 33710
813/822-8616

Headstart Books and Crafts
604 Flatbush Ave.
Brooklyn, NY 11225
718/469-4500

Heritage Books and Art
9700 Snowhill Rd.
Richmond, VA 23230
804/560-1644

Heritage Unlimited
216 Barclay Dr.
Stamford, CT 06903
203/322-3368

House of Our Own Bookstore
3920 Spruce St.
Philadelphia, PA 19143
215/748-2278

Hue-man Experience Bookstore
911 Park Ave. W
Denver, CO 80205-2601
303/293-2665

Insights
184 Due Dr.
Silver Spring, MD 20902
301/929-6598

J. R. Bookstore
10700 Macarthur Blvd.
Oakland, CA 94605
510/638-3864

Jackson's Books
320 Liberty St. SE
Salem, OR 97301
503/399-8694

Jacqueline's Black Art & Books
40 E. 3rd St.
Long Beach, CA 90802
310/435-8922

Jahi's Books & Things
2589 Sugarplum Dr.
San Jose, CA 95148
408/743-0357

The Jesus Shoppe
2210 W. 10th Ave.
Gary, IN 46404
219/944-7211

Khalil's Books and Cultural Shop
7 N. 2nd Ave.
Coatsville, PA 19320
215/384-3082

Kitabu Kingdom
609 Thurston Rd.
Rochester, NY 14619
716/328-1588

Know Bookstore
306 Dillard St.
Durham, NC 27701
919/682-0739

Know Thyself Bookstore
528 S. 52nd St.
Philadelphia, PA 19143
215/748-2278

Kum Ba Ya Christian Bookstore
1505 E. Livingston
Columbus, OH 43205
614/258-1334

Left Bank Books Inc.
399 N. Euclid St.
St. Louis, MO 63156
314/367-6731

Liberation Books
117 Hume Ave.
Alexandria, VA 22314
804/684-7750

Liberation Bookstore
421 Lexington Ave.
New York, NY 10037
212/281-4615

Liguorius Bookstore
Cheltenham Square Mall
Philadelphia, PA 19103
215/549-0995

Lodestar Books
2020 11th Ave. S
Birmingham, AL 35205
205/939-3356

Lushena Books
15 W. 24th St.
New York, NY 10010
212/989-0800

Marcus Books
1712 Fillmore St.
San Francisco, CA 94115
415/346-4222

Marcus Bookstore
3900 Martin Luther King Jr. Way
Oakland, CA 94609
510/652-2344

Marwil Bookstore
4870 Cass Ave.
Detroit, MI 48201
313/832-3078

McFarland Media
422 University Ave., #8
St. Paul, MN 55041
612/332-3344

My Solitude Books and More
6376 Germantown Ave.
Philadelphia, PA 19144
215/848-1255

Nefertiti Books and Gifts
3574 Chappi Way
Jacksonville, FL 32232
904/766-3830

News and Novels
4645C W. Market St.
Greensboro, NC 27407
919/275-2220

News Depot
207 Market Ave.
Canton, OH 44702
216/454-4441

Nkiru Books
68 St. Marks Ave.
Brooklyn, NY 11217
718/783-6306

Nokoa Bookstore
1205 E. 12th St.
Austin, TX 78702
512/499-8713

Nubian Bookstore
229 Pleasant Grove Shopping
   Center
Dallas, TX 75217
214/398-7697

Nubian Notion
617 Humboldt Ave.
Boston, MA 02119
617/442-4425

Odegard Books of Minneapolis
3001 Hennepin Ave. S
Minneapolis, MN 55408
612/831-9305

Omega Books
2226 Idlewood Ave.
Garland, TX 75040

Paperbacks Unlimited
2634 Woodward St.
Ferndale, MI 48220
313/546-3282

Pathfinder Bookstore
3284 23rd St.
San Francisco, CA 94110
415/282-6255

Positive Images Books and Gifts
3808 W. Burleigh St.
Milwaukee, WI 53210
414/873-8886

Positive Images Bookstore
65 Barclay Center
Cherry Hill, NJ 08034
609/486-2121

The Post Bookstore
597 Central Ave.
East Orange, NJ 07018
201/673-5892

Progressive Emporium Bookstore
6265 Delmar Blvd.
St. Louis, MO 63130
314/721-1344

Pyramid Books
220 Euclid Ave.
San Diego, CA 92114
619/266-8300

Pyramid Bookstore
2849 Georgia Ave. NW
Washington, DC 20001
202/328-0191

Rare Books and Things
1350 E. Livingston Ave.
Columbus, OH 43205
614/258-7576

Razzaq Books
23 West St.
Bordentown, NJ 08505
609/298-7696

Red and Black Books
432 15th Ave. E
Seattle, WA 98112
206/322-7323

Robin's Book Store
108 S. 13th St.
Philadelphia, PA 19107
215/735-9600

**Roots and Wings Cultural
  Bookplace**
1345 Carter Hill Rd.
Montgomery, AL 36106
205/262-1700

Savanna Books
858 Massachusetts Ave.
Cambridge, MA 02139
617/868-3423

Seven Rays Bookstore Inc.
508 Westcott St.
Syracuse, NY 13210
315/424-9137

Showcase Books
145 W. Market St.
Warren, OH 44481
216/392-7595

Shrine of the Black Madonna
13535 Livernois Ave.
Detroit, MI 48238
313/491-0777

Shrine of the Black Madonna
5317 Martin Luther King Jr. Blvd.
Houston, TX 77021
713/645-1071

Sisterhood Bookstore
1351 Westwood Blvd.
Los Angeles, CA 90024
310/477-7300

Somba Bookstore
1229 Albany Ave.
Hartford, CT 06112
203/728-5291

Soul Source Bookstore
118 James P. Brawley Dr. SW
Atlanta, GA 30314
404/577-1346

Southern Sisters
411 Morris St.
Durham, NC 27701
919/682-0739

Special Occasions
112 Martin Luther King Jr. Dr.
Winston-Salem, NC 27101
919/724-0344

Stick and Stones
110 DeKalb Ave.
Brooklyn, NY 11201
718/522-5383

Student Book Exchange
1806 N. High St.
Columbus, OH 43201
614/291-9528

Sunrise
608 W. 38th St.
Norfolk, VA 23508
804/625-3560

Sunrise African Gift Shop
88 Halsey St.
Newark, NJ 07102
201/504-9621

Sunset Card Shop Inc.
310 W. 125th St.
New York, NY 10027
212/666-0762

Tattered Cover Bookstore
2955 E. 1st Ave.
Denver, CO 80206
303/322-7727

**Tennessee Regular Baptist
Bookstore**
1055 S. Bellvue
Memphis, TN 38106
901/946-9669

Tut-Ra Ma Books
PO Box 757
Piscataway, NJ 08854
908/753-7142

Uhuru Books
3821 Clinton Ave., #2
Minneapolis, MN 55411
612/721-7113

**United Brothers and United Sisters
Books and Things**
1040 Settlers Landing Rd.
Hampton, VA 23669
804/724-2696

**Universal Books and Religious
Articles**
51 Court St.
White Plains, NY 10601
914/681-0484

Vertigo Books
1337 Connecticut Ave. NW
Washington, DC 20036
202/429-9272

Vision Books
532 River St.
Mattapan, MA 02126
617/298-1388

Western Book Distributors
2970 San Pablo Ave.
Berkeley, CA 94702
510/849-0100

Wilkie News Inc.
125 S. Ludlow
Dayton, OH 45402
513/429-1677

Wit and Wisdom
24031 Chagrin Blvd.
Beachwood, OH 44122
216/831-5035

X-Pressions
5912 N. College Ave.
Indianapolis, IN 46220
317/257-5448

Yawa Books and Gifts
22206 18th St. NW
Washington, DC 20009
202/483-6805

Zuri Art and Books
691 Water St.
Bridgeport, CT 06604
203/330-1037

THE VISUAL ARTS

FINE ARTISTS

Abayoni, Densua
PO Box 42544
Atlanta, GA 30311

Allen, Larry
11531 86th St. N
Birmingham, AL 35206

Amenra
231 Blvd. Granada SW
Atlanta, GA 30311

Anderson, Charles
3042 Wilshire
Markham, IL 60426

Antel, Derrick
PO Box 67094
Baltimore, MD 21215

Atkinson, Theresa
2603 P St. NW
Washington, DC 20781

Babatunde
1136 E. Montecito St.
Santa Barbara, CA 93103

Babhauddeen, Muneer
7472 N. 86th St.
Milwaukee, WI 53224

Beck, Stella
9353 S. Stewart Ave.
Chicago, IL 60620

Bernard
PO Box 451
Glenside, PA 19038

Bird, Stephanie
1007 S. Humphrey
Oak Park, IL 60304

Blanchard, Barbara
Dominique Clay Work
18818 Cedar Valley Way
New Hall, CA 91321

Bontemps, Jacqueline
1 Johnson Ct.
Hampton, VA 23669

Borden, Harold R.
1255½ S. Cochran Ave.
Los Angeles, CA 90019

Bowens, Margaret
Black Like Me
155 Lotus Dr.
Chula Vista, CA 91911

Branch, Plunky
2218 Rosewood Ave.
Richmond, VA 23220

Brother Luke
1037 Jefferson St.
Philadelphia, PA 19122

Brown, Larry "Poncho"
Melanin Graphics
2315 Hollins St.
Baltimore, MD 21223

Brown, Richard J.
2941 Fish Hatchery Rd., #9
Madison, WI 53713

Bustion, Nathaniel
Mattinni Studio
4414 N. Risinghill Rd.
Altadena, CA 91001

Camp, Kimberly
4069 S. Four Mile Run, #20
Arlington, VA 22204

Carter, William S.
116 W. Elm St., #1316
Chicago, IL 60610

Carty, Leo
PO Box 4132
Christianstead
St. Croix, VI 00822

Caton, Mitchell
5318 S. Maryland
Chicago, IL 60615

Clayton, Avery
3870 Crenshaw Blvd., #104-919
Los Angeles, CA 90008

Cliff, Clay
10605 Chester Ave.
Cleveland, OH 44106

Cooper, Emanuel
2645 Lockridge
Kansas City, MO 64128

Cornwell, Jean
862 Mariposa Pl.
San Diego, CA 92114

Crawford, A. Turner
4659 S. Drexel Blvd., #202
Chicago, IL 60653

Da Da
PO Box 257
Union, MI 49130

Damballah
6600 Luzon, #310
Washington, DC 20012

Davis, Alonzo
PO Box 6092
San Antonio, TX 78209

Davis, Harry L.
416 Crele Dr.
Wilmington, NC 28403

Daw'U
Gilbert House
1540 Beatie Ave.
Atlanta, GA 30310

Detry, Harry
8211 S. Exchange Ave.
Chicago, IL 60617

Develay, Lolita
615 N. Rossmore, #309
Los Angeles, CA 90004

Diagne, Aziz
509 Juniper Dr.
Pasadena, CA 91103

Dixon, Charles
423 E. Rosecrans Ave.
Compton, CA 90221

Donaldson, Jeff R.
Howard University
Washington, DC 20059

Duplessis, Laurel
250 Beaureguard Heights
Hampton, VA 23669

Edwards, Sherman L.
3307 Marlborough Ct.
Hampton, VA 23666

Feaman, Max
ImageMax
9630 S. Greenwood Ave.
Chicago, IL 60628

Featherstone, Billy
118 W. Mariposa St.
Altadena, CA 91001

Ferguson, Clarence
4505 Lincoln Ave.
Chicago, IL 60625

Garnes, Michael
5826 Hillside Cove
Alta Loma, CA 91701

Gillam, Sam
Nancy Drysdale Gallery
2103 O St. NW
Washington, DC 20037

Glenn, Beverly
3222 S. Prairie
Chicago, IL 60619

Gommillion, T. H.
7420 Calder Dr.
Capitol Heights, MD 20743

Goodnight, Paul
791 Tremont St., #307
Boston, MA 02118

Greer, Mary
1409 G St. NE
Washington, DC 20002

Gunn, Theodore
1368 Fulton St., 3rd Floor
Brooklyn, NY 11216

Hamilton, Pamela
PO Box 6272
FDR Station
New York, NY 10150-1902

Hammons, David
578 Broadway
New York, NY 10012

Hardison, Ineg
444 Central Park West, #4B
New York, NY 10025

Harper, Juana
168 Rockford Rd., 2nd Floor
Atlanta, GA 30317

Haywood, Wardell
La Collage Studios
1809 E. 71st St.
Chicago, IL 60649

Hill, Beverly
61 Halsey St.
Brooklyn, NY 11216

Howard, Marian
16 Crescent Ave.
Jersey City, NJ 07304

Hoyes, Bernard Stanley
985 Westchester Pl.
Los Angeles, CA 90019

Hunter, Candace
1800 E. 78th St.
Chicago, IL 60649

Iah, Jalil
1051 N. Wolcott
Chicago, IL 60622

Interp, Moja
5122 Gainor Rd.
Philadelphia, PA 19131

Iribhogbe, Bayo
EDO Studio
5750 S. Stony Island Ave.
Chicago, IL 60637

Jackson, Oliver L.
5525 Marshall St.
Oakland, CA 94608

Jarrell, Wadsworth A.
964 Watkins St. NW
Atlanta, GA 30318

Johnson, Darrell
728 W. College Ave., #10
State College, PA 16801-8738

Johnson, Jerome A.
2411 14th St. NE, #2
Washington, DC 20018

Johnson, Leroy
4946 N. Uber St.
Philadelphia, PA 19141

Jones, Calvin
925 W. Huron St., #103
Chicago, IL 60622

Joysmith, Brenda
PO Box 2276
Berkeley, CA 94702-0276

Kwamena-Poh, William
6751 S. Oglesby St., #1A
Chicago, IL 60649

Lane, Ronald L.
1022 Franklin Ave.
New Orleans, LA 70117

Lang, A. D.
394 4th St. NE
Atlanta, GA 30308

Laoye, Adedayo
5210 S. Harper Court
Chicago, IL 60615

Lawrence, Jacob
4316 37th Ave. NE
Seattle, WA 98105

Linton, Barbara
PO Box 2046
New York, NY 10027

Logan, Fern
1359 W. Estes St.
Chicago, IL 60620

Logan, Juan
30 Henry's Chapel Rd.
Belmont, NC 28012

Love, Ed
5138 Biscayne Ave.
Miami, FL 33137

Massey, Cal
509 Dawson St.
Moorestown, NJ 08057

Maynard, Joan
PO Box 120
St. John's Station
Brooklyn, NY 11213

McDaniel, Akua
266 Dodd St.
Atlanta, GA 30315

McNary, Oscar Lee
1308 Timberlake St.
Richardson, TX 75080

Mills, Charles
701 N.W. 214th St.
Miami, FL 33169

Morrison, Keith
3556 B St. NW
Washington, DC 20010

Murray, Joyce
PO Box 43452
Atlanta, GA 30336

Murrell, Robert
63 Walden St.
Cambridge, MA 02140

Nance, Marilyn
136 Cambridge Pl., #4R
Brooklyn, NY 11238

Nash, William
2015 S. Alston Ave.
Durham, NC 27707

Nock, George
Off the Wall of Time
PO Box 2848
Reston, VA 22090

Nottage, Ted
1403 W. 111th St., #1003
Chicago, IL 60643

Olomidun, Orisegun
4827 S. Vicennes Ave.
Chicago, IL 60615

O'Neal, Mary L.
440 Haddon Rd., #2
Oakland, CA 94606

Oti, Ni
6950 S. Yale St.
Chicago, IL 60621

Overstreet, Joe
214 E. 2nd St.
New York, NY 10003

Pannell, Patrick
830 5th Ave.
New York, NY 10021

Peters, K. Joy Ballard
1630 Stewart Ave. SW
Atlanta, GA 30310

Phillips, Ronnie
220 W. 50th St.
Atlanta, GA 30303

Powell, Rick
Department of Art and Art
    History
Duke University
Durham, NC 27008

Puryear, Martin
532 Broadway, 4th Floor
New York, NY 10012

Richardson, Frank
552 Baker St.
Baltimore, MD 21217

Roberts, Joseph M.
c/o Roberts and Roberts
12221 Quorn La.
Reston, VA 22091

Rozelle, John
37 S. Wabash St.
Chicago, IL 60602

Santos, Bakari
1276 Winsor Blvd.
Los Angeles, CA 90019

Satterfield, Floyd
1275 Walnut St.
Berkeley, CA 94709

Scott, JoAnne
c/o The School of the Art Institute
37 S. Wabash
Chicago, IL 60603

Seabrooke-Powell, Georgette
5203 New Hampshire Ave. NW
Washington, DC 20011

Sealy, Jackie
Dawn Graphics
4115 Wisconsin NW, #207
Washington, DC 20016

Searles, Chares R.
640 Broadway
New York, NY 10012

Shaw, Janathal
4207 28th Ave., #B2
Temple Hill, MD 20748

Simmons, John W.
3518 Cahuenga Blvd.
Los Angeles, CA 90068

Simpson, Merten
1063 Madison Ave.
New York, NY 10028

Smith, Charles
1410 Melrose St.
Mobile, AL 36605

Smith, Vernon
c/o Hobnail Gallery
4155 Lee St. E
St. Louis, MO 63115

Smith, Vincent
591 Broadway
New York, NY 10012

Taylor, William
634 North Carolina Ave SE
Washington, DC 20006

Terry, Evelyn
1119 Knapp St.
Milwaukee, WI 53202

Turner, Sandi
c/o Saturn Art Productions
924 Wissor St.
Reading, PA 19601

Vann, Bobb
c/o Vanngo Graphics
5306 Knox St.
Philadelphia, PA 19144

Ward-Brown, Denise
c/o Washington University
Campus Box 631
1 Brookings Dr.
St. Louis, MO 63130

Weiss, Roseann
Elliot Smith Gallery
360 N. Skinker Blvd.
St. Louis, MO 63130

Wider, James
c/o J. Clark Wider Studio
514 S. Weber
Colorado Springs, CO 80903

Williams, Bernard
209 W. Lake St., 4th Floor
Chicago, IL 60606

Williams, Grace
118 W. 120th St.
New York, NY 10027

Williams, Julian
1416 S. Michigan Ave.
Chicago, IL 60605

Williams, Michael K.
409 Edgecomb Ave.
New York, NY 10032

Williams-Boyd, Dawn
PO Box 7053
Denver, CO 80207-7053

Wilson, Midas
6420 S. Langley St.
Chicago, IL 60637

Woodson, Shirley
155 Woodward St.
Detroit, MI 48226

Young, Charles A.
8104 W. Beach Dr., NW
Washington, DC 20012

GALLERIES

Afriworks Inc.
2035 5th Ave.
New York, NY 10035
212/876-1447

Afrospectives
PO Box 13
Brooklyn, NY 11205
718/455-1825

Al Dogget Studios
1734 34th Ave.
Seattle, WA 98122
206/329-5563

Alex Cobbrey Prints
3451 Winton Wood Ct.
Marietta, GA 30062

Alex Graphic Design
311 Glenwood Rd.
Brooklyn, NY 11210
718/434-0040

Alitash Kebede Galleries
1310 N. Alta Vista
Los Angeles, CA 90046
213/874-6269

Annie Lee and Friends Art Gallery
3160 W. 175th St.
Hazelcrest, IL 60429
708/335-0908

Arabesque Studio
59 Armory St.
Boston, MA 02119
617/442-6577

Art Davo
1643 W. 80th St., #2
Los Angeles, CA 90047
213/758-8509

Art Without Walls
165 Clinton Ave.
Brooklyn, NY 11205
718/797-1696

Art'Frica Plus
PO Box 27687
San Antonio, TX 78227
800/358-4ART

Artistic Expressions
PO Box 15545
Richmond, VA 23227

Artistic Impressions
1642 Butler Pike, #106
Conshohocken, PA 19428

Artisan Emporium Gallery
18013 Euclid Ave.
Cleveland, OH 44112
216/383-0809

Artson Enterprises
1210 Fox Run Pl.
Woodbridge, VA 22191

Artware Chicago
8211 S. Exchange
Chicago, IL 60649
313/373-5900

Artwork
5300 S. Blackstone Ave.
Chicago, IL 60615
312/684-5300

Barton Prints
4340 S. Hopkins Ave.
Titusville, FL 32780

Bernice Steinbaum Gallery
132 Green St.
New York, NY 10012
212/431-4224

Black Gallery
107 Santa Barbara Plaza
Los Angeles, CA 90008
213/294-9024

Black Heritage Gallery
5408 Almeda Rd.
Houston, TX 77004
713/529-7900

Bomani Galleries
251 Post St.
San Francisco, CA 94109
415/296-8677

Brockman Gallery
4334 Degman Blvd.
Los Angeles, CA 90008
213/294-3766

Carribbean Art Gallery
Highway 59 S
Robertsdale, AL 36567
205/947-4813

CaSaj Art Gallery and Design Studio
2551 San Ramon Valley Blvd., #110
San Ramon, CA 94583
510/838-2323

Center for African Art
54 E. 68th St.
New York, NY 10021
212/861-1200

Cheick Souhanna
1212 S. Michigan Ave., #1410
Chicago, IL 60605
312/431-1005

Color Circle
PO Box 190763
Boston, MA 02119

Colors of Culture
PO Box 2444
Middlestown, CT 06470
203/632-1793

Cousen Rose Gallery
174 Circuit Ave.
Martha's Vineyard Island
Oak Bluffs, MA 02557
508/693-6656

Creative Concepts International
3870 Crenshaw Blvd., #104
Los Angeles, CA 90008
818/797-9871

Cultural Arts Institute
33 Lincoln Rd.
Brooklyn, NY 11225
718/287-2200

Dan Tighman Artworks
PO Box 69
Conshohocken, PA 19428
800/437-4770

Derrick Joshua Beard Fine Arts
1234 N. Ogden Dr.
West Hollywood, CA 90046
213/848-9488

Evans-Tibb Collection
1910 Vermont Ave. NW
Washington, DC 20001
202/234-8164

First Love Gallery
1455 Burnside Ave.
Los Angeles, CA 90019
213/939-8385

Focus-In-Print
494 Burnside Ave.
East Hartford, CT 06108
203/289-6105

**Fourth World Artisians
   Cooperatives**
3453 N. Southpoint
Chicago, IL 60657
312/561-3500

Gallery Antiqua
5138 Biscayne Blvd.
Miami, FL 33137
305/759-5355

Gallery at Hudson's Bay
1600 Stone St.
Denver, CO 80202
303/595-3600

Gallery 500
500 9th St. SE
Washington, DC 20003

Gallery LaTaj
1203 King St.
Alexandria, VA 22314
703/549-0508

Gallery Obiagali
296 New York Ave.
Brooklyn, NY 11216
718/978-4431

Gallery of Art
Morgan State University
1700 E. Cold Spring La.
Baltimore, MD 21239
410/319-3333

Gallery Plus
4333 Degan Blvd.
Los Angeles, CA 90008
213/296-2389

Gallery W
1309 Q St. NW
Washington, DC 20009
202/234-4427

Gamboa Publishing
31809 St. Pierre La.
Lake Elsinore, CA 92530

Graphitti Gems Gallery
10531 Storch Dr.
Seabrooke, MD 20746
301/794-8480

Grinnell Fine Art Collections
800 Riverside Dr., #5E
New York, NY 10022
212/927-7941

Handmasters Studio
5555 Germantown Ave., 2nd Floor
Philadelphia, PA 19133
215/844-8898

Hang It Up
13200 Morning Sky Ct.
Victorville, CA 92392
619/951-7981

Harriet Tubman Gallery and Resource Center
United South End Settlement
566 Columbus Ave.
Boston, MA 02118
617/536-8610

Hatch-Billops Collection
491 Broadway, 7th Floor
New York, NY 10012
212/966-3231

Howard University Gallery of Art
2455 6th St. NW
Washington, DC 20059
202/636-7047

Hughley Gallery and Objects
M2 Stovall St. SE
Atlanta, GA 30316
404/523-3201

Humorous Design Group
2300 Greenfield Rd., #206
Detroit, MI 48228
313/968-2346

Images By Owen
2302 N.E. 9th St.
Lawton, OK 73507
405/248-4762

Images of Us
Gallery of African American Art
1367 Fillmore Ave.
Buffalo, NY 14211
716/896-6440

Jazz 100
PO Box 1274
Corapolis, PA 15108
412/457-9923

JK Fine Art Editions Co.
600 Palisades Ave., 2nd Floor
Union City, NJ 07087
201/617-8840

Joy Company
1780 E. Hourn Ave.
Bronx, NY 10457
212/716-1605

Kathleen Atkins-Wilson and Associates
2024 W. Imperial Highway
Hawthorne, CA 90250

Kenkeleba Gallery
214 E. 2nd St.
New York, NY 10003
212/674-3939

Latasha Gallery
1705 Prairie Rd.
Severn, MD 21144
410/551-3145

Malcolm Brown Gallery
20100 Chagrin Blvd.
Shaker Heights, OH 44122
216/701-2955

Mirror Art Gallery
9 Blackpole Circle
Waldorf, MD 20602
301/843-3034

Miya Gallery
410 8th St. NW
Washington, DC 20004
202/347-6330

Mobile Art Gallery
PO Box 83893
San Diego, CA 92138
619/266-8496

Mocha Gallery
5445 Germantown Ave.
Philadelphia, PA 19144
215/844-3412

New Harlem Gallery
257 W. 117 St.
New York, NY 10026
212/749-7498

Nicole Gallery of the Art of Haiti
734 N. Wells St.
Chicago, IL 60610
312/787-7716

October Gallery
3805 Lancaster Ave.
Philadelphia, PA 19104
215/387-7177

Porter-Randall Gallery
5624 La Jolla Blvd.
La Jolla, CA 92037
619/551-8884

Pyramid Gallery
800 Riverside Dr., #B-1
New York, NY 10032
212/781-4585

**Renaissance Art and Design
Gallery**
35 Paisley Park
Boston, MA 02124
617/265-2902

Rising Star and Graphics
139 Fulton St., #803
New York, NY 10038
212/608-3661

Robert Cargo Folk Art Gallery
2314 6th St.
Tuscaloosa, AL 35401
205-758-8884

Russell W. Souhall Enterprises
PO Box 2276
Berkeley, CA 94702
510/540-1222

Shadow of the Bird Original Art
104 N. Stocton St.
Baltimore, MD 21223
410/566-7517

Spiral Gallery
637 Vanderbilt Ave.
Brooklyn, NY 11238
718/783-2891

Stephanie Honeywood Inc.
1185 South Victoria Ave.
Los Angeles, CA 90019
213/939-3705

Unique Artworks
PO Box 9193
New Haven, CT 06532
203/624-8367

Unique Cultural Arts Inc.
5 Cadwalader Dr.
Trenton, NY 08618
609/393-5245

Unity Gallery
2023 Walnut St., 1st Floor
Philadelphia, PA 19103
215/557-6694

Us Art Gallery
1012 E. Fairview
Montgomery, AL 36106
205/269-2550

Vargas and Associates
8240 Professional Pl., #200
Landover, MD 20785
301/731-5175

Wendell Street Gallery
17 Wendell St.
Cambridge, MA 02138
617/864-9294

Wild Strawberry/Muddy Wheel Gallery
4505 4th St. NW
Albuquerque, NM 87107
505/345-7671

Woodshop Art Gallery
441 E. 75th St.
Chicago, IL 60619
312/994-6666

Yocat Design
202 S. State St., #800
Chicago, IL 60604
312/271-9860

Zabezi Progressive Arts
7663 S. Chicago Ave.
Chicago, IL 60619
312/734-1858

GRAPHIC ARTISTS, PHOTOGRAPHERS, AND FASHION DESIGNERS

Adayemi, Bisi
663 Clifton Rd. NE
Atlanta, GA 30307
Fashion designer

Ademluyi, Mozella P.
c/o African Eye Inc.
2134 Wisconsin Ave. NW
Washington, DC 20007
Fashion designer

Ajanaku, Kenya
6265 Delmar Blvd.
St. Louis, MO 63130
Jewelry

Arsan, Ifama Diane
1035 Saux La.
New Orleans, LA 70114
Fiber artist

Baptiste, Aurora
PO Box 43486
Oakland, CA 94624
Fashion designer

Billingsley, Ray
c/o King Features Syndicate
235 East 45th St.
New York, NY 10017
Cartoonist

Boone, Angela
c/o Angela Boone Co.
2523 E. 73rd Pl.
Chicago, IL 60649
Interior designer

Branch, Harrison
c/o Oregon State University
Department of Art
Corvallis, OR 97331
Photographer, educator

Brandon, Barbara
Universal Press Syndicate
4900 Main St.
Kansas City, MO 64112
Cartoonist

Brawn, Bucky
c/o Playboy Magazine
680 N. Lakeshore
Chicago, IL 60611
Cartoonist

Briscoe, Zoe
c/o Mix Media Jewelry
405 Eccelston St.
Silver Spring, MD 20902
Jewelry designer

Carol, Phillip
5300 Hays St. NW
Albuquerque, NM 87120
Photographer

Coates, Doris
c/o Plum Dolls of Color
PO Box 2009
Sacramento, CA 95822
Doll maker

Colby, Osagebo
c/o Silver and Gold
2525 N. 46th St.
Milwaukee, WI 53210
Jewelry designer

Crusoe, Elena
c/o Elena Designs
1107 Parrish Dr.
Rockville, MD 20851
Fashion designer

Davis, Faith
7916 S. Kingston St.
Chicago, IL 60617
Jewelry designer

Diaz, Barbara
c/o Black Faces Are Beautiful
916 Prospect Pl.
Brooklyn, NY 11213
Jewelry designer

Dickerson-Thompson, Julee
c/o Julee Designs
3205 16th St. NE
Washington, DC 20018
Doll maker

Endesha, Johari
PO Box 100
St. Louis, MO 63112
Fashion designer

Ewa, Kathy
c/o Gotcha!
747 Fulton St.
Brooklyn, NY 11217
Fiber artist

Foreman, Rich
927 Noyes St.
Evanston, IL 60201
Photographer

Ghee, Samuel
17 Pearl St.
Atlanta, GA 30361
Graphic artist

Harris, Dwight
Studio D
PO Box 52292
New Orleans, LA 70152
Photographer

Hart, Victoria
c/o Shades of Blackness
PO Box 908
Industry, CA 91744
Fashion designer

Hassan, Askia
c/o The Defiant Ones
117-05 231 St.
Cambria Heights, NY 11411
Jewelry designer

Henderson, Gordon
450 W. 15th St.
New York, NY 10011
Fashion designer

Het Heru, Kaitha
155 Canal St., #9
New York, NY 10013
Fiber artist

Hicks, Jan
5517 S. Harper St.
Chicago, IL 60615
Fashion designer

Jarrell, Jae
3720 Blvd. Hills Rd.
Atlanta, GA 30318
Fashion designer

Jenkins, David
1416 S. Michigan Ave.
Chicago, IL 60606
Photographer

Jerome
456 E. 79th St.
Chicago, IL 60619
Photographer

Johnson, Harold
1416 S. Michigan Ave.
Chicago, IL 60605
Photographer

Jones, Brent
Brent Jones Stock and
    Assignment
9121 Meril Ave.
Chicago, IL 60617
Photographer

Joseph, Phillis
50 W. 97th St.
New York, NY 10025
Fashion designer

Kandirifu, Kamau
PO Box 49795
Chicago, IL 60649
Photographer

Kennedy, Kevin
1729 S. Holt Ave.
Los Angeles, CA 90035
Furniture designer

King, Jimi
7221 Melrose Ave., #32
Beverly Hills, CA 90046
Fiber artist

Lateef, Aziza
113 W. 120th St.
New York, NY 10027
Doll maker

Lunda, Ramu
6735 S. Cornell Ave.
Chicago, IL 60649
Fashion designer

Mainor, Paul
213 W. Institute Pl., #209
Chicago, IL 60610
Photographer

Malone, Maurice
c/o Maurice Malone Designs
15736 W. Seven Mile Rd.
Detroit, MI 48235
Fashion designer

Mandella, Ade'mola
59 John St.
New York, NY 10038
Fashion designer

McCannon, Dindga
c/o Pyramid Gallery
800 Riverside Dr., #B-1
New York, NY 10032
Fashion designer

Metu
139 Fulton St., #803
New York, NY 10038
Graphic artist

Moman, Lavern
6037 S. St. Lawrence St.
Chicago, IL 60637
Interior designer

Moutousamy-Ashe, Jean
c/o Random House
201 E. 50th St.
New York, NY 10022
Photographer, author

Mzuri
210 Garfield Pl.
Brooklyn, NY 11215
Fashion designer

Neals, Otto
138 Sullivan Pl.
Brooklyn, NY 11225
Graphic artist

Nesbit, Linda
c/o Printwear Graphic
375 Lincoln Pl.
Brooklyn, NY 11238
Fiber artist

Nicholson, Barbara R.
c/o Champagne and Grits
195 Linfield St.
Columbus, OH 43219
Fashion designer

Onli, Tutrel
5121 S. Ellis St.
Chicago, IL 60615
*Graphic artist, comic book
  publisher*

Rah Bird
2326 E. 70th St.
Chicago, IL 60649
Fiber artist

Reeves, Rosemary
c/o Road Designs
1 E. Delaware
Chicago, IL 60611
Fashion designer

Rojas, DeVorah
2102 E. 82nd St.
Chicago, IL 60649
Greeting card illustrator

Rome
7949 Justine St.
Chicago, IL 60620
Fashion designer

Sengstacke, Robert
1517 Western Ave., #206
Chicago, IL 60608
Photographer

Sherman, Ed
240 W. 139th St.
New York, NY 10030
Photographer

Simmons, Ken
3026 E. 80th St.
Chicago, IL 60617
Photographer

Simpson, Coreen
599 West End Ave.
New York, NY 10024
Jewelry designer

Sleet, Moneta J.
c/o Johnson Publishing Company
120 6th Ave.
New York, NY 10020
Photographer, journalist

Sleet, Thomas
608 N. 21st St.
St. Louis, MO 63103
Graphic artist

Smith, Charles
1410 Melrose St.
Mobile, AL 36605
Potter

Smith, Sumarah Karen
305 E. Philadelphia St.
Detroit, MI 48202
Graphic artist

Smith, Vernon
c/o Hobnail Gallery
4155 Lee St. E
St. Louis, MO 63115
Graphic artist

Sonli
64 St. Mark's Ave.
Brooklyn, NY 11217
Fashion designer

Taylor, Anthony
202 S. State St., #800
Chicago, IL 60604
Graphic artist

Taylor, Craig
202 S. State St., #800
Chicago, IL 60604
Graphic artist

Taylor, Raleigh
6736 S. Clyde St.
Chicago, IL 60649
Photographer

Wallace, Bill Onikwa
407 E. 25th St.
Chicago, IL 60616
Photographer

Wells, Yvonne T.
1922 42nd Ave.
Tuscaloosa, AL 35401
Collectible art

Werner, Eric
9407 S. Calumet Ave.
Chicago, IL 60619
Photographer

Windom, Alice M.
PO Box 4846
St. Louis, MO 63113
Photographer

Wise, Mark
c/o Jewelry by Moshe
4329 Chaplin St. SE
Washington, DC 20019
Jewelry designer

Yearwood, Lisa
101 Webster St.
Washington, DC 20009
Fashion designer

Young, Elaine
5802 Bartimer St.
St. Louis, MO 63112
Graphic artist

ARTS ORGANIZATIONS

African American Women on Tour
PO Box 15819
San Diego, CA 92175
619/560-2770

Art for Community Expressions
772 N. High St.
Columbus, OH 43215
614/252-3036

Artists Doing Business Worldwide
874 Brooklyn Ave.
Brooklyn, NY 11203
718/693-1274

Association for the Preservation and Presentation of the Arts
2011 Benning Rd. NE
Washington, DC 20002
202/529-3244

Black Artist Guild
306 Akin St.
Kinston, NC 28501
919/523-0003

Black Arts Alliance
1157 Navasota St.
Austin, TX 78702
512/477-9660

Black Arts National Diaspora Inc.
114–36 227th St.
Cambria Heights, NY 11411
718/528-5880

Creative Arts Foundation Inc.
7558 S. Chicago Ave.
Chicago, IL 60619
312/752-3955

**International Agency for Minority
   Artists' Affairs**
Adam Clayton Powell Jr. State
   Office Bldg.
163 W. 125th St., #909
New York, NY 10027
212/749-5298

Minority Arts Resource Council
1421 W. Girard Ave.
Philadelphia, PA 19130
215/236-2688

**Resident Art and Humanities
   Consortium**
1515 Linn St.
Cincinnati, OH 45214
513/381-0645

**Where We At: Black Women
   Artists**
154 Crown St.
Brooklyn, NY 11225
718/756-1897

SPORTS

THE PERSONALITIES

Aaron, Hank
PO Box 4064
Atlanta, GA 30302
Baseball player, team executive

Abderlnaby, Alaa
c/o Boston Celtics
150 Causeway St.
Boston, MA 02114
Basketball player

Abdul-Jabbar, Kareem
1170 Stone Canyon Rd.
Los Angeles, CA 90077
Basketball player (retired)

Adams, George
c/o New England Patriots
Sullivan Stadium
Rt. 1
Foxboro, MA 02035
Football player

Adams, Michael
c/o Washington Bullets
1 Harry S. Truman Dr.
Landover, MD 20786
Basketball player

Addison, Rafael
c/o New Jersey Nets
Brendan Byrne Arena
East Rutherford, NJ 07073
Basketball player

Agee, Thomas
c/o Dallas Cowboys
1 Cowboy Pkwy.
Irving, TX 75063
Football player

Aguire, Mark
c/o Los Angeles Clippers
3939 S. Figueroa St.
Los Angeles, CA 90037
Basketball player (retired)

Alexander, Hubbard
c/o Dallas Cowboys
1 Cowboy Pkwy.
Irving, TX 75063
Football coach

Alexander, Victor
c/o Golden State
Nimitz Freeway and
   Hegenberger Rd.
Oakland, CA 94621
Basketball player

159

Ali, Muhammad
PO Box 187
Berrien Springs, MI 49103
Former boxing champion

Allen, Marcus
1144 Rauol Dr.
Pacific Palisades, CA 90272
Football player

Alou, Felipe
c/o Montreal Expos
PO Box 500, Stadium M
Montreal, Quebec, H1V 3P2
Canada
Baseball manager

Alou, Moises
c/o Montreal Expos
PO Box 500, Stadium M
Montreal, Quebec, H1V 3P2
Canada
Baseball player

Ambrose, Ashley
c/o Indianapolis Colts
PO Box 535000
Indianapolis, IN 46254
Football player

Anderson, Alfred
c/o Minnesota Vikings
9520 Viking Dr.
Eden Prairie, MN 55344
Football player

Anderson, Flipper
c/o Los Angeles Raiders
332 Center St.
El Segundo, CA 90245
Football player

Anderson, Gary
c/o Tampa Bay Buccaneers
1 Buccaneer Plaza
Tampa, FL 33607
Football player

Anderson, Greg
c/o Milwaukee Bucks
1001 N. 4th St.
Milwaukee, WI 53203
Basketball player

Anderson, Kenny
c/o New Jersey Nets
Brendan Byrne Arena
East Rutherford, NJ 07073
Basketball player

Anderson, Nick
c/o Orlando Magic
1 Magic Pl.
Orlando, FL 32807
Basketball player

Anderson, Ron
c/o Philadelphia 76ers
PO Box 25040
Philadelphia, PA 19147
Basketball player

Anderson, Willie
c/o San Antonio Spurs
600 E. Market St., #102
San Antonio, TX 78205
Basketball player

Anderson, Willie Lee
c/o Los Angeles Rams
2327 W. Lincoln Ave.
Anaheim, CA 92801
Football player

Anthony, Eric
c/o Houston Astros
PO Box 288
Houston, TX 77001-0288
Baseball player

Anthony, Greg
c/o New York Knicks
4 Penn Plaza
New York, NY 10001
Basketball player

Arbuckle, Charles
c/o Indianapolis Colts
7001 W. 56th St.
PO Box 53500
Indianapolis, IN 46254
Football player

Archibald, Nate "Tiny"
c/o NBA Hall of Fame
PO Box 179
Springfield, MA 01101
Former basketball player

Armstrong, B. J.
c/o Chicago Bulls
980 N. Michigan Ave.
Chicago, IL 60611
Basketball player

Ashford, Evelyn
818 Plantation La.
Walnut, CA 91789
Track and field athlete

Askew, Vincent
c/o Golden State
Nimitz Freeway and
  Hegenberger Rd.
Oakland, CA 94621
Basketball player

Askins, Keith
c/o Miami Heat
Miami Arena
Miami, FL 33136
Basketball player

Augman, Stacy
c/o Atlanta Hawks
1 CNN Center
Atlanta, GA 30303
Basketball player

Austin, Isaac
c/o Utah Jazz
5 Triad Center
Salt Lake City, UT 84180
Basketball player

Avent, Anthony
c/o Milwaukee Bucks
1001 N. 4th St.
Milwaukee, WI 53203
Basketball player

Baerga, Carlos
c/o Cleveland Cavaliers
Cleveland Stadium
Cleveland, OH 44114
Basketball player

Bagley, John
c/o Boston Celtics
150 Causeway St.
Boston, MA 02114
Basketball player

Bailey, Thurl
c/o Minnesota Timberwolves
730 Hennepin Ave., #500
Minneapolis, MN 55403
Basketball player

Baines, Harold
c/o Baltimore Orioles
333 W. Camden St.
Baltimore, MD 21201
Baseball player

Baker, Dusty
c/o San Francisco Giants
Candlestick Park
San Francisco, CA 94124
Baseball player

Banks, Darren
c/o Boston Bruins
150 Causeway St.
Boston, MA 02114
Hockey player

Banks, Ernie
PO Box 24302
Los Angeles, CA 90024
Baseball coach, former player

Banks, Willie
501 Chicago Ave. S
Minneapolis, MN 55415
Baseball player

Barfield, Jesse
c/o New York Yankees
Yankee Stadium
Bronx, NY 10451
Baseball player

Barkley, Charles
c/o Phoenix Suns
2910 N. Central
PO Box 1369
Phoenix, AZ 85001
Basketball player

Barnes, Skeeter
c/o Detroit Tigers
Michigan and Trumbull Ave.
Detroit, MI 48216
Baseball player

Barros, Dana
c/o Seattle Supersonics
C Box 90011
Seattle, WA 98109
Basketball player

Baylor, Don
c/o Colorado Rockies
1700 Broadway, #2100
Denver, CO 80290
Baseball manager, former baseball player

Belle, Albert
c/o Cleveland Indians
Cleveland Stadium
Cleveland, OH 44114
Baseball player

Bennett, Cornelius
c/o Buffalo Bills
1 Bills Dr.
Orchard Park, NY 14127
Football player

Blackman, Rolando
c/o New York Knicks
4 Penn Plaza
New York, NY 10001
Basketball player

Blaylock, Mookie
c/o New Jersey Nets
Brendan Byrne Arena
East Rutherford, NJ 07073
Basketball player

Blue, Vida
Vida Blue Baseball Camp
PO Box 1449
Pleasanton, CA 94566
Former baseball player

Boggs, Wade
c/o Boston Red Sox
24 Yawkey Way
Boston, MA 02215
Baseball player

Bogues, Muggsy
c/o Charlotte Hornets
Hive Drive
Charlotte, NC 28217
Basketball player

Bol, Manute
c/o Philadelphia 76ers
PO Box 25040
Philadelphia, PA 19147
Basketball player

Bonds, Barry
c/o San Francisco Giants
Candlestick Park
San Francisco, CA 94124
Baseball player

Bonds, Bobby
c/o San Francisco Giants
Candlestick Park
San Francisco, CA 94124
Former baseball player, coach

Bones, Ricky
c/o Milwaukee Brewers
PO Box 3099
Milwaukee, WI 53201
Baseball player

Bonilla, Bobby
c/o New York Mets
126th and Roosevelt Ave.
Flushing, NY 11368
Baseball player

Bonner, Anthony
c/o New York Knicks
4 Penn Plaza
New York, NY 10001
Basketball player

Bosley, Thad
c/o Kansas City Royals
PO Box 419969
Kansas City, MO 64141
Baseball player

Boston, Daryl
c/o Colorado Rockies
1700 Broadway, #2100
Denver, CO 80290
Baseball player

Bowen, Ryan
c/o Florida Marlins
100 N.E. 3rd Ave.
Ft. Lauderdale, FL 33301
Baseball player

Bowie, Anthony
c/o Orlando Magic
1 Magic Place
Orlando, FL 32801
Basketball player

Bowie, Sam
c/o New Jersey Nets
Brendan Byrne Arena
East Rutherford, NJ 07073
Basketball player

Briscoe-Hooks, Valerie
World Class Management
PO Box 21053
Long Beach, CA 90801
Track and field athlete

Brooks, Kevin
c/o Denver Nuggets
PO Box 4658
Denver, CO 80204
Basketball player

Brown, Chad
c/o Pittsburgh Steelers
Three Rivers Stadium
300 Stadium Circle
Pittsburgh, PA 15212
Football player

Brown, Chucky
c/o New Jersey Nets
Brendan Byrne Arena
East Rutherford, NJ 07073
Basketball player

Brown, Dee
c/o Boston Celtics
150 Causeway St.
Boston, MA 02114
Basketball player

Brown, Jerry
c/o Florida Marlins
100 N.E. 3rd Ave.
Ft. Lauderdale, FL 33301
Baseball player

Brown, Jim
1851 Sunset Plaza River
Los Angeles, CA 90069
Football player (retired)

Brown, Mike
c/o Utah Jazz
5 Triad Center
Salt Lake City, UT 84180
Basketball player

Brown, Randy
c/o Sacramento Kings
1515 Sports Dr.
Sacramento, CA 95834
Basketball player

Brown, Tim
c/o Los Angeles Raiders
332 Center St.
El Segundo, CA 90245
Football player

Brown, Tony
c/o Seattle Supersonics
C Box 90011
Seattle, WA 98109
Basketball player

Browne, Jerry
c/o Oakland A's
Oakland-Alameda County
  Coliseum
Oakland, CA 94621
Baseball player

Bryant, Mark
c/o Portland Trailblazers
700 N.E. Multnomah St.
Portland, OR 97232
Basketball player

Burton, Willie
c/o Miami Dolphins
Miami Arena
Miami, FL 33136
Football player

Cage, Michael
c/o Seattle Supersonics
C Box 90011
Seattle, WA 98109
Basketball player

Calderon, Ivan
c/o Chicago White Sox
324 W. 35th St.
Chicago, IL 60616
Baseball player

Campbell, Elden
c/o Los Angeles Lakers
PO Box 10
Inglewood, CA 90306
Basketball player

Campbell, Tony
c/o New York Knicks
4 Penn Plaza
New York, NY 10001
Basketball player

Carew, Rod
1961 Miraloma
Placentia, CA 92670
Baseball player (retired)

Carr, Antoine
c/o San Antonio Spurs
600 E. Market St., #102
San Antonio, TX 78205
Basketball player

Carr, Chuck
c/o Florida Marlins
10 N.E. 3rd Ave.
Ft. Lauderdale, FL 33301
Baseball player

Carreker, Alphonso
c/o Denver Broncos
5700 Logan St.
Denver, CO 80216
Football player

Carrier, John
c/o Cleveland Browns
Cleveland Stadium
Cleveland, OH 44114
Football player

Carter, Anthony
c/o Minnesota Vikings
9520 Viking Dr.
Eden Prairie, MN 55344
Football player

Carter, Cari
c/o Green Bay Packers
1265 Lombardi Ave.
Green Bay, WI 54303
Football player

Carter, Chris
c/o Minnesota Vikings
9520 Viking Dr.
Eden Prairie, MN 55344
Football player

Carter, Joe
c/o Toronto Blue Jays
300 The Esplanade, #3
Toronto, Ontario M5V 3B3
Canada
Baseball player

Carter, Rodney
c/o Pittsburgh Steelers
Three Rivers Stadium
Pittsburgh, PA 15212
Football player

Carter, Wendell
c/o Los Angeles Rams
2327 W. Lincoln Ave.
Anaheim, CA 92801
Football player

Carthon, Maurice
c/o Giants Stadium
East Rutherford, NJ 07073
Football player

Cartwright, Bill
c/o Chicago Bulls
980 N. Michigan Ave., #1600
Chicago, IL 60611
Basketball player

Catledge, Terry
c/o Orlando Magic
1 Magic Pl.
Orlando, FL 32801
Basketball player

Causwell, Dwayne
c/o Sacramento Kings
1515 Sports Dr.
Sacramento, CA 95834
Basketball player

Ceeballos, Cedric
c/o Phoenix Suns
2910 N. Central
PO Box 1369
Phoenix, AZ 85001
Basketball player

Chamberlain, Wes
c/o Philadelphia 76ers
PO Box 7575
Philadelphia, PA 19101
Baseball player

Chamberlain, Wilt
15216 Antelo Pl.
Los Angeles, CA 90024
*Former basketball player, film
    producer*

Chambliss, Chris
c/o St. Louis Cardinals
250 Stadium Plaza
St. Louis, MO 63102
Former baseball player, coach

Charlton, Clifford
c/o Cleveland Browns
Cleveland Stadium
Cleveland, OH 44114
Football player

Cheaney, Calbert
c/o Washington Bullets
1 Harry S. Truman Dr.
Landover, MD 20786
Basketball player

Cheeks, Maurice
c/o Atlanta Hawks
1 CNN Center
Atlanta, GA 30303
Basketball player

Clancy, Sam
c/o Indianapolis Colts
PO Box 53500
Indianapolis, IN 46254
Football player

Clark, Gary
c/o Washington Redskins
PO Box 17247
Dulles International Airport
Washington, DC 20041
Football player

Clark, Jerald
c/o San Diego Padres
PO Box 2000
San Diego, CA 92120
Baseball player

Clayborn, Ray
c/o New England Patriots
Sullivan Stadium
Rt. 1
Foxboro, MA 02035
Football player

Clayton, Royce
c/o San Francisco Giants
Candlestick Park
San Francisco, CA 94124
Baseball player

Cobb, Reggie
c/o Tampa Bay Buccaneers
1 Buccaneer Plaza
Tampa, FL 33607
Football player

Cofer, Michael
Detroit Lions
PO Box 4200
Pontiac, MI 48057
Football player

Coffey, Richard
c/o Minnesota Timberwolves
500 City Pl., #730
Hennepin, MN 55403
Basketball player

Cole, Alexander
c/o Colorado Rockies
1700 Broadway, #2100
Denver, CO 80290
Baseball player

Coleman, Derrick
c/o New Jersey Nets
Brendan Byrne Arena
East Rutherford, NJ 07073
Basketball player

Coleman, Les
c/o National League of
    Professional Baseball Clubs
350 Park Ave.
New York, NY 10022
League president

Coleman, Monte
c/o Washington Redskins
PO Box 17247
Dulles International Airport
Washington, DC 20041
Football player

Coles, Bimbo
c/o Miami Heat
Miami Arena
Miami, FL 33136
Basketball player

Collins, Andre
c/o Washington Redskins
PO Box 17247
Dulles International Airport
Washington, DC 20041
Football player

Colter, Steve
c/o Washington Bullets
1 Harry S. Truman Dr.
Landover, MD 20786
Basketball player

Colton, Marcus
c/o Atlanta Falcons
Suwanee Road at I-85
Suwanee, GA 30174
Football player

Conley, Mike
1 Olympic Plaza
Colorado Springs, CO 80906
Track and field athlete

Connor, Lester
c/o Orlando Magic
1 Magic Pl.
Orlando, FL 32807
Basketball player

Cook, Anthony
c/o Denver Nuggets
PO Box 4658
Denver, CO 80204
Basketball player

Cooke, Anthony
c/o Denver Nuggets
PO Box 4658
Denver, CO 80204
Basketball player

Cooks, Johnnie
c/o Giants
Giants Stadium
East Rutherford, NJ 07073
Football player

Cooper, Duane
c/o Los Angeles Lakers
PO Box 10
Inglewood, CA 90306
Basketball player

Cooper, Tyrone
c/o Utah Jazz
5 Triad Center
Salt Lake City, UT 84180
Basketball player

Cooper, Wayne
c/o Portland Trailblazers
700 N.E. Multnomah St., #600
Portland, OR 97232
Basketball player

Corbin, Tyrone
c/o Utah Jazz
5 Triad Center
Salt Lake City, UT 84180
Basketball player

Cottingham, Robert
c/o U.S. Fencing Association
1750 E. Boulder St.
Colorado Springs, CO 80909-5774
Fencing champion

Cotto, Henry
c/o Florida Marlins
100 N.E. 3rd Ave.
Ft. Lauderdale, FL 33301
Baseball player

Croel, Mike
c/o Denver Broncos
5700 Logan St.
Denver, CO 80216
Football player

Cummings, Terry
c/o San Antonio Spurs
600 E. Market St., #102
San Antonio, TX 78205
Basketball player

Cunningham, Randall
c/o Philadelphia Eagles
Veterans Stadium
Philadelphia, PA 19148
Football player

Cunningham, Samuel
c/o New England Patriots
Sullivan Stadium
Rt. 1
Foxboro, MA 02035
Football player

Curry, Dell
c/o Charlotte Hornets
Hive Drive
Charlotte, NC 28217
Basketball player

Cuyler, Milton
c/o Detroit Tigers
Michigan and Trumbull Ave.
Detroit, MI 48216
Baseball player

Daniels, Lloyd
c/o San Antonio Spurs
600 E. Market St., #102
San Antonio, TX 78205
Basketball player

Davidson, Kenneth
c/o Pittsburgh Steelers
300 Stadium Circle
Pittsburgh, PA 15212
Football player

Davis, Alvin
c/o Oakland A's
PO Box 2000
Anaheim, CA 92803
Baseball player

Davis, Chili
c/o Oakland A's
PO Box 2000
Anaheim, CA 92803
Baseball player

Davis, Dale
c/o Oakland A's
PO Box 2000
Anaheim, CA 92803
Baseball player

Davis, Eric
c/o Detroit Tigers
Michigan and Trumbull Ave.
Detroit, MI 48216
Baseball player

Davis, Hubert
c/o New York Knicks
4 Penn Plaza
New York, NY 10001
Basketball player

Davis, Terry
c/o Miami Heat
Miami Arena
Miami, FL 33136
Basketball player

Davis, Wendell
c/o Chicago Bears
250 N. Washington Rd.
Lake Forest, IL 60045
Football player

Dawkins, Johnny
c/o Philadelphia 76ers
PO Box 25040
Philadelphia, PA 19147
Basketball player

Dawson, Andre
c/o Boston Red Sox
4 Yawkey Way
Boston, MA 02215
Baseball player

Dawson, James
c/o New England Patriots
Sullivan Stadium
Rt. 1
Foxboro, MA 02035
Football player

Dawson, Lin
c/o New England Patriots
Sullivan Stadium
Rt. 1
Foxboro, MA 02035
Football player

Day, Todd
c/o Milwaukee Bucks
1001 N. 4th St.
Milwaukee, WI 53203
Basketball player

Dent, Richard
c/o Chicago Bears
250 N. Washington Rd.
Lake Forest, IL 60045
Football player

De Shields, Delino
c/o Montreal Expos
PO Box 500, Station M
Montreal, Quebec, H1V 3P2
Canada
Baseball player

Destrade, Orestest
c/o Florida Marlins
100 N.E. 3rd Ave.
Ft. Lauderdale, FL 33301
Baseball player

Dickerson, Eric
c/o Indianapolis Colts
PO Box 53500
Indianapolis, IN 45254
Football player

Dixon, Floyd
c/o Philadelphia Eagles
Veterans Stadium
Philadelphia, PA 19148
Football player

Dixon, Hanford
c/o San Francisco 49ers
4949 Centennial Blvd.
Santa Clara, CA 95054
Football player

Dixon, James
c/o Dallas Cowboys
1 Cowboy Pkwy.
Irving, TX 75063
Football player

Donaldson, Ray
c/o Seattle Seahawks
11220 N.E. 53rd St.
Kirkland, WA 98033
Football player

Dorsey, Eric
c/o Giants
Giants Stadium
East Rutherford, NJ 07073
Football player

Doughtery, Brad
c/o Cleveland Cavaliers
2923 Streetsboro Rd.
Richfield, OH 44286
Basketball player

Douglas, Sherman
c/o Boston Celtics
150 Causeway St.
Boston, MA 02114
Basketball player

Dowdel, Marcus
c/o New Orleans Saints
6928 Saints Ave.
Metairie, LA 70003
Football player

Drexler, Clyde
c/o Portland Trailblazers
700 N.E. Multnomah St.
Portland, OR 97232
Basketball player

Duckworth, Kevin
c/o Portland Trailblazers
700 N.E. Multnomah St.
Portland, OR 97232
Basketball player

Dumars, Joe
c/o Detroit Pistons
1 Championship Dr.
Auburn Hills, MI 48057
Basketball player

Dumas, Richard
c/o Phoenix Suns
PO Box 1369
Phoenix, AZ 85001
Basketball player

Dunn, T. R.
c/o Denver Nuggets
PO Box 4658
Denver, CO 80204
Basketball player

Dunston, Shawon
c/o Chicago Cubs
1060 W. Addison St.
Chicago, IL 60613
Baseball player

Eackles, Ledell
c/o Washington Bullets
1 Harry S. Truman Dr.
Landover, MD 20786
Basketball player

Early, Quinn
c/o New Orleans Saints
6928 Saints Ave.
Metairie, LA 70003
Football player

Easley, Damon
c/o Oakland A's
PO Box 2000
Anaheim, CA 92803
Baseball player

Edmunds, Ferrell
c/o Seattle Seahawks
11220 N.E. 53rd St.
Kirkland, WA 98033
Football player

Edwards, Blue
c/o Milwaukee Brewers
1001 N. 4th St.
Milwaukee, WI 53203
Basketball player

Edwards, James
c/o Los Angeles Lakers
PO Box 10
Inglewood, CA 90306
Basketball player

Edwards, Kevin
c/o Miami Heat
Miami Arena
Miami, FL 33136
Basketball player

Elder, Lee
1725 K St., #1112
Washington, DC 20006
Professional golfer

Elewonibi, Mohammed
c/o Washington Redskins
PO Box 17247
Dulles International Airport
Washington, DC 20041
Football player

Elie, Mario
c/o Portland Trailblazers
700 N.E. Multnomah St.
Portland, OR 97232
Basketball player

Elkins, Michael
c/o Kansas City Chiefs
1 Arrowhead Dr.
Kansas City, MO 64141
Football player

Ellard, Henry
c/o Los Angeles Rams
2327 W. Lincoln Ave.
Anaheim, CA 92801
Football player

Elliot, Sean
c/o San Antonio Spurs
600 E. Market St., #102
San Antonio, TX 78205
Basketball player

Ellis, Dale
c/o San Antonio Spurs
600 E. Market St., #102
San Antonio, TX 78205
Basketball player

Ellison, Pervis
c/o Washington Bullets
1 Harry S. Truman Dr.
Landover, MD 20786
Basketball player

Erving, Julius
1420 Locust St., #12K
Philadelphia, PA 19102
*Retired basketball player,
    businessman*

Evans, Donald
c/o Pittsburgh Steelers
300 Stadium Circle
Pittsburgh, PA 15212
Football player

Ewing, Patrick
c/o New York Knicks
4 Penn Plaza
New York, NY 10001
Basketball player

Fenner, Derrick
c/o Seattle Seahawks
11220 N.E. 53rd St.
Kirkland, WA 98033
Football player

Ferrell, Duane
c/o Atlanta Hawks
1 CNN Center
Atlanta, GA 30303
Basketball player

Fielder, Cecil
c/o Detroit Tigers
Michigan and Trumbull Ave.
Detroit, MI 48216
Baseball player

Floyd, Sleepy
c/o Houston Rockets
The Summit
Houston, TX 77046
Basketball player

Foreman, George
7639 Pine Oak Dr.
Humble, TX 77397
Former boxer, actor

Fox, Rich
c/o Boston Celtics
150 Causeway St.
Boston, MA 02114
Basketball player

Francis, Ronald
New England Patriots
Foxboro Stadium
Rt. 1
Foxboro, MA 02035
Football player

Franco, Julio
1250 Copeland Rd., #4100
Arlington, TX 76011
Baseball player

Frazier, Joe
2917 N. Broad St.
Philadelphia, PA 19132
Former boxer

Frazier, Walt
675 Flamingo Dr.
Atlanta, GA 30311
*Former basketball player, radio
    commentator*

Frederick, Anthony
c/o Charlotte Hornets
Hive Drive
Charlotte, NC 29217
Basketball player

Fuhr, Grant
c/o Buffalo Sabres
140 Main St.
Buffalo, NY 14202
Hockey player

Garland, Winston
c/o Denver Nuggets
PO Box 4658
Denver, CO 80204
Basketball player

Garrick, Tom
c/o San Antonio Spurs
600 E. Market St., #102
San Antonio, TX 78205
Basketball player

Garrison, Zina
PO Box 272305
Houston, TX 77277
Tennis player

Gatling, Chris
c/o Golden State Warriors
Nimitz Freeway and
  Hegenberger Rd.
Oakland, CA 94621
Basketball player

Gattison, Kenny
c/o Charlotte Hornets
Hive Drive
Charlotte, NC 28217
Basketball player

Gault, Willie
7700 Sunset Blvd., #205
Los Angeles, CA 90046
Former football player

George, Tate
c/o New Jersey Nets
Brendan Byrne Arena
East Rutherford, NJ 07073
Basketball player

Gibson, Althea
275 Prospect St., #768
East Orange, NJ 07017
Former tennis player

Gill, Kendall
c/o Seattle Supersonics
C Box 90011
Seattle, WA 98109
Basketball player

Glass, Gerald
c/o Minnesota Timberwolves
730 Hennepin Ave., #500
Minneapolis, MN 55403
Basketball player

Gooden, Dwight
c/o New York Mets
126th and Roosevelt Ave.
Flushing, NY 11368
Baseball player

Gordon, Tom
c/o Kansas City Royals
1 Royal Way
Kansas City, MO 64141
Baseball player

Graham, Snoopy
c/o Atlanta Hawks
1 CNN Center
Atlanta, GA 30303
Basketball player

Grant, Gary
c/o Los Angeles Clippers
3939 S. Figueroa St.
Los Angeles, CA 90037
Basketball player

Grant, Greg
c/o Philadelphia 76ers
PO Box 25040
Philadelphia, PA 19147
Basketball player

Grant, Harvey
c/o Washington Bullets
1 Harry S. Truman Dr.
Landover, MD 20786
Basketball player

Grant, Horace
c/o Chicago Bulls
980 N. Michigan Ave.
Chicago, IL 60611
Basketball player

Grayer, Jeff
c/o Golden State Warriors
Nimitz Freeway and
   Hegenberger Rd.
Oakland, CA 94621
Basketball player

Green, A. C.
c/o Los Angeles Lakers
PO Box 10
Inglewood, CA 90306
Basketball player

Green, Sidney
c/o San Antonio Spurs
600 E. Market St., #102
San Antonio, TX 78205
Basketball player

Gregg, Eric Eugene
c/o National Baseball League
645 5th Ave.
New York, NY 10022
Major league umpire

Grier, Rosey
11656 Montana, #301
Los Angeles, CA 90049
*Former football player, gospel
   singer*

Griffey, Ken, Jr.
c/o Seattle Mariners
PO Box 4100
Seattle, WA 98104
Baseball player

Griffith-Joyner, Florence
11444 W. Olympic Blvd., 10th
   Floor
Los Angeles, CA 90064
Tack and field athlete

Grissom, Marquis
c/o Montreal Expos
PO Box 500, Station M
Montreal, Quebec, H1V 3P2
Canada
Baseball player

Gwynn, Chris
c/o Kansas City Royals
1 Royal Way
Kansas City, MO 64141
Baseball player

Gwynn, Tony
c/o San Diego Padres
PO Box 2000
San Diego, CA 92120
Baseball player

Hammond, Tom
c/o Charlotte Hornets
Hive Drive
Charlotte, NC 28217
Basketball player

Hardaway, Anfernee
c/o Orlando Magic
1 Magic Pl.
Orlando, FL 32801
Basketball player

Hardaway, Tim
c/o Golden State Warriors
Nimitz Freeway and
   Hegenberger Rd.
Oakland, CA 94621
Basketball player

Harlem Globetrotters
6121 Sunset Blvd.
Los Angeles, CA 90038
Comedy basketball team

Harper, Alvin
c/o Dallas Cowboys
1 Cowboy Pkwy.
Irving, TX 75063
Football player

Harper, Derek
c/o New York Knicks
4 Penn Plaza
New York, NY 10001
Basketball player

Harper, Ron
c/o Los Angeles Clippers
3939 S. Figueroa St.
Los Angeles, CA 90037
Basketball player

Harris, Lenny
c/o Los Angeles Dodgers
1000 Elysan Park Ave.
Los Angeles, CA 90012
Baseball player

Hatcher, Billy
c/o Boston Red Sox
4 Yawkey Way
Boston, MA 02215
Baseball player

Hawkins, Hershey
Philadelphia 76ers
PO Box 25040
Philadelphia, PA 19147
Basketball player

Hayes, Charlie
c/o Colorado Rockies
1700 Broadway, #2100
Denver, CO 80290
Baseball player

Hayley, Charles
c/o Dallas Cowboys
1 Cowboy Pkwy.
Irving, TX 75063
Football player

Hearns, Tommy
197 W. Twelve Mile Rd.
South Field, MI 48076
Former boxer

Henderson, Rickey
c/o Oakland A's
Oakland-Alameda County
    Stadium
Oakland, CA 94621
Baseball player

Herrera, Carl
c/o Houston Rockets
The Summit
Houston, TX 77046
Basketball player

Higgins, Rod
c/o Golden State Warriors
Nimitz Freeway and
    Hegenberger Rd.
Oakland, CA 94621
Basketball player

Higgins, Sean
c/o Los Angeles Lakers
PO Box 10
Inglewood, CA 90306
Basketball player

Hill, Drew
c/o Houston Oilers
6910 Fannin St.
Houston, TX 77030
Football player

Hill, Tyrone
c/o Golden State Warriors
Nimitz Freeway and
    Hegenberger Rd.
Oakland, CA 94621
Basketball player

Hinton Chris
c/o Atlanta Falcons
Suwanee Road at I-85
Suwanee, GA 30174
Football player

Hodge, Donald
c/o Dallas Mavericks
777 Sports St.
Dallas, TX 75207
Basketball player

Holmes, Jerry
c/o Green Bay Packers
1265 Lombardi Ave.
Green Bay, WI 54303
Football player

Holmes, Larry
413 N. Hampton St.
Easton, PA 18042
Former boxer

Holyfield, Evander
c/o Roll Wit It Entertainment
39510 Paseo Padre Pkwy., #250
Fremont, CA 94538
Boxer

Hopson, Dennis
c/o Sacramento Kings
1515 Sports Dr.
Sacramento, CA 95834
Basketball player

Howard, David
c/o Kansas City Royals
1 Royal Way
Kansas City, MO 64141
Baseball player

Howard, Thomas
c/o Cincinnati Reds
100 Riverfront Stadium
Cincinnati, OH 45202
Baseball player

Humphries, Jay
c/o Utah Jazz
6 Triad Center
Salt Lake City, UT 84180
Basketball player

Huskey, Butch
c/o New York Mets
126th and Roosevelt Ave.
Flushing, NY 11368
Baseball player

Irvin, Michael
c/o Dallas Cowboys
1 Cowboy Pkwy.
Irving, TX 75063
Football player

Jackson, Bo
PO Box 2517
Auburn, AL 36831
*Baseball player, former football
player*

Jackson, Chris
c/o Denver Nuggets
PO Box 4658
Denver, CO 80204
Basketball player

Jackson, Keith
c/o Miami Dolphins
2269 N.W. 199th St.
Miami, FL 33056
Football player

Jackson, Kenny
c/o Houston Oilers
6910 Fannin St.
Houston, TX 77030
Football player

Jackson, Mark
c/o Los Angeles Clippers
3939 S. Figueroa St.
Los Angeles, CA 90037
Basketball player

Jackson, Reggie
22 Yankee Hill
Oakland, CA 94616
*Former baseball player, sports
   administrator*

James, Rolando
c/o New England Patriots
Sullivan Stadium
Rt. 1
Foxboro, MA 02035
Football player

Jeffcoat, James
c/o Dallas Cowboys
1 Cowboy Pkwy.
Irving, TX 75063
Football player

Jefferson, Reggie
c/o Cleveland Indians
Cleveland Stadium
Cleveland, OH 44114
Baseball player

Jeffries, Haywood
c/o Houston Oilers
6910 Fannin St.
Houston, TX 77030
Football player

Jenkins, Chip
1 Olympic Plaza
Colorado Springs, CO 80909
Track and field athlete

Jenkins, Melvin
c/o Atlanta Falcons
Suwannee Road at I-85
Suwannee, GA 30174
Football player

Johnson, Avery
c/o Houston Rockets
The Summit
Houston, TX 77046
Basketball player

Johnson, Ben
62 Black Toft
Scarborough, Ontario, M1B 2N6
Canada
Track and field athlete

Johnson, Buck
c/o Houston Rockets
The Summit
Houston, TX 77046
Basketball player

Johnson, Eddie
c/o Seattle Supersonics
C Box 90011
Seattle, WA 98109
Basketball player

Johnson, Kevin
c/o Phoenix Suns
2910 N. Central
PO Box 1369
Phoenix, AZ 85001
Basketball player

Johnson, Lance
c/o Chicago Bulls
324 W. 35th St.
Chicago, IL 60616
Basketball player

Johnson, Larry
c/o Charlotte Hornets
Hive Drive
Charlotte, NC 28217
Basketball player

Johnson, Magic
12 Beverly Park
Beverly Hills, CA 90210
Former basketball player

Johnson, Victoria
Metro Fitness
PO Box 1744
Lake Oswego, OR 97035
Aerobics and fitness expert

Johnson, Vinnie
c/o San Antonio Spurs
600 E. Market St., #102
San Antonio, TX 78205
Basketball player

Jones, Esther B.
c/o Nike
1 Bowerman Dr.
Beaverton, OR 92005
Athlete

Jones, Sean
c/o Houston Oilers
6910 Fannin St.
Houston, TX 77030
Football player

Jordan, Michael
c/o Pro Serv
1101 Wilson Blvd.
Arlington, VA 22209
Basketball player (retired), baseball player, athletic company executive

Jordan, Ricky
c/o Philadelphia 76ers
PO Box 7575
Philadelphia, PA 19101
Baseball player

Jordan, Ryan
c/o St. Louis Cardinals
250 Stadium Plaza
St. Louis, MO 63102
Baseball player

Jose, Felix
c/o Kansas City Royals
1 Royal Way
Kansas City, MO 64141
Baseball player

Joyner-Kersee, Jackie
20214 Leadwell
Canoga Park, CA 91304
Track and field athlete

Justice, David
c/o Atlanta Braves
PO Box 4064
Atlanta, GA 30302
Baseball player

Kelly, Roberto
c/o Cincinnati Reds
100 Riverfront Stadium
Cincinnati, OH 45202
Baseball player

Kemp, Shawn
c/o Seattle Supersonics
C Box 90011
Seattle, WA 98109
Basketball player

Kennedy, Cortez
Seattle Seahawks
11220 N.E. 53rd St.
Kirkland, WA 98033
Football player

Kersey, Jerome
c/o Portland Trailblazers
700 N.E. Multnomah St.
Portland, OR 97232
Basketball player

Kimble, Bo
c/o Los Angeles Clippers
3939 S. Figueroa St.
Los Angeles, CA 90037
Basketball player

King, Don
c/o Don King Enterprises
32 E. 69th St.
New York, NY 10021
Boxing promoter and manager

Knight, Negele
c/o Phoenix Suns
PO Box 1369
Phoenix, AZ 85001
Basketball player

Landrum, Cedric
c/o New York Mets
126th and Roosevelt Ave.
Flushing, NY 11368
Baseball player

Lang, Andrew
c/o Philadelphia 76ers
PO Box 25040
Philadelphia, PA 19147
Basketball player

Larkin, Barry
c/o Cincinnati Reds
100 Riverfront Stadium
Cincinnati, OH 45202
Baseball player

Lemon, Meadowlark
PO Box 398
Sierra Vista, AZ 85635
Retired basketball player

Leonard, Sugar Ray
1505 Brady Ct.
Mitchellville, MD 20716
Former boxer, commentator

Lever, Lafayette "Fat"
c/o Dallas Mavericks
777 Sports St.
Dallas, TX 75207
Basketball player

Levingston, Cliff
c/o Chicago Bulls
980 N. Michigan Ave.
Chicago, IL 60611
Basketball player

Lewis, Albert
c/o Kansas City Royals
1 Arrowhead Dr.
Kansas City, MO 64129
Football player

Lewis, Carl
1801 Ocean Park Blvd., #112
Santa Monica, CA 90405
Track and field athlete

Lewis, Darren
c/o San Francisco Giants
Candlestick Park
San Francisco, CA 94124
Baseball player

Lewis, Ronald
c/o Green Bay Packers
1265 Lombardi Ave.
Green Bay, WI 54303
Football player

Liberty, Marcus
c/o Denver Nuggets
PO Box 4658
Denver, CO 80204
Basketball player

Lister, Alton
c/o Golden State Warriors
Nimitz Freeway and
    Hegenberger Rd.
Oakland, CA 94621
Basketball player

Lockhart, Eugene
c/o Dallas Cowboys
1 Cowboy Pkwy.
Irving, TX 75063
Football player

Long, Grant
c/o Miami Heat
Miami Arena
Miami, FL 33136
Basketball player

Long, Howard
c/o Los Angeles Raiders
332 Center St.
El Segundo, CA 90245
Football player

Lott, Ronnie
c/o New York Jets
598 Madison Ave.
New York, NY 10022
Football player

Lucas, John
PO Box 273023
Houston, TX 77277-3023
Coach, former basketball player

Malone, Jeff
c/o Utah Jazz
5 Triad Center
Salt Lake City, UT 84180
Basketball player

Malone, Karl
c/o Utah Jazz
5 Triad Center
Salt Lake City, UT 84180
Basketball player

Malone, Moses
c/o Milwaukee Bucks
1001 N. 4th St.
Milwaukee, WI 53203
Basketball player

Manning, Danny
c/o Los Angeles Clippers
3939 S. Figueroa St.
Los Angeles, CA 90037
Basketball player

Mariner, Jonathan
c/o Florida Marlins
100 N.E. 3rd Ave.
Ft. Lauderdale, FL 33301
Sports executive

Mashburn, Jamal
c/o Dallas Mavericks
777 Sports Dr.
Dallas, TX 75207
Basketball player

Mason, Anthony
c/o New York Knicks
4 Penn Plaza
New York, NY 10001
Basketball player

Mason, Mark
c/o Denver Nuggets
PO Box 4658
Denver, CO 80204
Basketball player

Maxwell, Vernon
c/o Houston Rockets
The Summit
Houston, TX 77046
Basketball player

May, Derrick
c/o Chicago Bulls
1060 W. Addison St.
Chicago, IL 60613
Basketball player

Mays, Travis
c/o Atlanta Hawks
1 CNN Center
Atlanta, GA 30303
Basketball player

Mays, Willie
3333 Henry Hudson Pkwy.
Bronx, NY 10463
Former baseball player

McCain, Bob
Minnesota Timberwolves
730 Hennepin Ave., #500
Minneapolis, MN 55403
Basketball player

McCray, Rodney
c/o Dallas Mavericks
777 Sports St.
Dallas, TX 75207
Basketball player

McDaniel, Xavier
c/o Boston Celtics
150 Causeway St.
Boston, MA 02114
Basketball player

McElroy, Chuck
c/o Chicago Bulls
1060 W. Addison St.
Chicago, IL 60613
Basketball player

McGee, Willie
c/o San Francisco Giants
Candlestick Park
San Francisco, CA 94124
Baseball player

McGriff, Fred
c/o San Diego Padres
PO Box 2000
San Diego, CA 92120
Baseball player

McKegney, Tony
5700 Oakland Ave.
St. Louis, MO 63110
Retired hockey player

McKey, Derek
c/o Seattle Supersonics
C Box 90011
Seattle, WA 98109
Basketball player

McMillan, Nate
c/o Seattle Supersonics
C Box 90011
Seattle, WA 98109
Basketball player

McRae, Brian
c/o Kansas City Royals
1 Royal Way
Kansas City, MO 64141
Baseball player

McRae, Hal
c/o Kansas City Royals
1 Royal Way
Kansas City, MO 64141
Baseball player

Metcalf, Eric
c/o Cleveland Browns
Cleveland Stadium
Cleveland, OH 44114
Football player

Meyers, Gerri
2852 Jefferson Davis Highway
Stafford, VA 22554
Gospel aerobics expert

Mills, Terry
c/o New Jersey Nets
Brendan Byrne Arena
East Rutherford, NJ 07073
Basketball player

Minor, Harold
c/o Miami Heat
Miami Arena
Miami, FL 33136
Basketball player

Mitchell, Kevin
c/o Cincinnati Reds
100 Riverfront Stadium
Cincinnati, OH 45202
Baseball player

Mitchell, Sam
c/o Minnesota Twins
730 Hennepin Ave., #500
Minneapolis, MN 55403
Basketball player

Monroe, Earl
113 W. 88th St.
New York, NY 10025
Former basketball player

Monroe, Rodney
c/o Atlanta Hawks
1 CNN Center
Atlanta, GA 30303
Basketball player

Moon, Warren
c/o Houston Oilers
7910 Fannin St.
Houston, TX 77030
Football player

Moore, Tracy
c/o Dallas Mavericks
777 Sports St.
Dallas, TX 75207
Basketball player

Morris, Chris
c/o New Jersey Nets
Brendan Byrne Arena
East Rutherford, NJ 07073
Basketball player

Morton, John
c/o Miami Heat
Miami Arena
Miami, FL 33136
Basketball player

Moses, Edwin
326 Otero
Newport Beach, CA 92660
Track and field athlete

Murdoch, Eric
c/o Milwaukee Bucks
1001 North St.
Milwaukee, WI 53203
Basketball player

Murray, Eddie
c/o New York Mets
126th and Roosevelt Ave.
Flushing, NY 11368
Baseball player

Mustaf, Jerrod
c/o Phoenix Suns
PO Box 1369
Phoenix, AZ 85001
Basketball player

Mutombo, Dikembe
c/o Denver Nuggets
PO Box 4658
Denver, CO 80204
Basketball player

Nance, Larry
c/o Cleveland Cavaliers
2923 Streetsboro Rd.
Richfield, OH 44286
Basketball player

Newman, Johnny
c/o New Jersey Nets
Brendan Byrne Arena
East Rutherford, NJ 07073
Basketball player

Nixon, Otis
c/o Atlanta Hawks
PO Box 4064
Atlanta, GA 30302
Baseball player

Noah, Yannick
Pro Serv Inc.
1101 Wilson Blvd., #1800
Arlington, VA 22209
Tennis player

Norman, Kenny
c/o Los Angeles Clippers
3939 S. Figueroa St.
Los Angeles, CA 90037
Basketball player

Norton, Ken
16 S. Peck Dr.
Laguna Niguel, CA 92607
Former boxer

Oakley, Charles
c/o New York Knicks
4 Penn Plaza
New York, NY 10001
Basketball player

Offerman, Jose
c/o Los Angeles Dodgers
1000 Elysan Park Ave.
Los Angeles, CA 90012
Baseball player

Olajuwon, Hakeem
c/o Houston Rockets
The Summit
Houston, TX 77046
Basketball player

Oliver, Brian
c/o Philadelphia 76ers
PO Box 25040
Philadelphia, PA 19147
Basketball player

O'Neal, Shaquille
c/o Orlando Magic
1 Magic Pl.
Orlando, FL 32801
Basketball player, rapper, actor

Owens, Billy
c/o Golden State Warriors
Nimitz Freeway and
  Hegenberger Rd.
Oakland, CA 94621
Basketball player

Owens, Keith
c/o Los Angeles Lakers
PO Box 10
Inglewood, CA 90306
Basketball player

Pach, Robert
c/o Portland Trailblazers
700 N.E. Multnomah St.
Portland, OR 97232
Basketball player

Parrish, Robert
c/o Boston Celtics
150 Causeway St.
Boston, MA 02114
Basketball player

Patterson, Floyd
PO Box 336
New Paltz, NY 12561
*Athletic commissioner, former
  heavyweight boxer*

Payne, Kenny
c/o Philadelphia 76ers
PO Box 25040
Philadelphia, PA 19147
Basketball player

Payton, Gary
c/o Seattle Supersonics
C Box 90011
Seattle, WA 98109

Peele, Rodney
c/o Detroit Tigers
PO Box 4200
Pontiac, MI 48057
Baseball player

Pele
75 Rockefeller Plaza
New York, NY 10019
Former soccer player

Pendleton, Terry
c/o Atlanta Braves
PO Box 4064
Atlanta, GA 30302
Baseball player

Perez, Melido
c/o New York Yankees
Yankees Stadium
Bronx, NY 10451
Baseball player

Perkins, Sam
c/o Seattle Supersonics
C Box 90011
Seattle, WA 98121
Basketball player

Perry, Gerald
c/o St. Louis Cardinals
250 Stadium Plaza
St. Louis, MO 63102
Baseball player

Perry, Tim
c/o Philadelphia 76ers
PO Box 25040
Philadelphia, PA 19147
Basketball player

Perry, William
c/o Chicago Bears
250 N. Washington Rd.
Lake Forest, IL 60645
Football player

Petra, Stanley
c/o Houston Oilers
6910 Fannin St.
Houston, TX 77030
Football player

Pierce, Ricky
c/o Seattle Supersonics
C Box 90011
Seattle, WA 98109
Basketball player

Pinckney, Ed
c/o Boston Celtics
150 Causeway St.
Boston, MA 02114
Basketball player

Pippen, Scottie
c/o Chicago Bulls
980 N. Michigan Ave.
Chicago, IL 60611
Basketball player

Porter, Terry
c/o Portland Trailblazers
700 N.E. Multnomah St.
Portland, OR 97232
Basketball player

Puckett, Kirby
c/o Minnesota Twins
501 Chicago Ave. S
Minneapolis, MN 55415
Baseball player

Quick, Mike
c/o Philadelphia Eagles
Veterans Stadium
Broad St. and Patterson
Philadelphia, PA 19148
Football player

Raines, Tim
c/o Chicago White Sox
324 W. 35th St.
Chicago, IL 60616
Baseball player

Randolph, Willie
c/o New York Mets
126th and Roosevelt Ave.
Flushing, NY 11368
Baseball player

Reid, J. R.
c/o Charlotte Hornets
Hive Drive
Charlotte, NC 28217
Basketball player

Reynolds, Jerry
c/o Orlando Magic
1 Magic Pl.
Orlando, FL 32801
Basketball player

Rice, Glen
c/o Miami Heat
Miami Arena
Miami, FL 33136
Basketball player

Rice, Jerry
c/o San Francisco 49ers
4949 Centennial Blvd.
Santa Clara, CA 95054
Football player

Richardson, Pooh
c/o Minnesota Timberwolves
730 Hennepin Ave., #500
Minneapolis, MN 55403
Basketball player

Richmond, Mitch
c/o Sacramento Kings
1515 Sports Dr.
Sacramento, CA 95834
Basketball player

Rison, Andre
c/o Atlanta Falcons
Suwanee Road at I-85
Suwanee, GA 30174
Football player

Rivers, Doc
c/o New York Knicks
4 Pennsylvania Plaza
New York, NY 10001
Basketball player

Roberts, Bip
c/o Cincinnati Reds
100 Riverfront Stadium
Cincinnati, OH 45202
Baseball player

Roberts, Stanley
c/o Orlando Magic
1 Magic Pl.
Orlando, Florida 32801
Basketball player

Robertson, Alvin
c/o Detroit Pistons
1 Championship Dr.
Auburn Hill, MI 48057
Basketball player

Robertson, Oscar
PO Box 179
Springfield, MA 01101
Former basketball player

Robinson, Cliff
c/o Portland Trailblazers
700 N.E. Multnomah St.
Portland, OR 97232
Basketball player

Robinson, David
c/o San Antonio Spurs
600 E. Market St., #102
San Antonio, TX 78205
Basketball player

Robinson, Rumeal
c/o Atlanta Hawks
1 CNN Center
Atlanta, GA 30303
Basketball player

Rodman, Dennis
c/o San Antonio Spurs
600 E. Market St., #102
San Antonio, TX 78205
Basketball player

Rogers, Rodney
c/o Denver Nuggets
PO Box 4658
Denver, CO 80204
Basketball player

Rollins, Wayne
c/o Orlando Magic
1 Magic Pl.
Orlando, FL 32801
Basketball player

Royal, Donald
c/o Orlando Magic
1 Magic Pl.
Orlando, FL 32801
Basketball player

Rudolph, Wilma
3500 Centennial Blvd.
Nashville, TN 37203
Track and field athlete

Russell, Bill
PO Box 58
Mercer Island, WA 98040
Former basketball player

Sanders, Barry
c/o Detroit Tigers
PO Box 4200
Pontiac, MI 48057
Football player

Sanders, Deion
521 Capitol Ave. SW
Atlanta, GA 30312-2303
Baseball and football player

Sanders, Jeff
c/o Atlanta Hawks
1 CNN Center
Atlanta, GA 30303
Basketball player

Sanders, Reggie
c/o Cincinnati Reds
100 Riverfront Stadium
Cincinnati, OH 45202
Baseball player

Savage, Reggie
c/o Washington Capitals
Capitol Center
Landover, MD 20786
Hockey player

Scott, Byron
c/o Los Angeles Lakers
PO Box 10
Inglewood, CA 90306
Basketball player

Scott, Dennis
c/o Orlando Magic
1 Magic Pl.
Orlando, FL 32801
Basketball player

Sellers, Brad
c/o Detroit Pistons
1 Championship Dr.
Auburn Hills, MI 48057
Basketball player

Shackleford, Charles
c/o Philadelphia 76ers
PO Box 25040
Philadelphia, PA 19147
Basketball player

Sharperson, Mike
c/o Los Angeles Dodgers
1000 Elysan Park Ave.
Los Angeles, CA 90012
Baseball player

Shaw, Brian
c/o Miami Heat
Miami Arena
Miami, FL 33136
Basketball player

Sheffield, Gary
c/o Florida Marlins
100 N.E. 3rd Ave.
Ft. Lauderdale, FL 33301
Baseball player

Shell, Art
308016 rue de la Pierre
Rancho Palos Verdes, CA 90274
Football coach

Sifford, Charlie
PO Box 109601
Palm Beach Gardens, FL 33418
Professional golfer

Simmons, Lionel
c/o Sacramento Kings
1515 Sports Dr.
Sacramento, CA 95834
Basketball player

Simmons, Ron
World Wrestling Foundation
1241 E. Main St.
Stamford, CT 06902
Professional wrestler

Simpson, O.J.
360 Rockingham Ave.
Brentwood, CA 94513
*Former football player,
   commentator, actor*

Smith, Anthony
c/o Los Angeles Raiders
332 Center St.
El Segundo, CA 90245
Football player

Smith, Charles
c/o New York Knicks
4 Penn Plaza
New York, NY 10001
Basketball player

Smith, Doug
c/o Dallas Mavericks
777 Sports Dr.
Dallas, TX 75207
Basketball player

Smith, Emmit
c/o Dallas Cowboys
1 Cowboy Pkwy.
Irving, TX 75063
Football player

Smith, Kenny
c/o Houston Rockets
The Summit
Houston, TX 77046
Basketball player

Smith, Lee
c/o St. Louis Cardinals
250 Stadium Plaza
St. Louis, MO 63102
Baseball player

Smith, Ozzie
c/o St. Louis Cardinals
250 Stadium Plaza
St. Louis, MO 63102
Baseball player

Smith, Steve
c/o Miami Heat
Miami Arena
Miami, FL 33136
Basketball player

Smith, Tony
c/o Los Angeles Lakers
PO Box 10
Inglewood, CA 90306
Basketball player

Spencer, Felton
c/o Minnesota Timberwolves
730 Hennepin Ave.
Minneapolis, MN 55403
Basketball player

Spinks, Leon
22 W. Ontario
Chicago, IL 60610
Former boxer

Spinks, Michael
20284 Archdale
Detroit, MI 48235
Former boxer

Stark, John
c/o New York Knicks
4 Penn Plaza
New York, NY 10001
Basketball player

Stith, Bryan
c/o Denver Nuggets
PO Box 4658
Denver, CO 80204
Basketball player

Strawberry, Darryl
4740 Zelzah Ave.
Encino, CA 91316
Baseball player

Strickland, Rod
c/o Portland Trailblazers
700 N.E. Multnomah St.
Portland, OR 97232
Basketball player

Struthers, Lamont
c/o Portland Trailblazers
700 N.E. Multnomah St.
Portland, OR 97232
Basketball player

Sutton, Greg
c/o San Antonio Spurs
600 E. Market St., #102
San Antonio, TX 78205
Basketball player

Swann, Lynn Curtis
c/o ABC News
47 W. 66th St.
New York, NY 10023
*Former football player, television
   commentator*

Tartabull, Danny
c/o New York Yankees
Yankees Stadium
Bronx, NY 10451
Baseball player

Thomas, Debi
c/o International Management
22 E. 71st St.
New York, NY 10021
Ice skater

Thomas, Derrick
c/o Kansas City Chiefs
1 Arrowhead Dr.
Kansas City, MO 64129
Football player

Thomas, Frank
c/o Chicago White Sox
324 W. 35th St.
Chicago, IL 60616
Baseball player

Thomas, Thurman
c/o Buffalo Bills
1 Bills Dr.
Orchard Park, NY 14127
Football player

Thomas, Isaiah
c/o Detroit Pistons
1 Championship Dr.
Auburn Hills, MI 48057
Basketball player

Thompson, John
c/o Georgetown University
   Basketball Program
Washington, DC 20057
Basketball coach

Thompson, Ryan
c/o New York Mets
126th and Roosevelt Ave.
Flushing, NY 11368
Baseball player

Thorpe, Otis
c/o Houston Rockets
The Summit
Houston, TX 77046
Basketball player

Threatt, Sedell
c/o Los Angeles Lakers
PO Box 10
Inglewood, CA 90306
Basketball player

Tisdale, Waymon
c/o Sacramento Kings
1515 Sports Dr.
Sacramento, CA 95834
Basketball player

Toon, Al
1000 Fulton Ave.
Hempstead, NY 11550
Retired football player

Townsend, Andre
c/o Denver Broncos
13655 Broncos Pkwy.
Englewood, CO 80112-4151
Football player

Townshend, Graeme
c/o Boston Bruins
150 Causeway St.
Boston, MA 02114
Hockey player

Tucker, Trent
c/o Chicago Bulls
980 N. Michigan Ave.
Chicago, IL 60611
Basketball player

Turner, John
c/o Houston Summit
The Summit
Houston, TX 77046
Basketball player

Tyson, Mike
922335 Regional Diagnostic
   Center
Plainfield, IN 46168
Former boxing champ

Vaughn, Greg
c/o Milwaukee Bucks
PO Box 3099
Milwaukee, WI 53201
Baseball player

Vaughn, Mo
c/o Boston Red Sox
4 Yawkey Way
Boston, MA 02215
Baseball player

Vaught, Loy
c/o Los Angeles Clippers
3939 S. Figueroa St.
Los Angeles, CA 90037
Basketball player

Vilgrain, Claude
c/o New Jersey Nets
Brendan Byrne Arena
East Rutherford, NJ 07073
Hockey player

Vincent, Sam
c/o Milwaukee Bucks
10001 N. 4th St.
Milwaukee, WI 53203
Basketball player

Walker, Chico
c/o New York Mets
126th and Roosevelt Ave.
Flushing, NY 11368
Baseball player

Walker, Darrell
c/o Chicago Bulls
980 N. Michigan Ave.
Chicago, IL 60611
Basketball player

Walker, Herschel
c/o Philadelphia Eagles
Veterans Stadium
Philadelphia, PA 19148
Football player

Walker, Reggie
c/o San Diego Padres
PO Box 2000
San Diego, CA 92120
Sports executive

Washington, Claudell
12 Charles Hill Rd.
Orinda, CA 94708
Baseball player

Webb, Spud
c/o Sacramento Kings
1515 Sports Dr.
Sacramento, CA 95834
Basketball player

Webber, Chris
c/o Golden State Warriors
Nimitz Freeway and
   Hegenberger Rd.
Oakland, CA 94621
Basketball player

West, Doug
c/o Minnesota Timberwolves
730 Hennepin Ave., #500
Minneapolis, MN 55403
Basketball player

West, Mark
c/o Phoenix Suns
PO Box 1369
Phoenix, AZ 85001
Basketball player

Whitaker, Lou
c/o Detroit Tigers
Michigan and Trumbull Ave.
Detroit, MI 48216
Baseball player

White, Bill
350 Park Ave.
New York, NY 10022
*Former president of the National
   League, former baseball player*

White, Randy
c/o Dallas Mavericks
777 Sports Dr.
Dallas, TX 75207
Basketball player

White, Reggie
c/o Green Bay Packers
1265 Lombardi Ave.
Green Bay, WI 54303
Retired football player

Whitmore, Daryl
c/o Florida Marlins
100 N.E. 3rd Ave.
Ft. Lauderdale, FL 33301
Baseball player

Wiggins, Mitchell
c/o Philadelphia 76ers
PO Box 25040
Philadelphia, PA 19147
Basketball player

Wiley, Morton
c/o Atlanta Hawks
1 CNN Center
Atlanta, GA 30303
Basketball player

Wilkins, Dominique
c/o Atlanta Hawks
1 CNN Center
Atlanta, GA 30303
Basketball player

Williams, Bernie
c/o New York Yankees
Yankees Stadium
Bronx, NY 10451
Baseball player

Williams, Brian
c/o Denver Nuggets
PO Box 4658
Denver, CO 80204
Basketball player

Williams, Brian
c/o Orlando Magic
1 Magic Pl.
Orlando, FL 32801
Basketball player

Williams, Buck
c/o Portland Trailblazers
700 N.E. Multnomah St.
Portland, OR 97232
Basketball player

Williams, Charlie
c/o National Baseball League
350 Park Ave.
New York, NY 10022
Major league baseball umpire

Williams, Herb
c/o New York Knicks
4 Penn Plaza
New York, NY 10001
Basketball player

Williams, Jayson
c/o Philadelphia 76ers
PO Box 25040
Philadelphia, PA 19147
Basketball player

Williams, John "Hot Rod"
c/o Cleveland Cavaliers
2923 Streetboro Rd.
Richfield, OH 44286
Basketball player

Williams, Reggie
c/o Denver Nuggets
PO Box 4658
Denver, CO 80204
Basketball player

Williams, Scott
c/o Chicago Bulls
980 N. Michigan Ave.
Chicago, IL 60611
Basketball player

Willis, Kevin
c/o Atlanta Hawks
1 CNN Center
Atlanta, GA 30303
Basketball player

Wilson, Nigel
c/o Florida Marlins
100 N.E. 3rd Ave.
Ft. Lauderdale, FL 33301
Baseball player

Wilson, Willie
c/o Chicago Cubs
1060 W. Addison St.
Chicago, IL 60613
Baseball player

Winfield, Dave
367 W. Forest St.
Teaneck, NJ 07666
Baseball player

Woolridge, Orlando
c/o Detroit Pistons
1 Championship Dr.
Auburn Hills, MI 48057
Basketball player

Worthen, Naz
c/o Kansas City Chiefs
1 Arrowhead Dr.
Kansas City, MO 64129
Football player

Worthy, James
c/o Los Angeles Lakers
PO Box 10
Inglewood, CA 90306
Basketball player

Wright, Alexander
c/o Dallas Cowboys
1 Cowboy Pkwy.
Irving, TX 75063
Football player

Yelding, Eric
c/o Chicago Bulls
1060 W. Addison St.
Chicago, IL 60613
Baseball player

Young, Anthony
c/o New York Mets
126th and Roosevelt Ave.
Flushing, NY 11368
Baseball player

Young, Danny
c/o Los Angeles Clippers
3939 S. Figueroa St.
Los Angeles, CA 90037
Basketball player

Young, Eric
c/o Colorado Rockies
1700 Broadway, #2100
Denver, CO 80290
Baseball player

Young, Gerald
c/o Colorado Rockies
1700 Broadway, #2100
Denver, CO 80290
Baseball player

Young, Kevin
Flavours Company Inc.
8860 Corbin Ave., #332
Northridge, CA 91334
Athlete

ORGANIZATIONS

**Afro-American Players
   Association**
161 Firing Center Rd.
Yakima, WA 98901
509/452-8080

Black Coaches Association
PO Box J
Des Moines, IA 52314
515/964-3550

Black Cowboys Association
4207 Whittle Ave.
Oakland, CA 94602
510/531-7583

Jackie Robinson Foundation Inc.
80 8th Ave.
New York, NY 10011
212/675-1511

Jesse Owens Foundations
401 N. Michigan Ave., #290
Chicago, IL 60601
312/527-3311

**National Association of Black
   Scuba Divers Association**
1605 Crittenden St. NE
Washington, DC 20017
800/521-6227

National Bowling Association
377 Park Ave. South, 7th Floor
New York, NY 10016
212/689-8308

National Brotherhood of Skiers
1525 E. 53rd St., #402
Chicago, IL 60615

Wilma Rudolph Foundation
3500 Centennial Blvd.
Nashville, TN 37203

HISTORY AND CULTURE

HISTORIANS

Berry, Mary Frances
Department of History
University of Pennsylvania
Philadelphia, PA 19104

Crew, Spencer
Director
American History Museum
Smithsonian Institution
100 Jefferson Dr. SW
Washington, DC 20560

Franklin, John Hope
c/o Department of History
Duke University
208C East Duke Bldg.
PO Box 90719
Durham, NC 27708

Moss, Alfred A.
c/o Department of History
University of Maryland
College Park, MD 20742

ORGANIZATIONS AND SOCIETIES

**African American Family History
  Association**
PO Box 115268
Atlanta, GA 30310
404/755-6391

**African American Holiday
  Association**
410 8th St. NW, #300
Washington, DC 20004
202/310-1430 or 202/737-1670

**African American Museums
  Association**
420 7th St. NW
Washington, DC 20004
202/783-7744

**Afro-American Historical and
  Cultural Society**
1841 Kennedy Blvd.
Jersey City, NJ 07305
201/546-5262

**Afro-American Historical and
  Genealogical Society Inc.**
PO Box 73086
Washington, DC 20056-3086
202/234-5350

**Afro-American Historical
  Association of the Niagara
  Frontier**
PO Box 63
Buffalo, NY 14216
716/878-5412

Association for Multicultural Counseling and Development
5999 Stevenson Ave.
Alexandria, VA 22302
703/823-9800

Association for the Study of Afro-American Life and History
Carter G. Woodson Center and Library
1407 14th St. NW
Washington, DC 20005
202/667-2822

Association of Black Anthropologists
c/o Department of Anthropology
University of Tennessee at Knoxville
252 South Stadium Hall
Knoxville, TN 37996-0720
615/974-4000

Black Focus
4115 Bridge Ave.
Cleveland, OH 44113
216/631-7660

Black Memorabilia Collector's Association
Hyattsville, MD
301/559-6363

Caribbean American Intercultural Organization
305 Webster St. NW
Washington, DC 20011
202/829-7468

National Association of Black Storytellers
PO Box 67722
Baltimore, MD 21215

Task Force on Historical Preservation and Minority Communities
500 N. 3rd St.
Richmond, VA 23219
804/788-1709

Women's Africa Committee of the African Institute
c/o African American Institute
833 United Nations Plaza
New York, NY 10017
212/949-5666

CULTURAL CENTERS

African American Archives
The Western Reserve Historical Society
10825 East Blvd.
Cleveland, OH 44106-1788
216/721-5722

African American Cultural Center
2560 W. 54th St.
Los Angeles, CA 90043
213/299-6124

African American Cultural Heritage Center
3700 Ross Ave., #147
Dallas, TX 75204
214/565-9026

African American Culture and Arts Network
2090 Adam Clayton Powell Jr. Blvd.
New York, NY 10027
212/749-4408

African American Heritage
4601 Market St.
Philadelphia, PA 19139
215/471-6609

African Cultural Art Forum
237 S. 60th St.
Philadelphia, PA 19139
215/476-0680

African Cultural Center
8226 Fenton St. S
Silver Spring, MD 20910
301/589-0454

African Cultural Center
350 Masten Ave.
Buffalo, NY 14208
716/884-2013

Afro-American Community Center
2560 W. 54th St.
Los Angeles, CA 90058
213/299-6124

Afro-American Cultural Center
Cleveland State University Black
   Studies Program
2121 Euclid Ave., UC 103
Cleveland, OH 44115
216/687-3655

Afro-American Cultural Center
401 N. Market St.
Spirit Square
Charlotte, NC 28202
704/371-1565

Afro-American Cultural Center
110 E. 7th Ave.
Charlotte, NC 28202
704/374-1565

Afro-American Cultural Center
1000 State St.
PO Box 374
Springfield, MA 01109
413/737-7000

Afro-American Cultural Center Inc.
2191 7th Ave.
New York, NY 10027
212/722-4900

Afro-American Research Center
Eastport
PO Box 4444
Anapolis, MD 21403
301/263-4844

Afro-Carib American Cultural Center
4511 N.W. 25th Pl.
Lauderhill, FL 33313
305/739-1015

Amistad Center
Tilton Hall
Tulane University
6823 St. Charles Ave.
New Orleans, LA 70118
504/865-5535

Beck Cultural Exchange Center Inc.
1927 Dandrige Ave.
Knoxville, TN 37915
615/524-8461

Bedford-Stuyvesant Restoration Cultural Affairs Center
1360 Fulton St., #4G
Brooklyn, NY 11216
718/636-7888

Black Archives of Mid-America Inc.
2033 Vine St.
Kansas City, MO 64108
816/483-1300

Black Archives Research Center and Museum
Florida A&M University
PO Box 809
Tallahassee, Florida 32307
904/599-3000

Black Cultural Center
2800 University Ave.
Grand Forks, ND 58203
701/777-4259

Black History Archives
1082 East Blvd.
Cleveland, OH 44092
216/721-5722

Black History Exhibit Center
106 N. Main St.
Hempstead, NY 11550
516/538-2274

Blues City Cultural Center
PO Box 14059
Memphis, TN 38114
901/525-3031

Caribbean Cultural Center
408 W. 58th St.
New York, NY 10019
212/307-7420

Center for African American Culture
210 S. Woodard, B-105
Florida State University
Tallahassee, FL 32303
904/644-3252

Center African Art
54 E. 68th St.
New York, NY 10021
212/861-1200

Center for African Studies
710 West End Ave.
New York, NY 10025
212/678-7184

Center for Southern Folklore Archives
1216 Peabody Ave.
PO Box 40105
Memphis, TN 38104
901/726-4205

Crispus Attucks Community Center
605 S. Duke St.
York, PA 17403
717/848-3610

Douglas-Truth Library
23000 E. Yesler Way
Seattle, WA 98122
206/684-4704

Frederick Douglass Creative Arts Center
168 W. 46th St.
New York, NY 10036
212/944-9870

Howard Tilton Library
Tulane University
Freret and Newcomb Pl.
New Orleans, LA 70118
504/865-5604

Langston Hughes Center for the Arts
1 Hilton St.
Providence, RI 02905
401/272-4400

Macon County Fine Arts Manifesto
104 Frazier St.
Tuskegee, AL 36083
205/727-3029

Madame Walker Urban Life Center
617 Indiana Ave.
Indianapolis, IN 46202
317/635-6915
317/236-2099

Martin Luther King Jr. Center for Nonviolent Social Changes
449 Auburn Ave. NE
Atlanta, GA 30312
404/524-1956

Mattye Reed African Heritage Center
North Carolina A&T State University
Greensboro, NC 27411
919/379-7874

Michigan Ethnic Heritage Studies Center
71 E. Perry St.
Detroit, MI 48202
313/832-7400

NAACP Historical and Cultural Project
441 Bergen Ave.
Jersey City, NJ 07304
201/596-6550

Operation Crossroads Africa
150 5th Ave., #310
New York, NY 10011
212/242-8550

Penn Center
PO Box 126
St. Helena Island, SC 29920
803/838-2432

Pillsbury House/Cultural Arts
3501 Chicago Ave. S
Minneapolis, MN 55407
612/824-0708

St. Louis Science Center
5050 Oakland Ave.
St. Louis, MO 63110
314/289-4400

Schomburg Center for Black Research in Black Culture
515 Malcolm X Blvd.
New York, NY 10037
212/491-2200

Southern Poverty Law Center
PO Box 2087
Montgomery, AL 36102
205/264-0286

University of Akron Black Cultural Center
Afro-American Studies
East Hall, #202
Akron, OH 44325

Vaughn Cultural Center
1408 N. Kings Highway, #205
St. Louis, MO 63113
314/361-0111

Young Men's Institute Cultural Center
PO Box 7301
Asheville, NC 28807
704/252-4614

Your Heritage House
110 E. Ferry
Detroit, MI 48202
313/871-1667

MUSEUMS

African American Library Museum
1765 Crawford Rd.
Cleveland, OH 44061
216/791-1700

African American Museum
PO Box 75315
Dallas, TX 73515
214/565-9026

African American Museum of Nassau County
110 N. Franklin St.
Hempstead, NY 11550
516/485-0470

African Arts Museum of S.M.A. Fathers
23 Bliss Ave.
Tenafly, NJ 07670
201/567-0450

Afro-American Heritage Museum Research Center
730 Martin Luther King Jr. Blvd.
Chattanooga, TN 37401
615/756-1076

Afro-American Historical and Cultural Museum
7th and Arch St.
Philadelphia, PA 19106
215/574-0380

Afro-American Museum of Detroit
301 Frederick Douglass Ave.
Detroit, MI 48202
313/833-9800

America's Black Holocaust Museum
2233 N. 4th St.
Milwaukee, WI 53212
414/264-2500

Anacosta Museum
1901 Florida Pl. SE
Washington, DC 20020
202/287-3306

Apex Museum
135 Auburn Ave. NE
Atlanta, GA 30303
404/521-2739

Appleton Museum of Art/Appleton Cultural Center
4333 E. Silver Springs Blvd.
Ocala, FL 32670
904/236-5050

Aunt Len's Doll and Toy Museum
6 Hamilton Terr.
New York, NY 10031
212/281-4143

Baltimore's Black American Museum
1769 Carswell St.
Baltimore, MD 21218
301/243-9600

Banneker-Douglass Museum
84 Franklin St.
Annapolis, MD 21401
301/974-2893

Bethune Museum-Archives
c/o National Historical Site
1318 Vermont Ave. NW
Washington, DC 20005
202/332-1233

Black American Western Museum and Historical Center
3091 California St.
Denver, CO 80205
303/292-2566

Black Fashion Museum
c/o Harlem Institute of Fashion
157 W. 126th St.
New York, NY 10027
212/666-1320

Black Filmmakers Hall of Fame
1100 Broadway, #3300
Oakland, CA 94607
415/465-0804

Black Heritage Museum
PO Box 570327
Miami, FL 33255
305/252-3535

Black Historical Museum and Cultural Center
122 W. Leigh St.
Richmond, VA 23220
804/780-9093

Black History Exhibit Center
106 N. Main St.
Hempstead, NY 11550
516/538-2274

Black Texas Cultural Museum and Hall of Fame
920 E. 11th St.
Austin, TX 70702
512/472-5731

Booker T. Washington National Monument
PO Box 310
Hardy, VA 24101
703/721-2094

California Museum of Afro-American History and Culture
4005 Crenshaw Blvd., 3rd Floor
Los Angeles, CA 90008
213/294-7071

Chattanooga Afro-American Museum and Research Center
200 E. Martin Luther King Jr. Blvd.
Chattanooga, TN 37402
615/267-1076

Cincinnati Art Museum
Eden Park
Cincinnati, OH 45202
513/721-5204

Downstate Afro-American Hall of Fame Museum
309 S. Dusable
Peoria, IL 61605
309/673-2206

Dunbar House
219 Summit St.
Dayton, OH 45407
513/224-7061

Dusable Museum of African American History
740 E. 56th Pl.
Chicago, IL 60637
312/947-0600

Ebony Museum of Art
1034 14th St.
Oakland, CA 94607
415/763-0141

Frederick Douglass Home
14 11th St. SE
Washington, DC 20001
202/426-5960

Genesis II Museum of International Black Culture
509 Cathedral Pkwy.
New York, NY 10025
212/666-7222

George Washington Carver Museum
PO Drawer 10
Tuskegee, AL 36088
205/727-3200

George Washington Carver Museum and Cultural Center
1165 Angelina St.
Austin, TX 78702
512/472-4809

Graystone International Jazz Museum
1521 Broadway
Detroit, MI 48226
313/963-3813

Great Blacks in Wax Museum Inc.
1601 E. North Ave.
Baltimore, MD 21213
410/563-3404 or 410/563-3414

Great Plains Black Museum
213 Lake St.
Omaha, NE 68110
402/345-2212

Harriet Tubman Historical and Cultural Museum
340 Walnut St.
Macon, GA 31208
912/743-8644

Harrison Museum of African American Culture
523 Harrison Ave.
Roanoke, VA 24016
703/345-4818

Herndon Home
587 University Pl. NW
Atlanta, GA 30314
404/581-9813

Howard University Museum—Moorland Springarn Research Center
500 Howard Pl. NW
Washington, DC 20059
202-636-7239

I. P. Stanbeck Museum and Planetarium
c/o South Carolina State College
Orangeburg, SC 29117
803/536-7174

James E. Lewis Museum of Art
c/o Morgan State University
Coldspring La. and Hilton Rd.
Baltimore, MD 21239
301/444-3030

Kirkpatrick Center Museum Complex
2100 N.E. 52nd St.
Oklahoma City, OK 73111
405/427-5461

Lillie Carroll Jackson Museum
1320 Eutaw Pl.
Baltimore, MD 21217
301/523-1208

Mann-Simons Cottage
1403 Richland St.
Orangeburg, SC 29201
803/252-1450 or 803/252-1770

Martin Luther King Jr. Museum of Black Culture
511 N. Henry St.
Eden, NC 27288

Martin Luther King Jr. National Historic Site and Preservation District
522 Auburn Ave. NE
Atlanta, GA 30312
404/331-5190

Maryland Museum of African Art
8510 Highridge Rd.
Columbia, MD 21044
301/461-6390 or 301/730-7105

Merabash Museum
PO Box 752
Willingsboro, NJ 08046
609/877-3177

Minority Arts Resource Council Studio Arts Museum
1421 W. Girard Ave.
Philadelphia, PA 19130
215/236-2688

Muddy Waters Museum
c/o Carnegie Public Library
114 Delta St.
Clarksdale, MS 38614
601/624-4461

Museum of African American Art
4005 Crenshaw Blvd., 3rd Floor
Los Angeles, CA 90008
213/294-7071

Museum of African American Art
2617 Lincoln Blvd., #207
Santa Monica, CA 90405
213/450-5045

Museum of African American Art
1308 N. Marion St.
Tampa, FL 33602
813/272-2466

**Museum of African and African
American Art and Antiquities**
1097 Ellicott St.
Buffalo, NY 14209-1935
716/882-7676

**Museum of African American
History**
301 Frederick Douglass St.
Detroit, MI 48202
313/833-9800

**Museum of African American Life
and Culture**
PO Box 26153
Dallas, TX 75226
214/565-9026 or 214/424-8204

Museum of Afro-American History
Abiel Smith School
46 Joy St.
Boston, MA 02114
617/742-1854 or 617/445-7400

**Museum of the National Center for
Afro-American Artists**
300 Walnut Ave.
Roxbury, MA 02119
617/442-8014

**NAACP Historical and Cultural
Project**
441 Bergen Ave.
Jersey City, NJ 07304
201/596-6550

**National Afro-American Museum
and Cultural Center**
PO Box 578
Wilberforce, OH 45384
216/791-1700

**National Civil Rights Museum at
the Lorraine Motel**
450 Mulberry St.
Memphis, TN 38103
901/521-9699

**National Museum of African
Art–Smithsonian Institution**
950 Independence Ave. SW
Washington, DC 20560
202/357-4876

Negro League Baseball Museum
1601 E. 18th St.
Kansas City, MO 64108
816/221-1920

Newark Museum
43-49 Washington St.
Newark, NJ 07101
201/596-6550

Old Slave Mart Museum
PO Box 446
Sullivan's Island, SC 29482
803/883-3797

**Parting Ways: The Museum of
Afro/American Ethno History**
130 Court St.
Plymouth, MA 02361
617/746-6028

**Resident Arts and Humanities
Consortium Black History
Museum**
1515 Linn St.
Cincinnati, OH 45214
513/381-0645

Sanamu African Art Museum
2100 N.E. 52nd St.
Oklahoma City, OK 73111
405/424-7760

**Simmons Collection African Arts
  Museum**
1063 Fulton St.
Brooklyn, NY 11238
718/230-0933

**Smith Robertson Museum and
  Cultural Center**
PO Box 3259
Jackson, MS 39207
601/960-1457

Storefront Museum
48 Alder Dr.
Mastic Beach, NY 11951
516/281-7585

Studio Museum in Harlem
144 W. 125th St.
New York, NY 10027
212/864-4500

Tunde Dada House of Africa Inc.
347 Main St.
Orange, NJ 07050
201/673-4446

Tuskegee Institute Historic Site
PO Box Drawer 10
Tuskegee, AL 36080
205-727-6390

Uncle Remus Museum
PO Box 3184
Eatonton, GA 31024
706/485-6856

**Virginia Museum for Black History
  and Archives**
PO Box 61052
Richmond, VA 23261
804/780-9093

**W. C. Handy Cabin Museum &
  Library**
620 West College St.
Florence, AL 35630
205/760-6434

THE SPIRITUAL LIFE

RELIGIOUS LEADERS

Adams, Charles G.
Hartford Memorial Baptist
  Church
18700 James Couzens Highway
Detroit, MI 48235

Adams, John H.
208 Auburn Ave. NE
Atlanta, GA 30303

Bailey, E. K.
Concord Baptist Church
3410 Polk St.
Dallas, TX 75224

Blake, Charles E.
West Angeles, Church of God in
  Christ
3045 Crenshaw Blvd.
Los Angeles, CA 90016

Booth, Charles E.
428 Main St.
Columbus, OH 43215

Brazier, Arthur
Apostolic Church of God
6326 S. Dorchester Ave.
Chicago, IL 60605

Brown, Amos
Third Baptist Church
1399 McAllister St.
San Francisco, CA 94115

Brown, Roy
Pilgrim Baptist Church
628 Central Ave.
Brooklyn, NY 11207

Bryant, John
400 S. Zang Blvd., #813
Dallas, TX 75208

Butts, Calvin
Abyssinian Baptist Church
132 Odell Park Pl. (W. 138 St.)
New York, NY 10030

Cannon, Katie Geneva
c/o Department of Religion
Temple University
646 Anderson Hall
Philadelphia, PA 19122-2228

Carpenter, Delores
Michigan Park Christian Church
1600 Taylor St. NE
Washington, DC 20005

Carter, Mack King
Mt. Olive Baptist Church
400 9th Ave. NW
Ft. Lauderdale, FL 33311

Clark, Caesar A. W.
Good Street Baptist Church
3100 Bonnie View Rd.
Dallas, TX 75215

Clements, George H.
PO Box N 8187
Nassau, Bahamas

Coleman, Caesar D.
2323 W. Illinois Ave.
Dallas, TX 75224

Coleman, Johnnie
Christ Universal Complex
11901 S. Ashland Ave.
Chicago, IL 60643

Cone, James
Union Theological Seminary
3041 Broadway
New York, NY 10027

Cousin, Phillip
c/o National Council of Churches
of Christ U.S.A.
475 Riverside Dr.
New York, NY 10115

Crayton, Spurgeon
Mt. Ollie Baptist Church
PO Box 285
Brooklyn, NY 11233

Dunston, Alfred G.
Presidential Commons
A521 City Line Ave.
Philadelphia, PA 19131

Eikerenkotter, Frederick II
(Rev. Ike)
PO Box 1000
Boston, MA 02103

Farrakhan, Louis
c/o Nation of Islam
734 W. 79th St.
Chicago, IL 60620

Forbes, Calvin
73 Arsdale Terr.
East Orange, NJ 07018

Franklin, Robert
Colgate Rochester Divinity
School
1100 S. Goodman St.
Rochester, NY 14620

Grant, Jacquelyn
671 Beckwith St. SW
Atlanta, GA 30314

Harris, Barbara C.
c/o Episcopal Diocese of
Massachusetts
138 Tremont St.
Boston, MA 02111

Hicks, H. Beecher
Metropolitan Baptist Church
1225 R St. NW
Washington, DC 20009

Hill, E. V.
Mt. Zion Baptist Church
3045 Crenshaw Blvd.
Los Angeles, CA 90016

Hooks, Benjamin
New Mt. Moriah Baptist Church
13100 Woodward St.
Highland Park, MI 48213

Jemison, T. J.
356 East Blvd.
Baton Rouge, LA 70802

Johnson-Cook, Suzanne
Mariner's Temple Baptist Church
3 Henry St.
New York, NY 10038

Jones, Edward E.
Galilee Baptist Church
1450 Pierre Ave.
Shreveport, LA 71107

Jones, William
Bethany Baptist Church
460 Summer Ave.
Brooklyn, NY 11216

Kilgore, Thomas
Second Baptist Church
241 Griffith Ave.
Los Angeles, CA 90011

King, Dr. Barbara
Hillside Chapel & Truth Center
2450 Cascade Rd. SW
Atlanta, GA 30311

Lockridge, S. M.
710 Crosby St.
San Diego, CA 92113

Lowe, Eugene
c/o Princeton University
308 W. College
Princeton, NJ 08544

Lowery, Joseph
334 Auburn Ave. NE
Atlanta, GA 30303

McKinney, Samuel
Mt. Zion Baptist Church
1634 19th St.
Seattle, WA 98122

Morton, Paul
Greater St. Stephen's Full Gospel
New Orleans, LA

Moss, Otis J.
8712 Quincy Ave.
Cleveland, OH 44106

Muhammad, Wallace D.
c/o MACA Fund
PO Box 1061
Calumet City, IL 60409

Murray, Cecil
First A.M.E. Church
2270 S. Harvard Blvd.
Los Angeles, CA 90018

Patterson, Gilbert
Temple of Deliverance Church of
    God in Christ
547 Mississippi Blvd.
Memphis, TN 38126

Patterson, Louis A.
Mt. Corinth Baptist Church
Church School Rd.
Houston, TX 77583

Perkins, James C.
Greater Christ Baptist Church
3544 Iroquois St.
Detroit, MI 48214

Price, Frederick K.
PO Box 90000
Los Angeles, CA 90009

Proctor, Samuel Dewitt
c/o Abyssinian Baptist Church
132 Odell Park Pl.
New York, NY 10030

Reid, Benjamin F.
First Church of God
9550 S. Crenshaw Blvd.
Inglewood, CA 90305

Richardson, Franklin
Grace Baptist Church
1 Grace Plaza
Mt. Vernon, NY 10550

Roberts, Joseph
Ebenezer Baptist Church
407 Auburn Ave.
Atlanta, GA 30303

Sampson, Frederick G.
Tabernacle Missionary Baptist
  Church
6125 Beachwood St.
Detroit, MI 48210

Scott, Manuel L.
St. John Missionary Baptist
  Church
2600 S. Marsalis Ave.
Dallas, TX 75216

Sharpton, Al
National Action Network
1133 Bedford Ave.
Brooklyn, NY 11216

Smith, J. Alfred
c/o Allen Temple
8500 A St.
Oakland, CA 94621

Streets, Frederick J.
University Chaplain
Yale University
PO Box 19A
Yale Station
New Haven, CT 06520-8020

Sullivan, Leon H.
c/o Progressive Plaza Shopping
  Center
1501 N. Broad St.
Philadelphia, PA 19122

Sullivan, Nelson H.
c/o New Pilgrim Baptist Church
708 Goldwire Pl.
Birmingham, AL 35211

Taylor, Gardner C.
Concord Baptist Church
833 Marcie Ave.
Brooklyn, NY 11216

Walker, Wyatt Tee
Canaan Baptist Church
132 W. 116th St.
New York, NY 10026

Watley, William
St. James African Methodist
  Episcopal Church
588 Martin Luther King Jr. Blvd.
Newark, NJ 07091

Williams, Cecil
Glide Memorial United
  Methodist Church
330 Ellis St.
San Francisco, CA 94102

Wilson, Willie F.
Union Temple Baptist Church
1225 W St. SE
Washington, DC 20009

Wright, Jeremiah A., Jr.
United Church of Christ
532 W. 95th St.
Chicago, IL 60620

Wynn, Prathia Hall
Mt. Sharon Baptist Church
1609 W. Gerard Ave.
Philadelphia, PA 19104

Young, Carmen
Hillside Chapel & Truth Center,
  Inc.
2450 Cascade Rd., SW
Atlanta, GA 30311

Youngblood, Johnny
St. Paul Community Baptist
  Church
859 Hendrix St.
Brooklyn, NY 11207

RELIGIOUS DENOMINATIONS AND ORGANIZATIONS

**African American Catholic
Congregation**
PO Box 91700
Washington, DC 20090-1700

**African American Women's
Clergy Association**
PO Box 1493
Washington, DC 20013
202/797-7460

**African Methodist Episcopal
Church**
1134 11th St. NW
Washington, DC 20001

**African Methodist Episcopal Zion
Church**
PO Box 23843
Charlotte, NC 28232

African Orthodox Church
c/o Rev. James A. Ford
137 Allston St.
Cambridge, MA 02139

**African People's Christian
Organization**
415 Atlantic Ave.
Brooklyn, NY 11217
718/596-1991

**African Union First Colored
Methodist Protestant Church**
602 Spruce St.
Wilmington, DE 19801

African Universal Church Inc.
2336 S.W. 48th Ave.
West Hollywood, FL 33023

**Afro-Am Social Research
Association**
PO Box 2150
Jacksonville, FL 32303

Ahmadiyya Anjuman
Ishaat Islam Lahore Inc.
36911 Walnut St.
Newark, CA 94560

**Ahmadiyya Movement in Islam
Inc. U.S.A.**
2141 Leroy Pl. NW
Washington, DC 20008

**Al-Hanif Madth-Hab Center,
Islamic Faith United States of
America, American Muslims**
7700 16th St. NW
Washington, DC 20012

**Alpha and Omega Pentacostal
Church of America Inc.**
c/o St. John Alpha and Omega
Pentacostal Church
1950 W. North Ave.
Baltimore, MD 21216

American Baptist Black Caucus
c/o Dr. Jacob L. Chatman
St. John Missionary Baptist
Church
34 W. Pleasant St.
Springfield, OH 45506

American Muslim Mission
7351 S. Stony Island Ave.
Chicago, IL 60649
312/667-7200

Ansaaru Allah Community
719 Bushwick Ave.
Brooklyn, NY 11221

**Apostolic Assemblies of Our Lord
and Savior Jesus Christ**
1200 W. Girard Ave.
Philadelphia, PA 19123
215/765-6305

Apostolic Church of Christ in God
c/o Bethlehem Apostolic Church
1217 E. 15th St.
Winston-Salem, NC 27105

Apostolic Church of Christ Inc.
2044 Martin Luther King Jr. Dr.
Winston-Salem, NC 27107

Apostolic Faith Church of God and True Holiness
801 South St.
Franklin, VA 23851

Apostolic Faith Churches Giving Grace Inc.
Rt. 3, Box 111G
Warrenton, NC 27589

Apostolic Faith Churches of a Living God Inc.
3416 Carver St.
Columbia, SC 29203

Apostolic Faith Churches of God Inc.
700 Charles St.
Franklin, VA 23851

Apostolic Faith Mission Church of God
3344 Pearl Ave. N
Birmingham, AL 35207

Apostolic Faith of God in Christ Inc.
330 King St.
Hertford, NC 27944

Apostolic Overcoming Holy Church of God
1120 N. 24th St.
Birmingham, AL 35234

Associated Churches of Christ
1302 E. Adams Blvd.
Los Angeles, CA 90011

Ausar Auset Society (sometimes known as Ra Un Nefer Amen)
PO Box 281
Bronx, NY 10462

Bibleway Church of Our Lord Jesus Christ Worldwide Inc.
1100 New Jersey Ave. NW
Washington, DC 20001

Black Methodist Clergy Association
Varick Memorial A.M.E. Zion Church
255 Anacostia Ave. NE
Washington, DC 20019

Black Primitive Baptists
c/o Primitive Baptist Library
Rt. 2
Elon College, NC 27244

Black Women in Church and Society
c/o Interdenominational Church Society
671 Beckwith St. SW
Atlanta, GA 30314
404/527-7740

Christian Methodist Episcopal Church
531 South Parkway E
Memphis, TN 38106

Church of Christ (Holiness) U.S.A.
329 E. Monument St.
Jackson, MS 39202

Church of God (Sanctified Church)
1037 Jefferson St.
Nashville, TN 37208

Church of God and Saints of Christ
3927 Bridge Rd.
Suffolk, VA 23435

Church of God in Christ
272 S. Main St.
Memphis, TN 38103

Church of God in Christ, Congregational
1905 Bond Ave.
East St. Louis, IL 62201

Church of God in Christ International
170 Adelphi St.
Brooklyn, NY 11205

Church of the Living God (Christian Workers for Fellowship)
434 Forest Ave.
Cincinnati, OH 45229

Church of the Living God, the Pillar & Ground of the Truth, Inc.
4520 Hydes Ferry Pike
PO Box 80735
Nashville, TN 37208

Church of Universal Triumph/The Dominion of God
8317 LaSalle Blvd.
Detroit, MI 48206

Churches of God's Holiness
170 Ashby St. NW
Atlanta, GA 30314

Commandment Keepers Congregation of the Living God
1 E. 123rd St.
New York, NY 10035

Congress of National Black Churches
1225 Eye Street NW, #750
Washington, DC 20005

Crenshaw Christian Center
PO Box 9000
Los Angeles, CA 90009

Deliverance Evangelistic Centers
505 Central Ave.
Newark, NJ 07107

Free Christian Zion Church of Christ
1315 Hutchinson
Nashville, TN 71852

General Assembly Churches of Christ (Disciples of Christ)
330 Warwick Ave.
Mt. Vernon, NY 10553

Gospel Mission
1637 S. Pulaski Rd.
Chicago, IL 60623

Gospel Music Workshop of America
PO Box 34635
Detroit, MI 48234
313/989-2340

Gospel Spreading Church
2030 Georgia Ave. NW
Washington, DC 20001

Highway Christian Church of Christ
436 W St. NW
Washington, DC 20001

Independence African American Catholic Church of St. Martin de Pores
PO Box 41449
Washington, DC 20018

International Council of Community Churches
7808 College Dr., #25E
Palos Heights, IL 60463

**International Evangelical Church
& Missionary Association**
c/o Evangelical Temple
13901 Central Ave.
Upper Marlboro, MD 20772

**Knights and Ladies of St. Peter
Claver**
Modern, Free and Accepted
Masons of the World Inc.
1825 Orleans Ave.
New Orleans, LA 70116-2894

**Lott Carey Baptist Foreign
Mission Convention**
150 11th St. NW
Washington, DC 20001

**Moorish Science Temple Divine
and National Movement of
North America Inc.**
PO Box 7213
Baltimore, MD 21218

**Moorish Science Temple of
America**
762 W. Baltimore St.
Baltimore, MD 21201

The Nation of Islam
PO Box 20083
Chicago, IL 60620

Nation of Islam
Temple #1
19920 Conat St.
Detroit, MI 48234

Nation of Yahweh
c/o Temple of Loe
2766 N.W. 62nd St.
Miami, FL 33147

**National Association of Black
Catholic Administrators**
50 N. Park Avenue
Rockville Centre, NY 11570

**National Association of Black
Seminarians**
1400 Shepard St. NE
Washington, DC 20010

**National Baptist Convention of
America Inc.**
1327 Pierre Ave.
Shreveport, LA 71103

**National Baptist Convention
U.S.A. Inc.**
1700 Baptist World Center Dr.
Nashville, TN 37207

**National Baptist Evangelical Life
and Soul Saving Assembly**
441-61 Monroe Ave.
Detroit, MI 48226

**National Baptist Publishing Board
Inc.**
6717 Centennial Blvd.
Nashville, TN 37209-1000

National Black Sisters Conference
2508 5th Ave.
Pittsburgh, PA 15213

**National Colored Spiritualist
Association of America**
14228 Wisconsin St.
Detroit, MI 48238

**National Colored Spiritualist
Association of Churches**
1245 W. Watkins Rd.
Phoenix, AZ 85007

**National Convention of Gospel
Choirs and Choruses Inc.**
650 Parkwood Dr.
Cleveland, OH 44108

National Convocation of the Christian Church (Disciples of Christ)
PO Box 1986
222 S. Downey Ave.
Indianapolis, IN 46206

National Missionary Baptist Convention
719 Crosby St.
San Diego, CA 92113
619/233-6487

National Office of Black Catholics
PO Box 29260
Washington, DC 20017

National Primitive Baptist Convention
PO Box 2355
Tallahassee, FL 32301

National United Church Usher's Association of America Inc.
1431 Shepard St. NW
Washington, DC 20011

Nubian Islamic Hebrews
719 Bushwick Ave.
Brooklyn, NY 11221

Original Hebrew Israelite Nation
c/o Communicators Press
PO Box 19504
Chicago, IL 60649

Original United Holy Church International
c/o Bishop H. W. Fields
PO Box 263
Durham, NC 27702

Peace Mission
c/o Divine International
Evangelical Peace Mission
Hotel
1808 Ridge Ave.
Philadelphia, PA 19130

Progressive National Baptist Convention Inc.
601 50th St. NE
Washington, DC 20019

Reformed Methodist Union Episcopal Church
1136 Brady Ave.
Charleston, SC 29407

Second Cumberland Presbyterian Church
226 Church St. NW
Huntsville, AL 35801

Shrines of the Black Madonna of the Pan-African Orthodox Christian Church
944 Gordan St. SW
Atlanta, GA 30310

Society of African Missions
23 Bliss Ave.
Tenafly, NJ 07670

Sunni Muslims
c/o Islamic Center
2551 Massachusetts Ave.
Washington, DC 20008

Union American Methodist Episcopal Church Inc.
772-74 Pine St.
Camden, NJ 08103

Union of Black Episcopalians National Cathedral
St. Albans Cathedral
Washington, DC 20016

Unitarian Universalist Association
Black Concerns Working Group
25 Beacon St.
Boston, MA 02108

United American Free Will Baptist Denomination Inc.
1011 University St.
PO Box 3303
Kinston, NC 28501

United Black Christians
2313 Aster Dr.
Greensboro, NC 27401

United Black Church Appeal
860 Forest Ave.
Bronx, NY 10456

United House of Prayer for All People
1721½ 7th St. NW
Washington, DC 20001

United Wesleyan Methodist Church of America
270 W. 126th St.
New York, NY 10027

Universal Foundation for Better Living
11901 S. Ashland Ave.
Chicago, IL 60643

Women Ministers of Greater Washington
624 17 St. NE
Washington, DC 20002

Women of Color Partnership Program of Religious Coalition
100 Maryland Ave. NE, #307
Washington, DC 20002

Yoruba Village of Oyotunji
PO Box 51
Sheldon, SC 29941

THE POLITICAL SCENE

POLITICIANS

Arrington, Richard, Jr.
7120 20th St.
North Birmingham, AL 35203
Mayor

Baker-Motley, Constance
U.S. Courthouse
Foley Square
New York, NY 10007
Senior federal court judge

Barnes, Thomas V.
Municipal Bldg.
401 Broadway
Gary, IN 46402
Mayor

Barthelemy, Sidney
City Hall, Civic Center
New Orleans, LA 70112
Mayor

Bishop, Sanford D. (GA-2nd)
1632 Longworth House Office
   Bldg.
Washington, DC 20510

Blackwell, Lucien
410 Cannon House Office Bldg.
Washington, DC 20510

Bond, Julian
6002 34th Pl. NW
Washington, DC 20015

Bradley, Tom
605 S. Irving Blvd.
Los Angeles, CA 90005
Former mayor

Brown, Corrine (FL-3rd)
1037 Longworth House Office
   Bldg.
Washington, DC 20510

Brown, Jesse
810 Vermont Ave. NW
Washington, DC 20420
Secretary of Veterans Affairs

Brown, Lee
Office of National Drug Control
   Policy
600 Vermont Ave. NW
Washington, DC 20420
Government official

Brown, Ron
430 S. Capitol St. SE
Washington, DC 20002
Secretary of Commerce

212

Chisolm, Shirley
Mt. Holyoke College
South Hadley, MA 01075
Former congresswoman

Cisneros, Henry
451 7th St. SW
Washington, DC 20410
*Housing and Urban Development
   secretary*

Clark-Taylor, Kristin
c/o Doubleday
1540 Broadway
New York, NY 10036
Former White House staffer, author

Clay, William (MO-1st)
2306 Rayburn House Office Bldg.
Washington, DC 20510

Clayton, Eva (NC-1st)
222 Cannon House Office Bldg.
Washington, DC 20510

Clyburn, James (SC-6th)
319 Cannon House Office Bldg.
Washington, DC 20510

Collins, Barbara Rose (MI-15th)
1108 Longworth House Office
   Bldg.
Washington, DC 20510

Collins, Cardiss (IL-7th)
2308 Rayburn House Office Bldg.
Washington, DC 20510

Conyers, John, Jr. (MI-14th)
2426 Rayburn House Office Bldg.
Washington, DC 20510

Daniels, John
950 Orange St.
New Haven, CT 06510
Mayor

Dinkins, David
City Hall
New York, NY 10007
Former mayor

Dixon, Julian (CA-32nd)
2400 Cannon House Office Bldg.
Washington, DC 20510
202/225-7924

Dixon, Richard C.
PO Box 22
Dayton, OH 45401
Mayor

Elders, Joycelyn
Secretary of Health and Human
   Services
Hubert H. Humphrey Bldg.
200 Independence Ave. SW
Washington, DC 20201
Surgeon General

Espy, Mike
14th and Independence Ave. SW
Washington, DC 20250
202/447-2791
Secretary of Agriculture

Fields, Cleo (4th)
513 Cannon House Office Bldg.
Washington, DC 20510

Flake, Floyd (NY-6th)
1035 Longworth House Office
   Bldg.
Washington, DC 20510

Ford, Harold (TN-9th)
2211 Rayburn House Office Bldg.
Washington, DC 20510

Ford, Johnny
101 Fonville St.
Tuskegee, AL 36083
Mayor

Franks, Gary (CT-5th)
435 Cannon House Office Bldg.
Washington, DC 20510

Fulani, Lenora
2032 5th Ave.
New York, NY 10035

Goode, Wilson
City Hall
Philadelphia, PA 19107
Mayor

Harris, Elinu
1 City Hall Plaza
Oakland, CA 94612
Mayor

Hastings, Alice (FL-23rd)
1039 Longworth House Office
   Bldg.
Washington, DC 20510

Herenton, W. W.
125 N. Mid-America Hall
Memphis, TN 38103
Mayor

Hilliard, Earl (AL-7th)
1007 Longworth House Office
   Bldg.
Washington, DC 20510

Holmes-Norton, Eleanor
1415 Longworth House Office
   Bldg.
Washington, DC 20510

Huntley-Cooper, Francis
2377 S. Fish Hatchery Rd.
Madison, WI 53711
Mayor

Jackson, Jesse
400 T St. NW
Washington, DC 20001
Rainbow Coalition head, minister,
   activist

Jackson, Maynard
City Hall, #2400
68th and Mitchell St.
Atlanta, GA 30335
Former mayor

Jefferson, William J. (LA-2nd)
42 Cannon House Office Bldg.
Washington, DC 20510
202/225-6636

Johnson, Eddie Bernice (TX-30th)
1725 Longworth House Office
   Bldg.
Washington, DC 20510

Jordan, Barbara
c/o University of Texas
Lyndon B. Johnson School of
   Public Affairs
Drawer Y
University Station
Austin, TX 78713
Politician, attorney, educator

Kenney, Walter
900 E. Broad St., #201
Richmond, VA 23219
Mayor

Lewis, John (GA-5th)
329 Cannon House Office Bldg.
Washington, DC 20510

McKinney, Cynthia (GA-11th)
124 Cannon House Office Bldg.
Washington, DC 20510

Meek, Carrie P. (FL-17th)
404 Cannon House Office Bldg.
Washington, DC 20510

Mfume, Kweisi (MD-7th)
2419 Rayburn House Office Bldg.
Washington, DC 20510

Mosely-Braun, Carole (IL)
708 Hart Senate Office Bldg.
Washington, DC 20510

O'Leary, Hazel
1000 Independence Ave. SW
Washington, DC 20585
Secretary of Energy

Owens, Major (NY-11th)
2305 Rayburn House Office Bldg.
Washington, DC 20510

Payne, Donald M. (NJ-10th)
417 Cannon House Office Bldg.
Washington, DC 20510

Pena, Frederico
400 7th St. SW
Washington, DC 20590
Secretary of Transportation

Perkins, Edward
United States Department of
  State
Washington, DC 20520
Diplomat

Perry, Carrie S.
City Hall
550 Main St.
Hartford, CT 06103
Mayor

Pratt Kelly, Sharon
1350 Pennsylvania Ave. NW, #520
Washington, DC 20004
Mayor

Rangel, Charles B. (NY-10th)
2252 Rayburn House Office Bldg.
Washington, DC 20510

Reynolds, Mel (IL-2nd)
514 Cannon House Office Bldg.
Washington, DC 20510

Rice, Norman B.
600 4th Ave.
Seattle, WA 98104
Mayor

Rush, Bobby (IL-1st)
1725 Longworth House Office
  Bldg.
Washington, DC 20510

Schmoke, Kurt
100 N. Holliday St.
Baltimore, MD 21202
Mayor

Scott, Robert C. (VA-3rd)
501 Cannon House Office Bldg.
Washington, DC 20510

Sharpe, James
920 Broadway St., #200
Newark, NJ 07102
Mayor

Stokes, Louis (OH-11th)
2365 Rayburn House Office Bldg.
Washington, DC 20510

Sullivan, Louis
Morehouse School of Medicine
830 Westview Dr. SW
Atlanta, GA 30314
Former Surgeon General

Thomas, Clarence
U.S. Supreme Court
1 1st St. NE
Washington, DC 20543
Supreme Court Justice

Townes, Edward (NY-10th)
2232 Rayburn House Office Bldg.
Washington, DC 20510

Tucker, Walter
205 S. Willowbrook
Compton, CA 90220
Mayor

Tucker, Walter, III (CA-37th)
419 Cannon House Office Bldg.
Washington, DC 20510

Tyson, Laura
Old Executive Office Bldg.
Executive Office to the President
Washington, DC 20506
Council of Economic Advisors

Vincent, Edward
1 Manchester Blvd. W.
Inglewood, CA 90301
Mayor

Washington, Craig A.
1711 Longworth House Office
Bldg.
Washington, DC 20510

Waters, Maxine (CA-35th)
1207 Longworth House Office
Bldg.
Washington, DC 20510

Watt, Melvin (NC-12th)
1232 Longworth House Office
Bldg.
Washington, DC 20510

Webb, Wellington E.
City and County Bldg., #305
Denver, CO 80202
Mayor

Wheat, Alan (MO-5th)
2334 Rayburn House Office Bldg.
Washington, DC 20510

White, Michael
601 Lakeside Ave.
Cleveland, OH 44114
Mayor

Wilder, Doug
State Capitol
Richmond, VA 33129
Former Virginia governor

Wright, Bruce
c/o Justice Supreme Court of
   New York
60 Centre St.
New York, NY 10007
Judge

Wynn, Albert (MD-4th)
423 Cannon House Office Bldg.
Washington, DC 20510
202/225-8699

Young, Andrew
1088 Veltrie Circle SW
Atlanta, GA 30311
Former ambassador

Young, Coleman
2 Woodward Ave.
Detroit, MI 48226
Former mayor

POLITICAL ORGANIZATIONS

**All-African People's Revolutionary
   Party**
1738 A St. SE
Washington, DC 20003

**American Association for
   Affirmative Action**
110 Administration Bldg.
Emory University
Atlanta, GA 30322

American Committee on Africa
198 Broadway
New York, NY 10038

America's Fund
2117 L St., #310
Washington, DC 20037
National fund-raising network

Anti-Repression Resource Team
PO Box 122
Jackson, MS 39205

Association for the Improvement of Minorities in Internal Revenue Services
PO Box 0497
Washington, DC 20044-0497

Association of Black Ambassadors
Washington, DC 20001

Black Citizens Fair Action Media
156-20 Riverside Dr., #131
New York, NY 10032

Black Women's Roundtable on Voter Participation
1430 K St. NW, #401
Washington, DC 20011

Congressional Park Associates Inc.
United States House of
Representatives, #1979
Longworth House Office Bldg.
Washington, DC 20515

Congressional Black Caucus
H2-344 House Annex #2
Washington, DC 20515
202/226-7790

Congressional Black Caucus Foundation
1004 Pennsylvania Ave., SE
Washington, DC 20003

Council for a Black Economic Agenda
1367 Connecticut Ave. NW
Washington, DC 20036

Democratic Council on Ethnic Americans
430 S. Capitol St. SE
Washington, DC 20002

Democratic National Committee Black Caucus
6700 Lincoln Dr.
Philadelphia, PA 19119

National African American Network
5113 Georgia Ave. NW
Washington, DC 20011

National Association of Black County Officials
440 1st St. NW, #500
Washington, DC 20001

National Association of Blacks within Government
1820 11th St. NW
Washington, DC 20001-5015

National Association of Minority Political Women, USA, Inc.
6120 Oregon Ave. NW
Washington, DC 20015

National Black Caucus of Local Elected Officials
1301 Pennsylvania Ave. NW, #400
Washington, DC 20004

National Black Caucus of State Legislators
444 N. Capitol St. NW, #206
Washington, DC 20001

National Black Independent Political Party
636 Alameda Ave.
Youngstown, OH 44504

National Black Republican Council
440 1st St. NW, #409
Washington, DC 20001

National Black Women's Political Caucus
1628 11th St. NW
Washington, DC 20001

National Black Women's Political Leadership Caucus
2705 30th St. NE
Washington, DC 20018

National Coalition on Black Voter Participation
1101 14th St. NW, #925
Washington, DC 20005

National Committee for Independent Political Action
PO Box 170610
Brooklyn, NY 11217

National Conference of Black Mayors
1422 W. Peachtree NW, #800
Atlanta, GA 30309

National Political Congress of Black Women
PO Box 411
Rancocas, NJ 08073

New Alliance Party
2032 5th Ave.
New York, NY 10035

North American Pan African Congress
PO Box 3687
Savannah, GA 31414

Pan American/Pan African Association
PO Box 143
Baldwinsville, NY 13027

Parker Coltrane Political Action Committee
2313 Rayburn House Office Bldg.
Washington, DC 20515

Trans Africa Forum
545 8th St. SE
Washington, DC 20003

Voter Education Project Inc.
604 Beckwith St.
Atlanta, GA 30314

World Conference of Mayors Inc.
101 Fonville St.
Tuskegee, AL 36083

ACTIVISTS

Abdullah, Al-Amin Janil (H. Rap Brown)
The Community Store
1128 Oak St. SW
Atlanta, GA 30310

Bates, Daisy
1510 Izard St.
Little Rock, AR 72202

Cameron, James
2233 N. 4th St.
Milwaukee, WI 53212

Chambers, Julius
99 Hudson St., 16th Floor
New York, NY 10013

Chavis, Ben
4805 Mt. Hope Dr.
Baltimore, MD 21215-3206

Cleaver, Eldridge
c/o Random House
201 E. 50th St.
New York, NY 10022

Daughtry, Herbert
415 Atlantic Ave.
Brooklyn, NY 11217

Davis, Angela
c/o Ethnic Studies Department
San Francisco, CA 94132

Dukes, Hazel
1501 Broadway
New York, NY 10036

Gregory, Dick
PO Box 3266
Tower Hill Farm
Plymouth, MA 02361

Hooks, Ben
260 5th Ave.
New York, NY 10001

Innis, Roy
30 Cooper Sq.
New York, NY 10003

Jacobs, John E.
500 E. 60th St.
New York, NY 10001

Jeffries, Leonard
African American Studies
   Department
City College of New York
138th and Convent Ave., #4150
New York, NY 10031

Jordan, Vernon, Jr.
1333 New Hampshire Ave. NW,
   #400
Washington, DC 20036

Karenga, Maulana
African American Studies
1250 Bellflower Blvd.
Long Beach, CA 90840

King, Coretta Scott
234 Sunset Ave. NW
Atlanta, GA 30314

Parks, Rosa
305 Federal Bldg.
231 W. Lafayette St.
Detroit, MI 48226

Robinson, Randall
545 8th St. SE, #200
Washington, DC 20003

Seale, Bobby
c/o African American Studies
   Department
Temple University
Philadelphia, PA 19122

Shabazz, Betty
Medgar Evers College
1659 Bedford Ave.
Brooklyn, NY 11225

Sharpton, Al
National Action Network
1133 Bedford Ave.
Brooklyn, NY 11216

**Toure, Kwame (Stokely
   Carmichael)**
c/o Random House
201 E. 50th St.
New York, NY 10022

Tutu, Desmond
PO Box 31190
Branfontein, Johannesburg
South Africa

CIVIL RIGHTS ORGANIZATIONS

American Association
1101 Administration Bldg.
Emory University
Atlanta, GA 30322
404/727-6017

American Association for Affirmative Action
11 E. Hubbard St., #200
Chicago, IL 60611
312/329-2512

Black American Response to the African Community
127 N. Madison Ave., #400
Pasadena, CA 91101
818/584-0303

Black Silent Majority Committee of the U.S.A.
PO Box 5519
San Antonio, TX 78201
210/340-2424

Congress of Racial Equality
1457 Flatbush Ave.
Brooklyn, NY 11210
718/434-3580

Council for African American Progress
PO Box 946
Little Rock, AR 72203-0946

Lawyer's Committee for Civil Rights Under Law
1400 I St. NW
Washington, DC 20005
202/371-1212

Leadership Conference on Civil Rights
1629 K St., #1010
Washington, DC 20036
202/667-1780

National Action Network
1133 Bedford Ave.
Brooklyn, NY 11216
718/398-1669

National Alliance of Black Organizations
3724 Airport Blvd.
Austin, TX 78722
512/478-9802

National Association for the Advancement of Colored People (NAACP)
4805 Mt. Hope Dr.
Baltimore, MD 21215
410/358-8900

National Association for the Southern Poor
712A 3rd St. SW
Washington, DC 20024-3104
202/554-3265

National Black on Black Love Campaign
401 N. Michigan Ave., 24th Floor
Chicago, IL 60611-4267
312/644-6610

National Black United Front
700 E. Oakwood Blvd.
Chicago, IL 60653
312/670-1784

National Urban Affairs Council
2350 Adam Clayton Powell Blvd.
New York, NY 10030
914/694-4000

National Urban Coalition
1120 G St. NW, #900
Washington, DC 20005
202/628-2990

National Urban League
500 E. 62nd St.
New York, NY 10021
212/310-9000

National Urban/Rural Fellows
570 7th Ave., #205
New York, NY 10018
212/221-7090

New African People's Organization
13206 Dexter St.
Detroit, MI 48238
313/883-3312

Operation Push Inc.
930 E. 50th St.
Chicago, IL 60615
312/373-3366

Southern Christian Leadership Conference
334 Auburn Ave. NE
Atlanta, GA 30312
404/522-1420

Universal Negro Improvement Association and African Communities League
1611 W. Columbia Ave.
Philadelphia, PA 19151
215/236-6063

Urban Network Coalition
Rockefeller Plaza
PO Box 4446
New York, NY 10185

EMBASSIES OF AFRICAN COUNTRIES

Embassy of Algeria
2118 Kalorama Rd. NW
Washington, DC 20008
202/265-2800

Embassy of Benin
2737 Cathedral Ave. NW
Washington, DC 20008
202/232-6656

Embassy of Botswana
3400 International Dr. NW, #7-M
Washington, DC 20008
202/244-4990

Embassy of Burundi
2233 Wisconsin Ave. NW, #212
Washington, DC 20007
202/342-2575

Embassy of Cameroon
2349 Massachusetts Ave. NW
Washington, DC 20008
202/265-8790

Embassy of Cape Verde
3415 Massachusetts Ave. NW
Washington, DC 20007
202/965-6820

Embassy of the Central African Republics
1618 22nd St. NW
Washington, DC 20008
202/483-7800

Embassy of Chad
2002 R St. NW
Washington, DC 20008
202/462-4009

Embassy of the People's Republic of the Congo
4891 Colorado Ave. NW
Washington, DC 20011
202/726-0825

Embassy of Djibouti
1430 K St. NW, #600
Washington, DC 20006
202/331-0270

Embassy of Egypt
2310 Decatur Pl. NW
Washington, DC 20008
202/232-5400

Embassy of Equatorial Guinea
2112 Leroy Pl. NW
Washington, DC 20008
202/483-9420

Embassy of Ethiopia
2134 Kalorama Rd., NW
Washington, DC 20008
202/234-2281

Embassy of Gabon
2034 20th St. NW
Washington, DC 20009
202/797-1000

Embassy of Ghana
3512 International Dr. NW
Washington, DC 20008
202/686-4520

Embassy of Guinea
2112 Leroy Pl. NW
Washington, DC 20008
202/483-9420

Embassy of Guinea-Bissau
918 16th St. NW
Washington, DC 20006
202/872-4222

Embassy of the Ivory Coast
2424 Massachusetts Ave. NW
Washington, DC 20008
202/483-2400

Embassy of Kenya
2249 R St. NW
Washington, DC 20008
202/387-6101

Embassy of Lesotho
2511 Massachusetts Ave. NW
Washington, DC 20008
202/797-5333

Embassy of the Republic of Liberia
5201 16th St. NW
Washington, DC 20011
202/291-0761

Embassy of Madagascar
2374 Massachusetts Ave. NW
Washington, DC 20008
202/265-5525

Embassy of Malawi
2408 Massachusetts Ave. NW
Washington, DC 20008
202/797-1007

Embassy of Mali
2130 R St. NW
Washington, DC 20008
202/332-2249

Embassy of Mauritania
2129 Leroy Pl. NW
Washington, DC 20008
202/232-5700

Embassy of Morocco
1601 21st St. NW
Washington, DC 20009
202/462-7979

Embassy of Mozambique
1990 M St. NW, #570
Washington, DC 20036
202/293-7146

Embassy of the Niger Republic
2204 R St. NW
Washington, DC 20008
202/483-4224

Embassy of Nigeria
2201 M St. NW
Washington, DC 20037
202/822-1500

Embassy of Rwanda
1714 New Hampshire Ave. NW
Washington, DC 20009
202/232-2882

Embassy of Senegal
2112 Wyoming Ave. NW
Washington, DC 20008
202/234-0540

Embassy of Seychelles
820 2nd Ave., #900F
New York, NY 10017
212/687-9766

Embassy of Sierra Leone
1701 19th St. NW
Washington, DC 20009
202/939-9261

Embassy of Sudan
2210 Massachusetts Ave. NW
Washington, DC 20008
202/338-8565

Embassy of Tanzania
2139 R St. NW
Washington, DC 20008
202/939-6125

Embassy of Togo
2208 Massachusetts Ave. NW
Washington, DC 20008
202/234-4212

Embassy of Tunisia
1515 Massachusetts Ave. NW
Washington, DC 20005
202/862-1850

Embassy of Uganda
5906 16th St. NW
Washington, DC 20011

Embassy of Upper Volta
2340 Massachusetts Ave. NW
Washington, DC 20008
202/332-5577

Embassy of Zaire
1800 New Hampshire Ave. NW
Washington, DC 20009
202/234-7690

Embassy of Zambia
2419 Massachusetts Ave. NW
Washington, DC 20008
202/265-9717

Embassy of Zimbabwe
2852 McGill Terr. NW
Washington, DC 20008
202/332-7100

EMBASSIES OF CARIBBEAN COUNTRIES AND TERRITORIES

Embassy of the Bahamas
2220 Massachusetts Ave. NW
Washington, DC 20008
202/319-2660

Embassy of the Barbados
2144 Wyoming Ave. NW
Washington, DC 20008
202/939-9200

Embassy of Belize
2535 Massachusetts Ave. NW
Washington, DC 20008
202/332-9636

Cuban Interest Section
2630 16th St. NW
Washington, DC 20009
202/797-8518

Embassy of the Dominican Republic
1715 22nd St. NW
Washington, DC 20008
202/332-6280

Embassy of Grenada
1701 New Hampshire Ave. NW
Washington, DC 20009
202/265-2561

Embassy of the Republic of Guyana
2490 Tracy Pl. NW
Washington, DC 20008
202/265-6900

Embassy of Haiti
2311 Massachusetts Ave. NW
Washington, DC 20008
202/332-4090

Embassy of Jamaica
1850 K St. NW, #355
Washington, DC 20006
202/452-0660

Embassy of Saint Lucia
2100 M St. NW, #309
Washington, DC 20037
202/463-7378

Embassy of Trinidad and Tobago
1708 Massachusetts Ave. NW
Washington, DC 20036
202/467-6490

THE ACADEMIC WORLD

EDUCATORS

Adkins, Gregory D.
Bluefield State College
219 Rock St.
Bluefield, WV 24701

Albright, Robert L.
Johnson C. Smith University
100 Beatties Ford Rd.
Charlotte, NC 28216

Barber, C. C.
Albany State University
PO Box 271
Montgomery, AL 36101

Barnes, George
Hinds Junior College
Utica, MS 39175

Beckley, David
Wiley College
711 Wiley Ave.
Marshall, TX 75670

Becton, Julius
Prairie View A&M University
PO Box 2610
Prairie View, TX 77446

Benson, Donna J.
North Carolina Central University
PO Box 19717
Durham, NC 27707

Brock, Annette
Savannah State College
James A. Colston Administration
  Bldg.
Savannah, GA 31404

Bronson, Oswald
Bethune-Cookman College
640 2nd Ave.
Daytona Beach, FL 32114

Bryan, Curtis E.
Denmark Technical College
PO Box 327
Denmark, SC 29042

Burnett, Calvin
Coppin State College
2500 W. North Ave.
Baltimore, MD 21216

Carpenter, Carl A.
South Carolina State College
PO Box 1628
Orangeburg, SC 29117

Carter, Hazo W.
West Virginia State College
Farrell Hall, #106
Institute, WV 25112

Carter, Stephen
Yale University Law School
Drawer 481A Station
New Haven, CT 06520

Chambers, Alex A.
Lane College
545 Lane Ave.
Jackson, TN 38301

Clark, Joe
366 S. Ridgewood Rd.
South Orange, NJ 07079

Cole, Johnetta
Spelman College
350 Spelman La. SW
Atlanta, GA 30314

Cole, Thomas
Clark Atlanta University
240 James P. Brawley Dr.
Atlanta, GA 30314

Coleman, Collie
Allen University
1530 Harden St.
Columbia, SC 29204

Collins, Marva
Westside Preparatory School
4146 Chicago Ave.
Chicago, IL 60651

Cooke, Sam
Dillard University
2601 Gentilly Blvd.
New Orleans, LA 70122

Cross, Dolores
Chicago State University
95th St. at King Dr.
Chicago, IL 60628

Davis, Laurence
University of Arkansas at Pine
  Bluff
PO Box 31
Pine Bluff, AR 71601

Dawson, B. W.
Selma University
1501 Lapsley St.
Selma, AL 36701

DeLauder, William B.
Delaware State College
1200 N. Dupont Highway
Dover, DE 19901

Edelman, Marian Wright
Children's Defense Fund
122 C St. NW
Washington, DC 20001

Fort, Edward B.
North Carolina State University
1601 E. Market St.
Greensboro, NC 27401

Francis, Norman C.
Xavier University
7325 Palmetto St.
New Orleans, LA 70125

Franklin, Bernard W.
Livingstone College
701 W. Monroe St.
Salisbury, NC 28144

Gates, Henry L.
c/o Brandt and Brandt Literary
  Agency
1501 Broadway
New York, NY 10036

Givens, Henry
Harris-Stowe State College
3026 Laclede Ave.
St. Louis, MO 63103

Gray, James E.
Natchez College
1010 N. Union St.
Natchez, MS 39120

Grigsby, Marshall
Office of the President
Benedict College
Harden and Blanding St.
Columbia, SC 29204

Guinier, Lani
University of Pennsylvania
Philadelphia, PA 19104

Hackley, Lloyd V.
Fayetteville State University
1200 Murchison Rd.
Fayetteville, NC 28301

Harris, William
Texas Southern University
3100 Clebourne Ave.
Houston, TX 77004

Harvey, William R.
Office of the President
Hampton University
Hampton, VA 23668

Hefner, James
Tennessee State University
PO Box 828
Nashville, TN 37203

Henderson, John
Wilberforce University
1055 N. Bickett Rd.
Wilberforce, OH 45384

Henson, David
Alabama A&M University
PO Box 285
Normal, AL 35762

Hill, Anita
300 Timberdell Rd.
Norman, OK 73019

Hodge, W. J.
Simmons Bible College
1811 Dumesnil St.
Louisville, KY 40210

Holloway, Ernest L.
Langston University
PO Box 728
Langston, OK 73050

Humphries, Frederick
Office of the President
Florida A&M University
Tallahassee, FL 32307

Jeffries, Leonard
Department of African American
    Studies
City College of New York
138th and Convent Ave., #4150
New York, NY 10031

Jenifer, Franklyn G.
Howard University
2400 6th St. NW
Washington, DC 20059

Jenkins, Jimmy
Elizabeth State University
PO Box 901
Elizabeth City, NC 27909

Jenkins, Sebetha
Jarvis Christian College
Highway 80 W, Drawer G
Hawkins, TX 75765

Johnson, Joseph
Talladega College
627 W. Battle St.
Talladega, AL 35160

Joiner, Burnett
807 Walker Ave.
Memphis, TN 38126

Keaton, William
Arkansas Baptist College
1600 High St.
Little Rock, AR 72202

Keith, Leroy
Morehouse College
830 Westview Dr.
Atlanta, GA 30314

Kennedy, Yvonne
Bishop State Community College
351 N. Broad St.
Mobile, AL 36690

Laston, James E.
Interdenominational Theological
  Center
671 Beckwith St. SW
Atlanta, GA 30314

Law, Thomas M.
St. Paul College
406 Windsor Ave.
Laurenceville, VA 23868

LeMelle, Tilden J.
University of Washington D.C.
4200 Connecticut Ave. NW
Washington, DC 20008

Lundy, Harold
Grambling State University
PO Box 864
Grambling, LA 71245

Lyons, James
Bowie State College
14000 Jericho Park Rd.
Bowie, MD 20715

McClure, Wesley Cornelius
Virginia State University
20708 4th Ave.
Petersburg, VA 23803

McMillan, Joseph T.
c/o Huston-Tillotson College
1820 E. 8th St.
Austin, TX 78702

McMillan, William A.
Rust College
150 Rust Ave.
Holly Springs, MS 38635

Mitchell, Katherine
Shorter College
604 N. Locust St.
North Little Rock, AR 72114

Mitchell, Robert L.
Edward Waters College
1658 Kings Rd.
Jacksonville, FL 22209

Moreland, Sallie V.
Clinton Junior College
1020 Crawford Rd.
Rock Hill, SC 29731

Morgan, Warren W.
Paul Quinn College
1020 Elm Ave.
Waco, TX 76704

Nuagbaraocha, Joel
Berber Scotia

Patten, A.C., Mitchell
Texas College
2404 N. Grand Ave.
Tyler, TX 74702

Patterson, Orlando
Harvard University
William Jame Hall, #520
Cambridge, MA 02138

Payton, Benjamin
Office of the President
Tuskegee University
Tuskegee, AL 36088

Ponder, Henry
Fisk University
1000 17th Ave. N
Nashville, TN 37203

Potts, Sammy
Mary Holmes Junior College
PO Box 1257
West Point, MS 39773

Prater, Oscar
Fort Valley State College
1005 State College Dr.
Fort Valley, GA 31030

Presley, Vivian M.
Coahoma Junior College
Rt. 1, PO Box 616
Clarksdale, MS 38614

Rayburn, Wendall G.
Lincoln University
820 Chestnut St.
Jefferson City, MO 65101

Reaves, Benjamin
Oakwood College
Oakwood Rd. NW
Huntsville, AL 35896

Reeves, Bennie L.
Florida Memorial College
15800 N.W. 42nd Ave.
Miami, FL 33054

Rice, Condoleeza
Political Science Department
Stanford University
Stanford, CA 94305-2044

Richardson, Earl S.
Morgan State University
Cold Spring La. and Hillen Rd.
Baltimore, MD 21239

Richardson, Luns C.
Morris College
100 W. College St.
Sumter, SC 29150

Robinson, Prezell
St. Augustine's College
1315 Oakwood Ave.
Raleigh, NC 27611

Satcher, David
Meharry Medical College
1005 D. B. Todd Blvd.
Nashville, TN 37208

Scott, Julius
Paul D. Camp Community College
College Dr.
Franklin, VA 23851

Shakir, Adbib
Office of the President
Tougaloo College
Tougaloo, MS 39174

Shaw, Talbert
Shaw University
118 E. South St.
Raleigh, NC 27611

Simmons, Charles W.
Sojourner-Douglass College
500 N. Caroline St.
Baltimore, MD 21205
College president

Sloan, Albert
Miles College
Bell Building
Birmingham, AL 35208

Smith, Calvert H.
Morris Brown College
643 Martin Luther King Jr. Dr.
   NW
Atlanta, GA 30314

**Sudarkasa, Niara (formerly known
   as Gloria A. Marshall)**
Lincoln University
Lincoln, PA 19352

Sutton, William W.
Office of the President
Mississippi Valley State
   University
Itta Bena, MS 38941

Swain-Cade, Valerie
Office of the President
Cheyney University
Cheyney, PA 19319
215/399-2000

Thomas, Arthur E.
Central State University
1400 Brush Row Rd.
Wilberforce, OH 45384

Thompson, Cleon F., Jr.
Winston-Salem University
601 Martin Luther King Jr. Dr.
   South
Winston-Salem, NC 27110

Thompson, Edwin A.
Atlanta Metro College
1630 Stewart Ave. SW
Atlanta, GA 30310

Titus, Myer
Philander-Smith College
812 W. 13th St.
Little Rock, AR 72202

Tolbert, Emory J.
Howard University
2400 6th St. NW
Washington, OH 20059

Turner, John
Knoxville College
901 College St. NW
Knoxville, TN 37921

Ward, Perry
Lawson State Community College
3060 Wilson Rd. SW
Birmingham, AL 35221

Washington, Walter
Alcorn State University
PO Box 359
Lorman, MS 39096

West, Cornell
Princeton University
104 Dickinson Hall
Princeton, NJ 08544

Wilson, Harrison B.
Norfolk State University
2401 Corprew Ave.
Norfolk, VA 23504

Wolfe, John T., Jr.
Kentucky State University
PO Box PG-92
Frankfort, KY 40601

Wynn, Cordell
Stillman College
PO Box 1430
Tuscaloosa, AL 35401

Yates, Marvin
Southern University and A&M
   College at Baton Rouge
Baton Rouge, LA 70813

EDUCATIONAL INSTITUTIONS

COLLEGES AND UNIVERSITIES

Alabama A&M University
PO Box 285
Normal, AL 35762
205/851-5200

Alabama State College
504 College Dr.
Albany, GA 31705-2794
912/430-4604

Albany State University
PO Box 271
Montgomery, AL 36101-0271
205/293-4100

Alcorn State University
PO Box 359
Lorman, MS 39096
601/877-6100

Allen University
1530 Harden St.
Columbia, SC 29204
803/254-4165

Arkansas Baptist College
1600 High St.
Little Rock, AR 72202
501/374-7856

Atlanta Metropolitan College
1630 Stewart Ave. SW
Atlanta, GA 30310
404/756-4000

Barber-Scotia College
145 Cabarrus Ave. W
Concord, NC 28025
704/786-5171

Benedict College
Harden and Blanding St.
Columbia, SC 29204
803/256-4220

Bennett College
900 E. Washington St.
Greensboro, NC 27402
919/273-4431

Bethune-Cookman College
640 2nd Ave.
Daytona Beach, FL 32114
904/253-5172

Bishop State Community College
351 N. Broad St.
Mobile, AL 36690
205/690-6416

Bluefield State College
Bluefield, WV 24701
304/327-4000

Bowie State College
Bowie, MD 20715
301/464-3000

Central State University
1400 Brush Row Rd.
Wilberforce, OH 45384
513/376-6332

**Charles R. Drew University of
    Medicine and Science**
1621 E. 120th St.
Los Angeles, CA 90059
213/563-4987

Cheyney University
Cheyney, PA 19319
215/399-2000

Chicago State University
95th St. at King Dr.
Chicago, IL 60628
312/995-2000

Claflin College
College Ave.
Orangeburg, SC 29115
803/534-2710

Clark Atlanta University
240 James P. Brawley Dr. SW
Atlanta, GA 30314
404/681-8017

Clinton Junior College
1020 Crawford Rd.
PO Box 968
Rock Hill, SC 29731
803/327-5587

Coahoma Junior College
Rt. 1, Box 616
Clarksdale, MS 38614
601/627-2571

Compton Community College
1111 E. Artesia Blvd.
Compton, CA 90221
213/637-2660

Concordia College
1804 Green St.
Selma, AL 36701
205/874-5736

Coppin State College
2500 W. North Ave.
Baltimore, MD 21216
301/333-5990

Cuyahoga Community College
700 Carnegie Ave.
Cleveland, OH 44115
216/987-6000

Delaware State College
1200 N. Dupont Highway
Dover, DE 19901
302/736-4917

Denmark Technical College
PO Box 327
Denmark, SC 29042
803/793-3301

Dillard University
2601 Gentilly Blvd.
New Orleans, LA 70122
504/283-8822

Edward Waters College
1658 Kings Rd.
Jacksonville, FL 22209
904/355-3030

Elizabeth State University
Weeksville Rd.
Elizabeth City, NC 27909
919/335-3305

Fayetteville State University
Fayetteville, NC 28301
919/486-1371

Fisk University
17th Ave. N
Nashville, TN 37203
615-329-8665

Florida A&M University
Tallahassee, FL 32307
904/599-3796

Florida Memorial College
15800 N.W. 42nd Ave.
Miami, FL 33054
305/625-4545

Fort Valley State College
Fort Valley, GA 31030
912/825-6211

Grambling State University
PO Box 864
Grambling, LA 71245
318/274-2435

Hampton University
Hampton, VA 23668
804/727-5328

Harris-Stowe State College
3026 Laclede Ave.
St. Louis, MO 63103
314/533-3000

Highland Park Community College
Glendale at 3rd
Highland Park, MI 48203
313/252-0436

Hinds Junior College
Utica, MS 39175
601/885-6062

Howard University
2400 6th St. NW
Washington, DC 20059
800/822-6363

Huston-Tillotson College
900 Chicon St.
Austin, TX 78702-2793
512/476-7421

J. F. Drake State Technical College
Huntsville, AL 35811
205/539-8161

Jackson State University
1400 John R. Lynch St.
Jackson, MS 39217
601/968-2100

Jarvis Christian College
Hawkins, TX 75765
214/769-2174

Johnson C. Smith University
100 Beatties Ford Rd.
Charlotte, NC 28216
704/378-1010

Kentucky State University
Frankfort, KY 40601
800/325-1716

Knoxville College
901 College St.
Knoxville, TN 37921
615/524-6525

LaGuardia Community College
31-10 Thompson Ave.
Long Island City, NY 11101
718/482-5050

Lane College
545 Lane Ave.
Jackson, TN 38301
901/424-4600

Langston University
PO Box 728
Langston, OK 73050
405/466-2231

Lawson State Community College
360 Wilson Rd.
Birmingham, AL 35221
205/925-1666

Le Moyne-Owen College
807 Walker St.
Memphis, TN 38126
901/942-7302

Lincoln University
820 Chestnut St.
Jefferson City, MO 65101
314/681-5599

Lincoln University
Lincoln, PA 19352
215/932-8300

Livingstone College
701 W. Monroe St.
Salisbury, NC 28144
704/638-5502

Mark Holmes Junior College
PO Box 1257
West Point, MS 39773
601/494-6820

Martin Community College
Williamston, NC 27892
919/792-1521

Medgar Evers College
(City University of New York at
   Medgar Evers College)
1650 Bedford Ave.
Brooklyn, NY 11225
718/270-4900

Meharry Medical College
1005 Doctor D. B. Todd Blvd.
Nashville, TN 37208
615/327-6223

Miles College
Birmingham, AL 35208
205/923-2771

Mississippi Valley State University
Itta Bena, MS 38941
601/254-9041

Morehouse College
830 Westview Dr. SW
Atlanta, GA 30314
404/681-2800

Morehouse School of Medicine
720 Westview Dr. SW
Atlanta, GA 30310
404/681-2800

Morgan State University
Cold Spring La. and Hillen Rd.
Baltimore, MD 21239
301/444-3430

Morris Brown College
643 Martin Luther King Jr. Dr.
   NW
Atlanta, GA 30311
404/525-7831

Morris College
N. Main St.
Sumter, SC 29150
803/775-9371

Morristown College
417 N. Games St.
Morristown, TN 37814
615/586-5262

Natchez College
1010 N. Union St.
Natchez, MS 39120
601/445-9702

Norfolk State University
2401 Corprew Ave.
Norfolk, VA 23504
804/683-8391

**North Carolina A&T State
   University**
Greensboro, NC 27401
919/334-7946

North Carolina Central University
PO Box 19717
Durham, NC 27707
919/560-6326

Oakwood College
Oakwood Rd. NW
Huntsville, AL 35896
205/837-1630

Paine College
1235 15th St.
Augusta, GA 30910
404/722-4471

Paul D. Camp Community College
College Dr.
Franklin, VA 23851
804/562-2171

Paul Quinn College
Waco, TX 76704
817/753-6415

Philander-Smith College
Little Rock, AR 72202
501/375-9845

Prairie View A&M University
PO Box 2818
Prairie View, TX 77446
409/857-2618

Rust College
1-A Rust Ave.
Holly Springs, MS 38635
601/252-4661

St. Augustine's College
Raleigh, NC 27611
919/828-4451

St. Paul College
406 Windsor Ave.
Laurenceville, VA 23868
804/848-3984

Savannah State College
Savannah, GA 31404
912/356-2181

Selma University
Selma, AL 36701
205/872-2533

Shaw College at Detroit
7351 Woodward Ave.
Detroit, MI 48202
313/873-7920

Shaw University
Raleigh, NC 27611
919/755-4804

Shorter College
604 North Locust St.
North Little Rock, AR 72114
501/374-6305

Simmons Bible College
1811 Dumesnil St.
Louisville, KY 40210
502/776-1443

Sojourner-Douglass College
500 N. Caroline St.
Baltimore, MD 21205
410/276-0306

South Carolina State College
PO Box 1628
Orangeburg, SC 29117
803/536-7013

Southern University and A&M College at Baton Rouge
Baton Rouge, LA 70813
504/771-2430

Southwestern Christian College
PO Box 10
Terrell, TX 75160
214/563-3341

Spelman College
350 Spelman La. SW
Atlanta, GA 30314
800/241-3421

Stillman College
PO Box 1430
Tuscaloosa, AL 35403
800/841-7522

Talladega College
627 W. Battle St.
Talladega, AL 35160
205/362-0206

Tennessee State University
PO Box 828
Nashville, TN 37203
615/320-3420 or 615/320-3035

Texas College
Tyler, TX 75702
214/593-8311

Texas Southern University
3100 Clebourne Ave.
Houston, TX 77004
713/527-7070

Tougaloo College
Tougaloo, MS 39174
601/956-4941

Tuskegee University
Tuskegee, AL 36088
205/727-8500

University of Arkansas at Pine Bluff
Pine Bluff, AR 71601
501/541-6559

University of D.C.
200 Connecticut Ave. NW
Washington, DC 20008
202/282-3200

University of the Virgin Islands
St. Thomas, U.S. Virgin Islands
 00802
809/776-9200

Virginia Seminary and College
Garfield and Dewitt St.
Lynchburg, VA 24501
804/528-5276

Virginia State University
Petersburg, VA 23803
804/524-5900

Virginia Union University
1500 N. Lombardy St.
Richmond, VA 23220
800/368-3227

Voorhees College
Voorhees Road
Denmark, SC 29042
803/793-3351

Wayne County Community College
Detroit, MI 48226
313/496-2500

West Virginia State College
Institute, WV 25112
304/766-3000

Wilberforce University
1055 N. Bickett Road
Wilberforce, OH 45384
800/367-8565

Wiley College
711 Wiley Ave.
Marshall, TX 75670
214/938-8341

Winston-Salem University
601 Martin Luther King Jr. Dr.
 South
Winston-Salem, NC 27110
910/750-2000

Xavier University
New Orleans, LA 70125
504/486-7411

INSTITUTES

African American Institute
833 United Nations Plaza
New York, NY 10017
212/949-5666

African Scientific Institute
527 32nd St.
Oakland, CA 94609
510/653-7027

Arthur Ashe Institute for Urban Health
State University of New York at Brooklyn College
Health Science Center
Brooklyn, NY 11212
718/951-5000

Avery Research for Afro-American History and Culture
College of Charleston
66 George St.
Charleston, SC 29401
803/792-5742

Birmingham Civil Rights Institute
520 16th St. N
Birmingham, AL 35203
205/328-9696

Black Child Development Institute Inc.
1028 Connecticut Ave. NW, #514
Washington, DC 20036
202/659-4010

Black Film Institute
University of Columbia
Carnegie Building
8th St. and Mt. Vernon Pl. NW
Washington, DC 20001
202/727-2396

Black Leadership Development Institute
334 E. 37th St.
Chicago, IL 60653-1346
312/548-6000

Black Military History Institute of America
PO Box 4134
Fort Meade, MD 20755
410/757-4250

Black Think Tank
1801 Bush St. #127
San Francisco, CA 94109
415/474-4701

Colored Performing Arts Institute
1920 18th Ave.
Meridian, MS 39301
601/462-8456

Crenshaw Christian Center School of Ministry
PO Box 90000
Los Angeles, CA 90009
213/758-3777

Harlem School of the Arts
645 St. Nicolas Ave.
New York, NY 10030
212/926-4100

Howard University Press Book Publishing Institute
1240 Randolph NE
Washington, DC 20017
202/806-4938

Institute for Independent Education
1313 N. Capitol St. NE
Washington, DC 20002
202/745-0500

Institute for the Advanced Study of Black Family Life and Culture
175 Filbert St., #202
Oakland, CA 94607
510/836-3245

Institute of Jazz Studies
135 Broadway Hall
Newark, NJ 07102
201/648-5595

Institute of New Cinema Artists Inc.
407 E. 25th St., 6th Floor
Chicago, IL 60616
312/225-3400

Interdenominational Theological Center
671 Beckwith St. SW
Atlanta, GA 30314
404/527-7709

Joint Center for Political and Economic Studies
1090 Vermont Ave. NW, #1100
Washington, DC 20005-4961
202/789-3500

Langston Hughes Institute
25 Hugh St.
Buffalo, NY 14203
716/881-3266

Mary MacCleod Bethune Institute
2560 W. 54th St.
Los Angeles, CA 90043
213/299-6124

National Black Child Development Institute
1023 45th St. NW, #600
Washington, DC 20005
202/234-4738

National Center for Urban Environmental Studies
James Office Bldg., #405
Annapolis, MD 21401
301/841-3612

Potomac Institute
1785 Massachusetts Ave. NW, #401
Washington, DC 20036
202/332-5566

Prentiss Normal and Industrial Institute
PO Box 1107
Prentiss, MS 39474
601/792-5175

St. Paul's Bible Institute
37 W. 116 St.
New York, NY 10026
212/722-5488

Sammy Davis Jr. National Liver Institute
Medical Science Bldg., #1-506
185 S. Orange Ave.
Newark, NJ 07103-2757
201/456-4535

Universal Bible Institute and Training School
19-23 Park St.
Orange, NJ 07050
201-673-4424

W. E. B. Du Bois Institute for Afro-American Research
Harvard University
44 Brattle St.
Cambridge, MA 02138
617/495-4113

Wajumbe Cultural Institute Inc.
762 Fulton St.
San Francisco, CA 94402
415/563-3519

Watkins Academy of Cultural Arts
724 Mineola Ave. —
Akron, OH 44320
216/864-0673

World Institute of Black Communications
463 7th Ave.
New York, NY 10018
212/714-1508

Young Men's Institute Cultural Center
PO Box 7301
Asheville, NC 28802
704/252-4614

EDUCATIONAL ORGANIZATIONS

A Better Chance Inc.
419 Boylston St.
Boston, MA 02115
617/421-0950

African Studies Association
c/o Dr. Edna Bay
Credit Union Building
Emory University
Atlanta, GA 30322
404/329-6410

American Association of Community and Junior Colleges
National Council on Black American Affairs
1 DuPont Circle NW
Washington, DC 20036
202/728-0200

American Association of University Women
1111 16th St. NW
Washington, DC 20036
202/685-7700

American Foundation of Negro Affairs
1700 Market St.
Philadelphia, PA 19103
215/563-1248

Assault on Illiteracy Program (AOIP)
231 W. 29th St., #1205
New York, NY 10001
212/967-4008

Association of African Studies Programs
c/o Thomas A. Hale
Pennsylvania State University
French Department
University Park, PA 16802
814/865-8481

Association of Black Admissions and Financial Aid Officers of Ivy League and Sister Schools Inc.
c/o Lloyd Peterson
Admissions Office
Yale University
149 Elm St.
New Haven, CT 06520
203/432-1916

Association of Black Sociologists
c/o Howard University
PO Box 302
Washington, DC 20059
202/806-6853

Association of Black Women in Higher Education
c/o Lenore R. Gall
234 Hudson Ave.
Albany, NY 12210
518/472-1791

Association of Caribbean Studies
PO Box 22202
Lexington, KY 40522
606/257-6966

Big Eight Council on Black Student Government
Minority Student Services
Hester Hall, #213
731 Elm Ave.
University of Oklahoma
Norman, OK 73019

Black Student Fund
3636 16th St. NW, #AG15
Washington, DC 20010
202/387-1414

Black Student Organization for Communication
University of Illinois at Chicago
PO Box 4348
Chicago, IL 60680
312/996-2408

Black Women Organized for Educational Development
518 17th St., #202
Oakland, CA 94612
510/763-9501

Black Women's Educational Alliance
6625 Greene St.
Philadelphia, PA 19119

Blacks and Mathematics
Wentworth Institute of Technology
550 Huntington Ave.
Boston, MA 02115
617/442-9010

Caribbean Studies Association
c/o Department of Social Sciences
Interamerican University of Puerto Rico
PO Box 5100
San German, PR 00683
809/264-1912

Center for Urban Black Studies
Graduate Theological Union
2465 Leconte Ave.
Berkeley, CA 91709
510/841-8401

Charles D. Smith Jr. Educational Center
755 Central Ave.
Bridgeport, CT 06607
203/334-1461

Cleveland Foundation
c/o Alicia M. Cilberto
1400 Hanna Building
Cleveland, OH 44115

Concerned Educators of Black Students
School of Education
Fayetteville, NC 28301
919/486-1181

Council of 1890 College Presidents
Langston University
PO Box 907
Langston, OK 73050
405/466-2231

Council of Independent Black Institutions
PO Box 40519
Pasadena, CA 91103
818/798-5406

Council of National Alumni Association
c/o Bobbie Jones
Delaware State College
Dover, DE 19901
904/561-2408

Golden State Minority Foundation
1999 W. Adams Blvd.
Los Angeles, CA 90018
213/731-7771

The Honorable Elijah Muhammad Educational Foundation
813 E. Broadway
Phoenix, AZ 85040

Independent School Alliance for Minority Affairs
110 S. La Brea Ave., #265
Inglewood, CA 90301
213/672-5544

Luster Education Foundation
401 N. Michigan Ave.
Chicago, IL 60611
312/225-0787

National Alliance of Black School Educators
2816 Georgia Ave. NW
Washington, DC 20001
202/483-1549

National Association for Equal Opportunity in Higher Education
400 12th St. NE, 2nd Floor
Washington, DC 20002
202/543-9111

National Association for the Advancement of Blacks in Vocational Education
4000 Stuyvesant St.
Detroit, MI 48201
313/935-1513

National Association of Black Professors
PO Box 526
Crisfield, MD 21817
410/968-2393

National Association of Black Reading and Language Educators
PO Box 51556
Palo Alto, CA 94303

National Association of College Deans, Registrars & Admissions Officers
917 Dorsett Ave.
Albany, GA 31701
912/435-4945

National Association of State Universities and Land Grant Colleges
1 DuPont Circle NW
Washington, DC 20036-1191
202/778-0818

National Association of University Women
1553 Pine Forest Dr.
Tallahassee, FL 32381
904/878-4660

National Black Alliance for Graduate Level Education
c/o Dr. John W. Wilson
University of Akron
Spicer Hall
Akron, OH 44325
216/972-7066

National Black Christian Student's Conference
PO Box 4311
Chicago, IL 60680
312/722-1441

National Black College Alumni Hall of Fame Foundation
818 Washington St., #E-18
Atlanta, GA 30315
404/658-6617

National Black Law Student's Association
1225 11th St. NW
Washington, DC 20001
202/842-3900

National Black MBA Association
180 N. Michigan Ave., #1515
Chicago, IL 60601
312/236-2622 or 312/644-6610

National Black Youth Leadership
250 W. 54th St., #800
New York, NY 10019
212/541-7600

**National Coalition for Quality
Integrated Education**
1201 16th St. NW, #424
Washington, DC 20036
202/822-7708

**National Conference of Black
Political Scientists**
Albany State College
Department of History and
Political Science
Albany, GA 31705
912/430-4870

**National Consortium for Graduate
Degrees for Minorities in
Science & Engineering**
PO Box 537
Notre Dame, IN 46556
219/287-1097

**National Consortium of Arts and
Letters for Historically Black
Colleges and Universities**
PO Box 10933
Washington, DC 20004
202/223-4060

National Council for Black Studies
Memorial Hall
Indiana University
Bloomington, IN 47405
812/335-6581

**National Organization of Black
College Alumni**
4 Washington Square Village,
#15E
New York, NY 10012
212/982-7726

**Nigerian Students Union in the
Americas**
654 Girard St. NW, #512
Washington, DC 20001
202/462-9124

**Office for the Advancement of
Public Black Colleges of the
National Association of State
Universities and Land Grant
Colleges**
1 DuPont Circle NW, #710
Washington, DC 20036
202/778-0818

Project on Equal Rights
c/o Now LDEF
1333 H St. NW, 11th Floor
Washington, DC 20005
202/682-0940

**Southern Coalition for
Educational Equality**
PO Box 22904
Jackson, MS 39225
601/355-7398

Southern Education Foundation
135 Auburn Ave. NE, 2nd Floor
Atlanta, GA 30303-2503
404/523-0001

**Student National Medical
Association Inc.**
1012 10th St. NW, #1000
Washington, DC 20001
202/371-1616

21st Century Foundation
c/o Phelps-Stokes Fund
10 E. 87th St.
New York, NY 10128
212/427-8100

United Negro College Fund
500 E. 62nd St.
New York, NY 10021
212/326-1118

Visions Foundation
1538 9th St. NW
Washington, DC 20001
202/462-1779

**Whitney M. Young Jr. Memorial
Conference**
The Wharton School of the
University of Pennsylvania
216 Vance Hall
Philadelphia, PA 19104
215/898-6180

SCHOLARSHIPS

The following is a list of organizations offering scholarships specifically intended for African-American and minority students. Write, or call where telephone numbers are provided, for more information.

**African Methodist Episcopal
Church**
2311 North St. NW
Washington, DC 20037
202/337-3930

**African Methodist Episcopal Zion
Church**
1200 Windmere Dr.
Pittsburgh, PA 15218
412/242-5842

**Allied Daily Newspaper
Foundation**
Journalism Scholarship for
Minority Students
PO Box 11410
Tacoma, WA 98411
206/272-3611

**Allied Daily Newspaper
Scholarship Program**
Scholarship Committee
PO Box 11128
Tacoma, WA 98411-0128
206/272-3611

Alpha Kappa Alpha Sorority Inc.
5211 S. Greenwood Ave.
Chicago, IL 60615
312/684-1282

Alpha Phi Alpha Fraternity Inc.
4432 S. Martin Luther King Jr.
Dr.
Chicago, IL 60653
312/373-1819

**American Association of
Respiratory Therapy**
11030 Adles La.
Dallas, TX 75229
214/243-8892

**American Foundation for Negro
Affairs**
New Access Routes to
Professional Careers
1700 Market St.
Philadelphia, PA 19103
215/563-1248

American Fund for Dental Health
Director of Public Affairs
211 E. Chicago Ave.
Chicago, IL 60611
312/787-6270

American Geological Institute
American Geological Institute
  Minority Participation
Director of Education
4220 King St.
Alexandria, VA 22302
703/379-2480

**American Home Economics
  Association**
2010 Massachusetts Ave. NW
Washington, DC 20036-1028
202/682-8300

American Institute of Architects
Minority Disadvantaged
  Scholarship Program
Educational Programs Director
1735 New York Ave. NW
Washington, DC 20006
202/785-7350

**American Institute of Certified
  Public Accountants**
Scholarships for Minority
  Undergraduate Accounting
  Majors
1211 Avenue of the Americas
New York, NY 10036
212/575-6200

American Library Association
50 E. Huron St.
Chicago, IL 60611
312/944-6780

American Nurses Association
Clinical Fellowship Program for
  Ethnic/Racial Minorities
Ethnic/Racial Minority
  Fellowship Program
2420 Pershing Rd.
Kansas City, MO 64108
816/474-5720

**American Nurses Association
  Minority Fellowship Program**
Kellog Leadership Grant
1030 15th St. NW, #716
Washington, DC 20005
202/789-1234

American Physical Society
Corporate Sponsored
  Scholarships for Minority
  Undergraduate Students in
  Physics
335 E. 45th St.
New York, NY 10017
212/682-7341

American Planning Association
Director of Council Programs
1776 Massachusetts Ave. NW
Washington, DC 20036
202/872-0611

**American Political Science
  Association**
1527 New Hampshire Ave. NW
Washington, DC 20036
202/482-2512

American Psychology Association
Minority Fellowship Program
1200 17th St. NW
Washington, DC 20036
913/864-3881

American Society for Microbiology
Public Affairs Director
1325 Massachusetts Ave. NW
Washington, DC 20005
202/833-9680

American Society of Newspaper Editors
Minority Affairs Director
PO Box 17004
Washington, DC 20041
703/620-6087

American Sociological Association
Minority Fellowship Program
1722 N St. NW
Washington, DC 20036
202/833-3410

American Speech, Language & Hearing Foundation
Scholarship Committee
10801 Rockville Pike
Rockville, MD 20852
301/897-5700

Arby's Foundation
Hank Aaron Scholarship
10 Piedmont Center
Atlanta, GA 30305

Aristo Club of Boston
193 Fayerweather St.
Cambridge, MA 02138

ARMCO Insurance Group
Minorities Engineering Scholarships
703 Curtis St.
Middleton, OH 45043
513/425-5293

Army ROTC Quality Enrichment Program
11499 Chester St., #403
Cincinnati, OH 45246
513/772-6135

Aspira of New York
332 E. 149th St.
New York, NY 10451
212/564-6880

Association of Black Journalists Scholarship
St. Louis Area Chapter
Martin Luther King Jr. Dr.
St. Louis, MO 63106
314/535-5185

California Library Association
717 K St., #300
Sacramento, CA 95814-3324
916/447-8541

California State Library
Library Development Services
1001 6th St., #300
Sacramento, CA 95814-3324
916/323-4400

California Teacher's Association
Human Rights Department
1705 Murchison Dr.
PO Box 921
Burlingame, CA 94011-0921
415/697-1400

Career Opportunities Through Education
Equal Opportunity Publications
Scholarship Program
PO Box 2810
Cherry Hill, NJ 08034
609/795-9634

Central Florida Association of Blacks in Criminal Justice
PO Box 866
Orlando, FL 32803

Charles Drew Scholarship Loan Fund Inc.
PO Box 431427
Los Angeles, CA 90043

Chicago Association of Black Journalists
Department of Journalism
Northern Illinois University
DeKalb, IL 60115
815/753-7017

Coalition of Black Members of the American Lutheran Church
422 S. 5th St.
Minneapolis, MN 55415
612/330-3100

Committee on Institute Cooperation
Minorities Fellowship
Kirkwood Hall, #114
Indiana University
Bloomington, IN 47405
800/457-4420

Council on Career Development for Minorities
Julius A. Thomas Fellowship
Program Manager
1341 W. Mockingbird La.
Dallas, TX 75247
214/631-3677

Courier-Journal and The Louisville Times Internship
Human Resources Department
The Courier-Journal and The
  Louisville Times
525 W. Broadway
Louisville, KY 40202
502/582-4803

Cox Enterprises
Cox Newspapers Minority
  Journalism Scholarship
Scholarship Officer
PO Box 4689
Atlanta, GA 30302
404/526-5091

Daily Press Inc.
Daily Press Scholarships for
  Black Journalists
7505 Warwick Blvd.
PO Box 746
Newport News, VA 23607
804/244-8421

Dallas–Fort Worth Association of Black Communicators
400 Records St., Belo Bldg., #343
Dallas, TX 75265

Dart and Kraft/National Urban League Scholarship
Director of Education
500 E. 62nd St.
New York, NY 10021
212/310-9000

Delaware Valley Club Scholarship
Scholarship Chairperson
2324 47th St.
Pennsauken, NJ 08110
609/662-8739

Delta Sigma Theta Sorority Inc.
1707 New Hampshire Ave. NW
Washington, DC 20009
202/483-5460

Digital Equipment Corp. Minorities and Women Engineers
Scholarship Program
  Administration
1 Federal St.
Springfield, MA 01005

District of Columbia Metro Organization
D.C. Public Schools Division of
  Student Services
415 12th St. NW
Washington, DC 20004

Earl Warren Legal Training Program
99 Hudson St., #1600
New York, NY 10013
212/219-1900

Educational and Cultural Fund of the Electrical Industry
Dr. Martin Luther King Jr.
  Memorial Scholarship Award
Electric Industry Center
158–11 Jewel Ave.
Flushing, NY 11365

Educational Assistance Program
Racine Environment Committee
  Educational Fund
316 5th St.
Racine, WI 53403
414/637-8893

Equal Opportunity Publications Scholarship Program
Career Opportunities Through
  Education
PO Box 2810
Cherry Hill, NJ 08034
609/795-9634

Florida Society of Newspaper Editors
Florida Society of Newspaper
  Editors Journalism Scholarship
Managing Editor
The Tampa Tribune
202 Parkway St.
Tampa, FL 33606

Ford Foundation Postdoctoral Fellowship for Minorities
National Research Council Office
  Fellowship Office
2101 Constitution Ave. NW
Washington, DC 20418

Foundation for Exceptional Children Scholarships
Scholarship Committee
1920 Association Dr.
Reston, VA 22091
703/620-1054

Freedom House
Scholarship Coordinator
14 Crawford St.
Roxbury, MA 02121
617/445-3700

Fund for Theological Education
421 Wall St.
Princeton, NJ 08540
609/924-0004

George Washington Carver Scholarships
626-B E. De LaGuerra
Santa Barbara, CA 93103

Golden State Minority Scholarships
Golden State Minority
  Foundation
1999 W. Adams Blvd.
Los Angeles, CA 90018
213/731-7771

Golub Corporation
The Tillie Golub-Schwartz
  Memorial Scholarship
Scholarship Committee
PO Box 1074
Schenectedy, NY 12301

Grandmet/National Urban League, Essay Contest
Deputy Director
Northern Virginia Beach Branch
  Washington Urban League Inc.
901 N. Washington St., #202
Alexandria, VA 22314
703/836-2858

Improved Benevolent Protective Order of Elks of the World
Elks National Foundation
  Scholarship
PO Box 159
Winton, NC 29786
919/358-7661

Inner City Scholarship
1011 1st Ave.
New York, NY 10003
212/753-8583

Inroads/Nashville Inc. Internships
PO Box 3111
Nashville, TN 37219
615/255-7397

**Jackie Robinson Education and
  Leadership Development
  Program**
80 8th Ave.
New York, NY 10011

Kappa Alpha Psi Fraternity Inc.
2320 N. Broad St.
Philadelphia, PA 19132
215/228-7184

Kodak Minority Academic Awards
Scholarship Officer
Eastman Kodak Company
343 State St.
Rochester, NY 14650
716/724-3127

Lee Elder Scholarship Fund
1725 K St. NW, #1201
Washington, DC 20006

Lincoln National Life Insurance
Thomas A. Watson Scholarship
1300 S. Clinton St.
PO Box 1110
Fort Wayne, IN 46801

Links Inc.
Boston Chapter
46 Brockton St.
Mattapan, MA 02126

Lutheran Church Women
Kemp Scholarship
2900 Queen La.
Philadelphia, PA 19129
215/438-2200

**McDonald's Crew College
  Education Program**
Paragon Public Relations
3951 Snapfinger Pkwy., #345
Decatur, GA 30035

Medical Library Association
919 N. Michigan Ave., #3208
Chicago, IL 60611
312/266-2456

**Minority Research Enhancement
  Award**
Manpower Development National
  Institute of Health
Westwood Building, #7A03
Bethesda, MD 20892
301/496-3461

Minority Scholarship Program
3040 Market St.
Camp Hill, PA 17011-4591
717/737-0421

NAACP
Agnes Jones Jackson
  Undergraduate Scholarship
Roy Wilkins Education
  Scholarship
Director of Education
4805 Mt. Hope
Baltimore, MD 21215
301/358-8900

**NAACP Legal Defense and
  Educational Fund Inc.**
Herbert Lehman Education Fund
10 Columbus Circle, #2030
New York, NY 10019
212/219-1900

**National Achievement Scholarship
  Program for Outstanding
  Negro Students**
National Merit Scholarship
  Corporation
1 American Plaza
Evanston, IL 60201
312/866-5100

National Action Council for Minorities in Engineering Inc.
3 W. 35th St.
New York, NY 10001
212/279-2626

National Association of Black Accountants
300 I St. NE, #107
Washington, DC 20002
202/543-6656

National Association of Black Journalists
PO Box 17212
Washington, DC 20041

National Association of Black Women Attorneys
1325 18th St. NW, #210
Washington, DC 20036

National Association of Colored Women's Clubs
Hallie Q. Brown Scholarship Fund
5808 16th St. NW
Washington, DC 20011
202/726-2044

National Black Caucus of Librarians
Rollins Scholarship Committee
6914 S. Morgan St.
Chicago, IL 60621
312/874-7534

National Black Police Association
1100 17th St. NW, #1000
Washington, DC 20036
202/457-0563

National Broadcasting Company (NBC)
Scholarship and Intern Program
30 Rockefeller Plaza
New York, NY 10020

National Cancer Institute
Comprehensive Minority Biomedical Program
Bldg. 31, #10A04
Bethesda, MD 20892
301/496-7344

National Heart, Lung and Blood Institute
Research Training and Development
Westwood Bldg., #640
Bethesda, MD 20892
301/496-7668

National Institute of Health Research Apprentice Program for Minority High School Students
Bldg. 31, #5B23
Bethesda, MD 20892
301/496-6743

National Newspaper Publisher's Association
c/o The Louisville Defender
1720 Dixie Highway
Louisville, KY 40210
502/772-2591

National Pharmaceutical Foundation Inc.
Ethnic Minority Pharmacy Scholarships
1728 17th St. NE
Washington, DC 20002
202/829-5008

National Press Photographers Association
Joseph Ehreneich Scholarship
PO Box 1146
Durham, NC 27702
219/489-3700

National Scholarship Service and Fund for Minority Students
322 8th Ave.
New York, NY 10001

National Science Foundation
Data Support Services
Postdoctoral Doctorate for
Science/English Education
Washington, DC 20550

National Society of Professional Engineers Racial Minority Grants
2029 K St. NW
Washington, DC 20006
202/463-2300

National Student Nurses Association
555 W. 57th St.
New York, NY 10019

National Student Nurses' Association
Breakthrough to Nursing
Scholarship
10 Columbus Circle
New York, NY 10019
212/581-2211

National Technical Association
PO Box 27787
Washington, DC 20038
202/829-6100

National Urban League
Duracell/National Urban League
Scholarship and Intern
Program
500 E. 62nd St.
New York, NY 10021

Negro Educational Emergency Drive
2003 Law and Finance Bldg.
429 4th Ave.
Pittsburgh, PA 15219
412/566-2760

New Jersey Department of Higher Education
PO Box 1417
Trenton, NJ 08625
609/292-4368

New Mexico Commission of Higher Education
1068 Cerrillos Rd.
Santa Fe, NM 87503
505/827-8300

New York Philharmonic
Music Assistance Fund
Scholarship Program
Avery Fisher Hall
Broadway at 65th St.
New York, NY 10023
212/580-8700

New York State Department of Education
Regents Professional Opportunity
Scholarships
Professional Educational Testing
Bureau Cultural Center
Albany, NY 12230

Newspaper Fund Scholarship/ Internship Contest
PO Box 300
Princeton, NJ 08540
609/452-2820

North Carolina Education Assistance Program
Minority Presence Doctoral
Program
PO Box 2688
Chapel Hill, NC 27515

Northern Virginia Branch Washington Urban League Essay
Deputy Director
901 N. Washington St., #202
Alexandria, VA 22314

**Northside Association—
Educational Advancement
Scholarship**
Local High School Counselors
Kalamazoo, MI 49008
616/375-0960

Northwood Institute
Private Donor Scholarship Office
3225 Cook Rd.
Midland, MI 48640-2398
517/832-4279

Nurses Educational Fund
555 W. 57th St.
New York, NY 10019
212/582-8820

Omega Phi Psi Fraternity Inc.
International Headquarters
2714 Georgia Ave. NW
Washington, DC 20001
202/667-7158

Omega Wives Scholarship
William Penn High School
Broad and Masters St.
Philadelphia, PA 19122

Pacific Gas and Electric Company
77 Beale St., #F-1500
San Francisco, CA 94106
415/972-1338

Phi Beta Sigma Fraternity Inc.
1327 R St. NW
Washington, DC 20011
202/726-5434

Presbyterian Church
Financial Aid for Studies
475 Riverside Dr., #430
New York, NY 10115-0094

Presbyterian Church
Student Opportunity
Scholarships Financial Aid for
Studies
Church Vocations Unit
100 Witherspoon St.
Louisville, KY 40202-1396
502/569-5735

**Professional Opportunity
Scholarship**
State Education Department
Cultural Education Center
Empire State Plaza
Albany, NY 12230

**Racine Environment Committee
Educational Fund**
310 5th St., #101
Racine, WI 53403
414/631-5600

Reformed Church of America
Minority Education Fund
Office of Human Resources
475 Riverside Dr., #1819
New York, NY 10027
212/870-3071

**Registered Nurse Fellowship
Program for Ethnic/Racial
Minorities**
1030 15th St. NW, #716
Washington, DC 20005
202/789-1334

Robert Wood Johnson Foundation
College Rd.
PO Box 2316
Princeton, NJ 08543-2316
609/452-8701

**Sachs Foundation Undergraduate
Scholarships**
418 1st National Bank Bldg.
Colorado Springs, CO 80903
303/633-2353

St. Thomas Church
11 Placid La.
Willingboro, NJ 08046

Scripps Howard Foundation Scholarship
PO Box 5380
Cincinnati, OH 45201

Sigma Gamma Rho Sorority Inc.
840 E. 87th St.
Chicago, IL 60619
312/873-9000

Society of Actuaries
Scholarship Committee
500 Park Blvd.
Itasca, IL 60143
313/773-3010

Stanley E. Jackson Scholarship Award for Minority Handicapped Students
Foundation for Exceptional Students
1920 Association Dr.
Reston, VA 22091
703/630-3660

Student Assistant Commission
Minority Teacher Scholarship
964 N. Pennsylvania St.
Indianapolis, IN 46204
317/232-2350

Tennessee Student Assistance
Program Administrator
404 James Robertson Pkwy., #1950
Nashville, TN 37243
615/741-1346

Texas State Scholarship Program for Ethnic Recruitment
Texas Higher Education Coordinating Board
PO Box 12788
Capitol Station
Austin, TX 78711

United Church of Christ Commission for Racial Justice
Special Higher Education
105 Madison Ave.
New York, NY 10016
212/533-7370

United Methodist
Mission Person
Resources Department
General Board of Global Ministers Crusade Scholarship Desk
475 Riverside Dr., #1470
New York, NY 10115

United Methodist Ethnic Ministry
PO Box 871
Nashville, TN 37202
615/327-2700

United Methodist Publishing House
Office and Loans Scholarship Program
PO Box 871
Nashville, TN 37202

United Negro College Fund
Michael Jackson Scholarship
Johnson and Johnson Leadership Award
RJR Nabisco Scholarship Program
500 E. 62nd St.
New York, NY 10021
212/644-9712

United Presbyterian Church in the U.S.A.
475 Riverside Dr., #430
New York, NY 10115
212/870-2618

Virgil Hawkins Fellowship
Administration Department of Higher Education
Office of Student Financial Assistance
Tallahassee, FL 32310

Washington Council for Postsecondary Education
Washington State Need Grant
908 E. 5th St.
Olympia, WA 98504
206/753-3571

Washington Urban League Essay
Deputy Director
901 N. Washington St., #202
Alexandria, VA 22314

Wisconsin Minority Student Grant Program
Higher Education Aids Board
PO Box 7885
Madison, WI 53707
608/266-1954

YMCA–Kate H. Atherton Scholarship
Hawaiian Trust Company Ltd.
PO Box 3170
Honolulu, HI 96802
808/525-8511

Zeta Phi Beta Sorority Inc.
1734 New Hampshire Ave. NW
Washington, DC 20009
202/387-3103

THE BUSINESS WORLD

BUSINESS EXECUTIVES

Amos, Wally
PO Box 897
Kailua, HI 96734

Anderson, Warren
The Anderson-Dubose Co.
6575 Davis Industrial Pkwy.
Solon, OH 44139

Barden, Don H.
Barden Communications Inc.
243 W. Congress St., 10th Floor
Detroit, MI 48226

Bing, David
The Bing Group
1130 W. Grand Blvd.
Detroit, MI 48208

Brooks, Frank B.
Brooks Sausage Co., Inc.
7600 95th St.
Kenosha, WI 53142

Brown, John E.
Am-Pro Protective Agency Inc.
PO Box 23829
Columbia, SC 29224

Burrell, Thomas J.
Burrell Communications Group
20 N. Michigan Ave.
Chicago, IL 60602

Calhoun, Greg
Calhoun Enterprises
4155 Lomac St., #G
Montgomery, AL 36106

Chatman, James I.
Technology Applications Inc.
6101 Stevenson Ave.
Alexandria, VA 22304

Chennault, Kenneth
President of Travel Related
  Services
American Express
Amex Tower
New York, NY 10047

Cook, Levi, Jr.
Advantage Enterprises, Inc.
5030 Advantage Blvd.
Toledo, OH 43612

Cornwell, Don
Granite Broadcasting
Dag Hammarskjold Plaza
New York, NY 10017

Cottrell, Comer J.
Pro-Line Corp.
2121 Panoramic Circle
Dallas, TX 75212

Davidson, Robert C.
Surface Protection Industries Inc.
3411 E. 15th St.
Los Angeles, CA 90023

Davis, William E.
Pulsar Systems Inc.
2 Reads Way, #218
New Castle, DE 19720

Dodd, Geralda L.
Integrated Steel Inc.
12301 Hubbell St.
Detroit, MI 48227

Dudley, Joe L.
Dudley Products Inc.
7856 McCloud Rd.
Greensboro, NC 27409

Farrington, Thomas A.
Input Output Computer Services
400 Totten Pond Rd.
Waltham, MA 02254

Ford, Vernon R.
President's Office
Vancouver Extension Co. Inc.
5509 N.W. Lower River Rd.
PO Box 970
Vancouver, WA 98666

Gardner, Edward G.
Soft Sheen Products, Inc.
1000 E. 87th St.
Chicago, IL 60619

Gidron, Richard
Dick Gidron Cadillac Inc.
696 E. Fordham Rd.
Bronx, NY 10459

Gillespie, Tom P.
Gillespie Ford Inc.
3333 Grant St.
Box M-89
Gary, IN 46408

Goldston, Nathaniel R.
The Gourmet Companies
1100 Spring St., #450
Atlanta, GA 30309

Grady, Glenn G.
Cimarron Express Inc.
21883 State Rt. 51
PO Box 185
Genoa, OH 43430

Graves, Earl G.
Earl G. Graves Ltd.
130 5th Ave.
New York, NY 10011

Griffey, Dick
African Development Public
    Investment Corp.
1635 N. Cahuenga Blvd.
Hollywood, CA 90028

Grimes, Calvin M.
Grimes Oil Company Inc.
165 Norfolk St.
Boston, MA 02124

Guthrie, Carlton L.
Trumark Inc.
1820 Sunset Ave.
Lansing, MI 48917

Holemes, Arthur
Automated Sciences Group Inc.
1010 Wayne Ave., #700
Silver Spring, MD 20910

Huggins, David W.
RMS Technologies Inc.
5 Eves Dr.
Marlton, NJ 08053

Johnson, Joan
Chairman of the Board
Johnson Products Co.
8522 S. Lafayette Ave.
Chicago, IL 60620

Johnson, John H.
Johnson Publishing Company
820 S. Michigan Ave.
Chicago, IL 60605

Johnson, Robert
Black Entertainment Television
1700 N. Moore St.
Rosslyn, VA 22209

Johnson-Rice, Linda
Johnson Publishing Company
820 S. Michigan Ave.
Chicago, IL 60605

Jones, Carl
Threads 4 Life Corp.
PO Box 91-1091
Commerce, CA 90091

Lewis, Byron
Uniworld Group Inc.
100 Avenue of the Americas
New York, NY 10013

Lewis, Delano E.
President
National Public Radio
635 Massachusetts Ave., NW
Washington, DC 20001

Lewis, Edward
Essence Communications
1500 Broadway
New York, NY 10036

Liautaud, Jim
Capsonic Group
460 S. 2nd St.
Elgin, IL 60123

Llewellyn, J. Bruce
Philadelphia Coca-Cola Bottling
Co., Inc.
725 E. Erie Av.
Philadelphia, PA 19134

Luster, Jory
Luster Products Co.
1625 S. Michigan Ave.
Chicago, IL 60616

Mays, William G.
Mays Chemical Co. Inc.
7760 E. 89th St.
Indianapolis, IN 46256

McHenry, Emmit J.
Network Solutions, Inc.
505 Huntmar Park Dr.
Herndon, VA 22070

Metters, Samuel
Metters Industries, Inc.
8200 Greensboro Dr., #500
McLean, VA 22102

Mitchell, Roderick B.
Restoration Supermarket Corp.
1360 Fulton St.
Brooklyn, NY 11216

Mullens, Delbert W.
Wesley Industries Inc.
c/o Flint Coatings Inc.
40221 James P. Cole Blvd.
Flint, MI 48505

Neloms, Henry
Premium Distributors Inc. of
  Washington, DC
3350 New York Ave. NE
Washington, DC 20002

Pearson, Drew
Drew Pearson Marketing
15006 Beltway Dr.
Addison, TX 75244

Poe, Alfred
Campbell Soup Company
President Meal Enhancement
  Group
Campbell Pl.
Camden, NJ 08103

Powers, Mamom
Powers & Sons Construction Co.,
  Inc.
2636 W. 15th St.
Gary, IN 46404

Russell, Herman J.
c/o H. J. Russell & Co.
504 Fair St. SW
Atlanta, GA 30313

Smith, Joshua I.
The Maxima Corp.
4200 Parliament Pl.
Lanham, MD 20706

Smith, Oscar A.
Community Foods Inc.
2936 Remington Ave.
Baltimore, MD 21211

Sutton, Percy
c/o Inner City Broadcasting
801 2nd Ave.
New York, NY 10017

Thacker, Floyd G.
Thacker Engineering Inc.
101 Marietta St. NW, #3402
Atlanta, GA 30303

Thomas, Earl
Gold Line Refining Ltd.
7324 Southwest Freeway, #600
Houston, TX 77074

Valentine, Herman
Systems Management American
  Corp.
254 Monticello Ave.
Norfolk, VA 23510

Wise, Warren C.
Wise Construction Co. Inc.
1705 Guenther Rd.
Dayton, OH 45417

Yancy, Earl
Yancy Minerals
1768 Litchfield Turnpike
Woodbridge, CT 06525

BLACK-OWNED BUSINESSES

Advanced Systems Technology Inc.
3490 Piedmont Rd. NE
Atlanta, GA 30305-4810
404/240-2930
Computer systems services

Advantage Enterprises Inc.
5030 Advantage Blvd.
Toledo, OH 43612
419/727-0027
*Project integrator for health care
  and construction*

Advantage Enterprises Inc.
5030 Advantage Blvd.
Toledo, OH 43612
419/727-0027
*Project integrator for health care
and construction*

**African Development Public
Investment Corp.**
1635 N. Cahuenga Blvd.
Hollywood, CA 90028
213/461-0330
*African commodities and charter
service*

Am-Pro Protective Agency Inc.
PO Box 23829
Columbia, SC 29224
803/741-0287
Security guard services

Amsco Wholesalers Inc.
6525 Best Friend Rd., #A
Norcross, GA 30071
404/447-5100
*Wholesale distributor to apartment
industry*

Anderson-Dubose Co.
6575 Davis Industrial Pkwy.
Solon, OH 44139
216/248-8800
Food distributor

Automated Sciences Group Inc.
1010 Wayne Ave., #700
Silver Spring, MD 21910
301/587-8750
*Maker of information and sensor
technology*

Barden Communications Inc.
243 W. Congress, 10th Floor
Detroit, MI 48226
313/963-5010
*Communications and real estate
development*

Beauchamp Distributing Company
1911 S. Santa Fe Ave.
Compton, CA 90221
310/639-5320
Beverage distributor

The Bing Group
1130 W. Grand Blvd.
Detroit, MI 48208
313/895-3400
*Steel processing and metal
stamping distribution*

Bronner Brothers
600 Bronner Brothers Way
Atlanta, GA 30310
404/577-4321
Hair care products manufacturer

Brooks Sausage Co. Inc.
7600 95th St.
Kenosha, WI 53142
414/947-0320
Sausage manufacturer

Burns Enterprises
822 S. 125th St.
Louisville, KY 40210
502/585-0400
*Janitorial services and
supermarkets*

Burrell Communications Group
20 N. Michigan Ave.
Chicago, IL 60602
312/443-8600
*Advertising, public relations,
consumer promotions*

C. H. James and Co.
3990 Dunbar Ave.
Dunbar, WV 25064
304/744-0880
Wholesale food distributor

Calhoun Enterprises
4155 Lomac St., #G
Montgomery, AL 36106
205/272-4400
Supermarket chain

Capsonic Group
460 S. 2nd St.
Elgin, IL 60123
708/888-7300
*Composite components for auto
and computer control systems*

Cimarron Express Inc.
21883 State Rt. 51
PO Box 185
Genoa, OH 43430
419/855-7012
Interstate trucking company

Community Foods Inc.
2936 Remington Ave.
Baltimore, MD 21211
410/235-9800
Supermarket chain

Consolidated Beverage Corp.
235 W. 154th St.
New York, NY 10039
212/926-5865
Beverage importer and exporter

Crest Computer Supply
7855 Grosftpoint Rd.
Skokie, IL 60077
708/982-1030
*Computer hardware and software
supplier*

D-Orum Hair Products
1075 Grant St.
Gary, IN 46404
219/882-2922
Hair care products manufacturer

Drew Pearson Marketing
15006 Beltway Dr.
Addison, TX 75244
214/702-8055
*Sports licensing and sportswear
manufacture*

Dual Inc.
2101 Wilson Blvd., #600
Arlington, VA 22201
703/527-3500
Engineering and technical services

Dudley Products Inc.
7856 McCloud Rd.
Greensboro, NC 27409
919/668-3000
Beauty products manufacturer

Earl G. Graves Ltd.
130 5th Ave.
New York, NY 10011
212/242-8000
Magazine publishing company

Essence Communications Inc.
1500 Broadway
New York, NY 10036
212/642-0600
Magazine publishing company

Garden State Cable TV
PO Box 5025
Cherry Hill, NJ 08034
609/354-1660
Cable television operator

Gold Line Refining Ltd.
7324 S.W. Freeway, #600
Houston, TX 77074
713/271-3550
Oil refinery

The Gourmet Companies
1100 Spring St., #450
Atlanta, GA 30309
404/876-5700
*Food service, golf facilities
management*

Granite Broadcasting Corp.
1767 3rd Ave., 28th Floor
New York, NY 10017
212/826-2530
Network TV affiliates

Grimes Oil Co., Inc.
165 Norfolk St.
Boston, MA 02124
617/825-1200
Petroleum products distributor

H. F. Henderson Industries
45 Fairfield Pl.
West Caldwell, NJ 07006
201/227-9250
*Industrial process controls and
electronics*

H. J. Russell and Co.
504 Fair St. SW
Atlanta, GA 30313
404/330-1000
*Construction and development,
food services*

Inner City Broadcasting Corp.
801 2nd Ave.
New York, NY 10017
212/661-3311
Radio, television, cable franchises

**Input Output Computer Services
Inc.**
400 Totten Pond Rd.
Waltham, MA 02254
617/890-2299
*Computer software and systems
integrations*

Integrated Steel Inc.
12301 Hubbell St.
Detroit, MI 48227
313/273-4020
*Automotive stamping and steel
sales and processing*

Integrated Systems Analysts Inc.
Shirlington Rd., #1100
Arlington, VA 22206
703/824-0700
*Systems engineering, computer
systems services*

J. E. Ethridge Construction Inc.
5270 E. Pine St.
Fresno, CA 93727
209/454-0500
Commercial construction

Johnson Publishing Company Inc.
820 S. Michigan Ave.
Chicago, IL 60605
312/322-9200
*Publishing, broadcasting,
television production, hair care
manufacturer, and cosmetics*

Lockhart and Pettus
79th 5th Ave., 10th Floor
New York, NY 10003
212/366-3200
Advertising agency

Luster Products Inc.
1625 S. Michigan Ave.
Chicago, IL 60616
312/431-1150
*Hair care products manufacturer
and distributor*

The Maxima Corp.
4200 Parliament Pl.
Lanham, MD 20706
301/459-2000
*Systems engineering and computer
facilities management*

Mays Chemical Co., Inc.
7760 E. 89th St.
Indianapolis, IN 46256
317/842-8722
Industrial chemical distributors

Metters Industries Inc.
8200 Greensboro Dr., #500
McLean, VA 22102
703/821-3300
*Systems engineering,
telecommunications*

Mid-Delta Home Health Inc.
PO Box 373
Belzoni, MS 39038
601/247-1254
*Home health care medical
equipment and supplies*

The Mingo Group
228 E. 45th St., 2nd Floor
New York, NY 10017
212/697-4515
*Advertising and public relations
agency*

Minority Entity Inc.
PO Box 397
Norco, LA 70079
504/287-8561
Janitorial and food services

Network Solutions Inc.
505 Huntmar Park Dr.
Herndon, VA 22070
703/742-0400
Systems integration

Ozone Construction Co., Inc.
1635 E. 25th St.
Cleveland, OH 44114
216/696-2876
*General construction and
construction management*

Parks' Sausage Company
3330 Henry G. Parks Circle
Baltimore, MD 21215
410/664-5050
Sausage manufacturer

Pepsi-Cola of Washington
PO Box 10520
Washington, DC 20020
202/337-3774
Soft drink distributor

**Premium Distributors Inc. of
Washington, D.C.**
3350 New York Ave. SE
Washington, DC 20002
Beverage distributor

Pro-Line Corp.
2121 Panoramic Circle
Dallas, TX 75212
214/631-4247
*Hair care products manufacturer
and distributor*

Pulsar Systems Inc.
2 Reads Way, #218
New Castle, DE 19720
302/325-3484
*Systems integration office
automation computer resaler*

Queen City Broadcasting, Inc.
7 Broadcast Plaza
Buffalo, NY 14202
716/845-6190
Network television affiliates

R. O. W. Sciences Inc.
1700 Research Blvd., #400
Rockville, MD 20850
301/294-5400
Biomedical and health services

Restoration Supermarket Corp.
1360 Fulton St.
Brooklyn, NY 11216
Supermarket and drugstore

RMS Technologies Inc.
5 Eves Dr.
Marlton, NJ 08053
609/596-5775
Computer and technical services

RPM Supply Co. Inc.
621 N. 2nd St.
Philadelphia, PA 19123
215/627-7106
General supply company

Rush Communications Inc.
298 Elizabeth St.
New York, NY 10001
212/388-0012
Music publishing, television, film, radio production

Soft Sheen Products
1000 E. 87th St.
Chicago, IL 60619
312/978-0700
Hair care products manufacturer and distributor

Solo Construction Corp.
15251 N.E. 18th Ave., #12
North Miami, FL 33162
305/944-3922
General engineering construction

Specialized Packaging International Inc.
3190 Whitney Ave., Bldg. 1
Hamden, CT 06518
203/287-8561
Packaging design, engineering brokerage

Stephens Engineering Company
4601 Forbes Blvd., #300
Lanham, MD 20706
301/306-9355
Engineering firm

Stop, Shop and Save
770 W. North Ave.
Baltimore, MD 21217
410/225-7900
Supermarket chain

Surface Protection Industries Inc.
3411 E. 15th St.
Los Angeles, CA 90023
213/269-9224
Paint and specialty coatings manufacturer

Systems Engineering and Management Associates Inc.
2000 N. Beauregard St., #600
Alexandria, VA 22311
703/845-1200
Technical support services

Systems Management American Corp.
254 Monticello Ave.
Norfolk, VA 23510
804/627-9331
Systems management, technical support services

Technology Applications Inc.
6101 Stevenson Ave.
Alexandria, VA 22304
703/461-2000
Systems integration and software engineering

Terry Manufacturing Co. Inc.
PO Box 648
Roanoke, VA 36274
205/863-2171
Apparel manufacturing

Thacker Engineering Company
10 Marietta St. NW, #3402
Atlanta, GA 30303
404/223-3404
Construction management

Threads 4 Life Corp.
PO Box 91-1091
Commerce, CA 90091
213/890-4700
Apparel manufacturer

TLC Beatrice International Holdings Inc.
9 W. 57th St.
New York, NY 10019
212/756-8900
International food processor and distributor

Tresp Associates Inc.
4900 Seminary Rd., #700
Alexandria, VA 22311
703/845-9400
Military logistics systems, engineering computers

Trumark
1820 Sunset Ave.
Lansing, MI 48917
Metal stampings manufacturing, welding

UBM Inc.
212 W. Van Buren St., 8th Floor
Chicago, IL 60607
312/226-1696
General contracting and construction management

Uniworld Communications Group
100 Avenue of the Americas
New York, NY 10013
212/219-1600
Advertising agency

Urban Organization
4128 N. Miami Ave.
Miami, FL 33127
305/576-1408
General contracting and construction management

Watiker and Sons Inc.
PO Box 2688
Zanesville, OH 43702
614/454-7958
Heavy highway bridges, mine reclamation

Wesley Industries Inc.
c/o Flint Coatings Inc.
40221 James P. Cole Blvd.
Flint, MI 48505
Makers of industrial and foundry products

William-Russell and Johnson Inc.
771 Spring St. NW
Atlanta, GA 30308
404/853-6800
Engineers, architect, and planners

Wise Construction Co. Inc.
1705 Guenther Rd.
Dayton, OH 45417
513/854-0281
Construction company

Yancy Minerals
1768 Litchfield Turnpike
Woodbridge, CT 06525
203/624-8067
Industrial metals, minerals, and coal distributor

FINANCIAL INSTITUTIONS

Advance Federal Savings & Loan Association
1405 E. Cold Spring La.
Baltimore, MD 21239
301/323-9570

American Federal Savings & Loan Association
701 E. Market St.
Greensboro, NC 20071
919/273-9753

American State Bank
PO Box 6389
Tulsa, OK 74148
918/428-2211

American State Bank
PO Box 12348
Portland, OR 97212
503/282-2216

Berean Federal Savings Bank
5228 Chestnut St.
Philadelphia, PA 19139
215/472-4545

Boston Bank of Commerce
133 Federal St.
Boston, MA 02110
617/457-4400

**Broadway Federal Savings &
Loan Association**
4501 S. Broadway
Los Angeles, CA 90037
213/232-4271

**Carver Federal Savings & Loan
Association**
75 W. 125th St.
New York, NY 10027
212/876-4747

Carver State Bank
701 Martin Luther King Jr. Blvd.
Savannah, GA 31401
912/233-9971

Citizens Bank
401 Charlotte St.
Nashville, TN 37219
615/256-6193

Citizens Federal Savings Bank
300 N. 18th St.
Birmingham, AL 35201

Citizens Federal Savings Bank
1728 3rd Ave. N
Birmingham, AL 35203
205/328-2041

Citizens Trust Bank
PO Box 4485
Atlanta, GA 30302
404/659-5959

City National Bank of New Jersey
900 Broad St.
Newark, NJ 07102
201/624-0865

**Columbia Savings & Loan
Association**
2000 W. Fond du Lac Ave.
Milwaukee, WI 53202
414/374-0486

Commonwealth National Bank
2214 St. Stephens Rd.
Mobile, AL 36601
205/476-5938

Community Bank of Lawndale
1111 S. Homan Ave.
Chicago, IL 60624
312/533-6900

**Community Federal Savings &
Loan Association**
4490 Main St.
Bridgeport, CT 06606

Development Bank of Washington
2000 L St. NW, #702
Washington, DC 20036
202/332-9333

The Douglass Bank
1314 N. 5th St.
Kansas City, KS 66101
913/321-7200

Drexel National Bank
3401 S. King Dr.
Chicago, IL 60616
312/225-9200

Dwelling House Savings & Loan Association
501 Herron Ave.
Pittsburgh, PA 15219
412/683-5116

Emerald City Bank
2320 E. Union St.
Seattle, WA 98122
206/329-3434

Enterprise Savings & Loan Association
1219 E. Rosecrans Ave.
Compton, CA 90282
213/591-5641

Family Savings & Loan Association
3683 Crenshaw Blvd.
Los Angeles, CA 90016
213/295-3381

First Commerce Savings Bank
PO Box 3199
Jackson, MS 39205

First Federal Savings & Loan
7990 Scenic Highway
Baton Rouge, LA 70874
504/775-6133

First Independence National Bank
44 Michigan Ave.
Detroit, MI 48226
313/256-8250

First Southern Bank
PO Box 1019
Lithonia, GA 30058
404/987-3511

First State Bank
PO Box 640
Danville, VA 24543
804/793-4611

First Texas Bank
PO Box 29775
Dallas, TX 75229
214/243-2400

Founders National Bank of Los Angeles
3910 W. Martin Luther King Jr. Blvd.
Los Angeles, CA 90008
213/295-3161

Gateway National Bank
3412 Union Blvd. N
St. Louis, MO 63115
314/389-3000

Golden Coin Savings & Loan Association
170 Columbus Ave., #210
San Francisco, CA 94133

Greensboro National Bank
PO Box 22046
Greensboro, NC 27420
919/373-8500

Harbor Bank of Maryland
21 W. Fayette St.
Baltimore, MD 21201
410/528-1800

Heritage National Bank
6393 Penn Ave.
Pittsburgh, PA 15206

Highland Community Bank
1701 W. 87th St.
Chicago, IL 60620
312/881-6800

Home Federal Savings Bank
9108 Woodward Ave.
Detroit, MI 48202
313/873-3310

Ideal Federal Savings Bank
1629 Druid Hill Ave.
Baltimore, MD 21217
301/669-1629

Imperial Savings & Loan Association
211 Fayette St.
Martinsville, VA 24114
703/638-7545

Independence Bank of Chicago
7936 S. Cottage Grove
Chicago, IL 60619
312/487-4700

Independence Federal Savings & Loan Association
1229 Connecticut Ave. NW
Washington, DC 20036

Industrial Bank of Washington
4812 Georgia Ave. NW
Washington, DC 20011
202/722-2014

Liberty Bank & Trust Company
3939 Tulane Ave.
New Orleans, LA 70160
504/483-6601

Life Savings Bank
7990 Scenic Highway
PO Box 74108
Baton Rouge, LA 70874

Mechanics & Farmers Bank
PO Box 1932
Durham, NC 27702
919/683-1521

Metro Savings Bank
715 Goldwin Ave.
Orlando, FL 32805

Mutual Federal Savings & Loan Association
205 Auburn Ave. NE
Atlanta, GA 30303
404/659-0701

Mutual Savings & Loan Association
112 W. Parrish St.
Durham, NC 27701
919/688-1308

New Age Federal Savings & Loan Association
1401 N. Kings Highway Blvd.
St. Louis, MO 63113
314/361-4100

New Atlantic Bank
415 St. Paul's Blvd.
Norfolk, VA 23510
804/623-6155

North Milwaukee State Bank
5630 W. Fond du Lac Ave.
Milwaukee, WI 53216
414/466-2344

Omnibank
10474 W. Jefferson Ave.
River Rouge, MI 48218
313/843-8856

Peoples National Bank of Commerce
3275 N.W. 79th St.
Miami, FL 33147
305/686-0700

People's Savings & Loan Association
101 N. Armistead Ave.
Hampton, VA 23669
804/722-2575

Seaway National Bank of Chicago
645 E. 87th St.
Chicago, IL 60619
312/487-4800

**Sound Savings and Loan
  Association**
1006 2nd Ave.
Seattle, WA 98114

**Standard Savings & Loan
  Association**
PO Box 8806
Houston, TX 77288
713/529-9133

**Tuskegee Federal Savings & Loan
  Association**
301 N. Elm St.
Tuskegee, AL 36088
205/727-2560

United Bank & Trust Company
2714 Canal St.
New Orleans, LA 70119
504/827-0060

United National Bank
PO Box 1450
137 Gillespie St.
Fayetteville, NC 28302
919/483-1131

**United National Bank of
  Washington**
3940 Minnesota Ave. NE
Washington, DC 20006
202/828-4300

Unity National Bank
2602 Blodgett St.
Houston, TX 77004
713/526-3971

Victory Savings Bank
1545 Sumter St.
Columbia, SC 29201
803/733-8100

**Washington Shores Federal
  Savings & Loan Association**
715 Goldwin Ave.
Orlando, FL 32805
305/293-7320

INSURANCE COMPANIES

Atlanta Life Insurance Company
PO Box 897
Atlanta, GA 30301

**Benevolent Life Insurance
  Company**
1624 Milam St.
Shreveport, LA 71103

**Booker T. Washington Insurance
  Company**
PO Box 697
Birmingham, AL 35201
205/328-5454

**Central Life Insurance Company
  of Florida**
PO Box 3286
Tampa, FL 33607
813/251-1897

Chicago Metropolitan Assurance Company
4455 Martin Luther King Jr. Dr.
Chicago, IL 60653
312/285-3030

George F. Carter Insurance Agency, Inc.
PO Box 12337
Jacksonville, FL 32209
904/764-0025

Gertrude Geddes Willis Life Insurance Company
2128 Jackson Ave.
New Orleans, LA 70153
504/522-2525

Golden Circle Life Insurance Company
39 Jackson Ave.
Bronsville, TN 38012

Golden State Mutual Life Insurance Company
PO Box 2332
Terminal Annex
Los Angeles, CA 90018

Goodrich Johnson Brokerage
271 W. 125th St., #208
New York, NY 10027
212/865-5606

Lighthouse Life Insurance Company
1544 Milam St.
Shreveport, LA 71103

Lovett's Life and Burial Insurance Company
PO Box 364
Mobile, AL 36603

Majestic Life Insurance Company
1833 Dryades St.
New Orleans, LA 70113

Mammoth Life and Accident Insurance Company
PO Box 2099
Louisville, KY 40201

MCAP Bonding and Insurance Company
89-50 164th St., #2B
Jamaica, NY 11432
718/657-6444

National Service Industrial Life Insurance Company
1716 N. Claiborne Ave.
New Orleans, LA 70116

North Carolina Mutual Life Insurance Company
Mutual Plaza
Durham, NC 27701
919/682-9201

People's Progressive Insurance Company
109 Harrison St.
Rayville, LA 71269

Pilgrim Health and Life Insurance Company
PO Box 1897
Augusta, GA 30901

Protective Industrial Insurance Company of Alabama, Inc.
PO Box 2744
Birmingham, AL 35204

Purple Shield Life Insurance Company
PO Box 3157
Baton Rouge, LA 70802

Reliable Life Insurance Company
108 N. 23rd St.
Monroe, LA 71201

Security Life Insurance of the South
PO Box 159
Jackson, MS 39203

**Southern Aid Life Insurance
Company**
PO Box 12024
Richmond, VA 23241

**Supreme Life Insurance Company
of America**
3501 Martin Luther King Jr. Dr.
Chicago, IL 60714
312/538-5100

**United Mutual Life Insurance
Company**
310 Lenox Ave.
New York, NY 10027
212/369-4200

Universal Life Insurance Company
PO Box 241
Memphis, TN 38101

**Winston Mutual Life Insurance
Company**
PO Box 998
Winston-Salem, NC 27102

**Wright Mutual Insurance
Company**
2995 E. Grand Blvd.
Detroit, MI 48202

RESTAURANTS

Aunt Gussy's Pl.
205 N. Los Robles Ave.
Pasadena, CA 91101
818/794-7400

B. Smith's
771 8th Ave.
New York, NY 10017
212/247-2222

Bentley's
25 E. 40th St.
New York, NY 10016
212/684-2540

Cafe Beaulah
39 E. 19th St.
New York, NY 10003
212/777-9700

Caribbean Sunset
60 Upper Alabama St. SW
Atlanta, GA 30303
404/659-4587

Charlie Trotters
816 W. Armitage Ave.
Chicago, IL 60605
312/248-6228

Copeland's
547 W. 145th St.
New York, NY 10031

Dooky Chase's Restaurant
2301 Orleans Ave.
New Orleans, LA 70119
504-821-0535

Jezebel's
630 9th Ave.
New York, NY 10017
212/582-1045

Kwanzaa
19 Cleveland St.
New York, NY 10003

The Living Room Lounge
1365 Mayson Tuyner Rd.
Atlanta, GA 30303
404/892-8345

London and Son Wing House Company
3740 Martin Luther King Jr. Dr.
St. Louis, MO 63113
314/371-4925

Mama's Kountry Kitchen
15250 W. Mile Rd.
Detroit, MI 48207
313/342-6120

Mr. Leo's
17 W. 27th St.
New York, NY 10001
212/532-6673

New Orleans Jazz Club
828 Royal St., #265
New Orleans, LA 70116
504/455-6847

The Praline Connection
542 Frenchman St.
New Orleans, LA 70116
800/392-0362

Restaurant 2110
2110 N. Charles St.
Baltimore, MD 21202
410/528-1655

The Retreat
605 E. 111th St.
Chicago, IL 60628
312/568-6000

Roscoe's Chicken and Waffles
5006 W. Pico Blvd.
Los Angeles, CA 90028
213/466-7453

The Serving Spoon Restaurant
1403 Centinela St.
Inglewood, CA 90301
310/412-3927

The Shark Bar
307 Amsterdam Ave.
New York, NY 10019
212/874-8500

Sylvia's Restaurant and Food Products
332 Lenox Ave.
New York, NY 10027
212/996-0660

T. J.'s Southern Gourmet
92 Chambers St.
New York, NY 10007
212/406-3442

Two Pardners Restaurant
144 Robert B. Cullen Ave.
Dallas, TX 77535
214/421-5387

Vee's on Peachtree
320 Peachtree
Atlanta, GA 30365
404/522-3021

Vernon's Jamaican Jerk Paradise
252 W. 29th St.
New York, NY 10003
212/268-7020

Well's
2247 Adam Clayton Powell Blvd.
New York, NY 10027
212/234-0700

Zulu's Cafe
1260 Amsterdam Ave.
New York, NY 10027
212/663-1670

BUSINESS AND TRADE ORGANIZATIONS

Action Alliance of Black Managers
PO Box 15636
Columbus, OH 43215
614/860-9388

African Business Association
271 Madison Ave., #908
New York, NY 10016
212/576-1219

Afro-Am Police League
PO Box 49122
Chicago, IL 60649
312/568-7329

Alliance of Black Technicians
1869 Buckingham Rd.
Los Angeles, CA 90019
213/933-0746

Alliance of Minority Women for Business and Political Development
c/o Brenda Alford
PO Box 13933
Silver Spring, MD 20911-3933
301/565-0258

American Association of Black Women Entrepreneurs
PO Box 13933
Silver Spring, MD 20911
301/565-0258

American Association of Blacks in Energy
801 Pennsylvania Ave. SE, #250
Washington, DC 20003
202/547-9378

American Association of Minority Veterans
c/o Cuyahoga Community College
2900 Community College Ave.
Cleveland, OH 44115
216/987-4203

American Health and Beauty Aid Institute (AHBAI)
401 N. Michigan Ave., 25th Floor
Chicago, IL 60611
312/644-6610

American League of Financial Institutions
1709 New York Ave. NW, #801
Washington, DC 20006
202/628-5624

Association of Black Certified Public Accountant Firms
1101 Connecticut Ave. NW, #700
Washington, DC 20036
202/857-1100

Association of Black Women Entrepreneurs
PO Box 49368
Los Angeles, CA 90049
213/624-8639

Black Affairs for Training and Organizational Development
10918 Jarboe Ct.
Silver Spring, MD 20901
301/681-9822

Black Business Alliance
PO Box 26443
Baltimore, MD 21207
410/467-7427

Black Caucus of American Library Association
c/o Dr. Alex Boyd
Newark Public Library
5 Washington St.
Newark, NJ 07101
201/733-7780

Black Creative Professional Association
PO Box 34272
Los Angeles, CA 90034
213/964-3550

Black Data Processing Associates
PO Box 7466
Philadelphia, PA 19101
215/843-9120

Black Entertainment and Sports Lawyers Association
PO Box 508067
Chicago, IL 60461
708/386-8338

Black Executive Exchange Program
c/o National Urban League
500 E. 62nd St.
New York, NY 10021

Black Professional Secretaries Association
PO Box 4486
Atlanta, GA 30302
404/578-5005

Black Professionals in International Affairs
PO Box 11675
Washington, DC 20008-0875
301/953-0815

Black Retail Action Group
PO Box 1192
Rockefeller Center Station
New York, NY 10185
212/308-6017

Black Veterans for Social Justice Inc.
686 Fulton St.
Brooklyn, NY 11217
718/935-1116

Blacks in Government
1820 11th St. NW
Washington, DC 20001
202/667-3280

Blacks in Law Enforcement
256 E. McLemore Ave.
Memphis, TN 38106-2833
901/774-1118

Carribbean-American Chamber of Commerce and Industry Inc.
Brooklyn Navy Yard, Bldg. #5
Brooklyn, NY 11205
718/834-4544

Coalition of Black Trade Unionists
PO Box 73120
Washington, DC 20056-3120
202/429-1203

Conference of Minority Public Administrators
1120 G St. NW, #700
Washington, DC 20005
202/393-7878

Council on Career Development for Minorities
1341 W. Mockingbird La., #412-E
Dallas, TX 75277
214/631-3677

Federation of Southern Cooperatives and Land Assistance Fund
100 Edgewood Ave., #814
Atlanta, GA 30303
404/524-6882

InterAmerican Travel Agents Society
Alameda Travel Inc.
1020 Holcombe Ave., #1306
Houston, TX 77030
713/799-1001

International Association of African and Black Business People
18900 Schoolcraft St.
Detroit, MI 48223

International Association of Black Business Educators
915 S. Jackson St.
Montgomery, AL 36195
205/931-4124

International Association of Black Professional Fire Fighters
1025 Connecticut Ave. NW, #610
Washington, DC 20036
202/296-0157

International Black Toy Manufacturers Association
PO Box 348
Springfield Gardens, NY 11434

Interracial Council for Business Opportunity
51 Madison Ave., #2212
New York, NY 10010
212/779-4360

Minority Agricultural Resources Center
817 14th St., #300A
Sacramento, CA 95814
916/444-2924

Minority Business Enterprise Legal Defense and Education Fund
220 I St., #280
Washington, DC 20002
202/513-0010

National Action Council for Minorities in Engineering
3 W. 35th St.
New York, NY 10001
212/279-2626

National Association for Black Veterans
2201 N. Martin Luther King Jr. Dr.
Milwaukee, WI 53212
414/265-8940

National Association for Sickle Cell Disease Inc.
3345 Wilshire Blvd., #1106
Los Angeles, CA 90010
213/736-5455

National Association of African American Entrepreneurs
PO Box 1191
Indianapolis, IN 42606
317/841-3717

National Association of Black Accountants
220 I St. NE
Washington, DC 20002
202/546-6222

National Association of Black Consulting Engineers
6406 Georgia Ave. NW
Washington, DC 20012
202/291-3550

National Association of Black Geologists & Geophysicists
PO Box 720157
Houston, TX 77272

National Association of Black Manufacturers
1910 K St. NW
Washington, DC 20006
202/785-5133

National Association of Black Real Estate Professionals
PO Box 21421
Alexandria, VA 22320
703/920-7661

National Association of Black Sales Professionals
PO Box 5303
River Forest, IL 60305
708/445-1010

National Association of Black Women Attorneys
3711 Macomb St. NW, #4
Washington, DC 20016
202/298-5931

National Association of Black Women Entrepreneurs Inc.
PO Box 1375
Detroit, MI 48231
313/341-7400

National Association of Blacks in Criminal Justice
PO Box 9499
Washington, DC 20016
301/681-2365

National Association of Investment Companies
1111 14th St. NW, #700
Washington, DC 20005
202/289-4336

National Association of Management Consultants
3101 Euclid Office Plaza, #501
Cleveland, OH 44115
216/431-0303

National Association of Market Developers Inc.
PO Box 4446
Rockefeller Center Station
New York, NY 10186
212/355-1732

National Association of Minority Contractors
1333 F. St. NW, #500
Washington, DC 20004
202/347-8259

National Association of Minority Women in Business
906 Grand Ave., #200
Kansas City, MO 64106
816/421-3335

National Association of Negro Business and Professional Women's Club
1806 New Hampshire Ave. NW
Washington, DC 20009
202/483-4206

National Association of Securities Professionals
1360 Peachtree St. NE, #800
Atlanta, GA 30309
404/875-2161

National Association of Urban Bankers Inc.
810 1st St. NE, #530
Washington, DC 20002
301/892-1433

National Bankers Association
122 C St. NW, #580
Washington, DC 20009
202/588-5432

National Bar Association
1225 11th St. NW
Washington, DC 20001
202/842-3900

National Beauty Culturists League
25 Logan Circle NW
Washington, DC 20005
202/332-2695

National Black Chambers of Commerce
5741 Telegraph Ave.
Oakland, CA 94609
510/601-5741

National Black Coalition of Federal Aviation Employees
9470 Timberleaf St.
Dallas, TX 75243
214/343-2668

National Black Leadership Roundtable
2135 Rayburn House Office Bldg.
Washington, DC 20515
202/331-2030

National Black Police Association
3251 Mt. Pleasant St. NW
Washington, DC 20010
202/982-2070

National Black Public Relations Society of America
6565 Sunset Blvd., #301
Los Angeles, CA 90028
213/856-0827

National Black Staff Network
213 S. Adams St.
Tallahassee, FL 32301
904/222-5820

National Business League
1629 K St. NW, #605
Washington, DC 20006
202/466-5483

National Center for Neighborhood Enterprise
1367 Connecticut Ave. NW
Washington, DC 20036
202/331-1103

National Coalition of Black Meeting Planners
10320 Little Patuxent Pkwy., #1106
Columbia, MD 20144
202/628-3952

National Conference of Black Lawyers
126 W. 119th St.
New York, NY 10026
212/864-4000

National Consortium for Black Professional Development
2210 Goldsmith Office Center, #228-A
Louisville, KY 40218
502/451-8199

National Council for Equal Business Opportunity
7932 W. Branch Dr.
Washington, DC 20012
202/723-8348

National Council of Black Engineers and Scientists
1525 Aviation Blvd., #C424
Redondo Beach, CA 90278
213/896-9779

National Development Council
41 E. 42nd St.
New York, NY 10017
212/682-1106

National Economic Association
c/o Dr. Gus T. Ridgel
Southern University
Baton Rouge, LA 70813
504/771-5020

National Florist Association
PO Box 90776
Washington, DC 20013
716/235-3370

National Forum for Black Public Administrators
777 N. Capitol St. NE, #807
Washington, DC 20002
202/408-9300

National Funeral Directors and Morticians Association
1800 E. Linwood Blvd.
Kansas City, MO 64109
816/921-1800

National Insurance Association
PO Box 53230
Chicago, IL 60653-0230
312/924-3308

National Minority Business Council
235 E. 42nd St.
New York, NY 10017
212/573-2385

National Minority Supplier Development Council Inc.
15 W. 39th St., 9th Floor
New York, NY 10018
212/944-2430

National Naval Officers Association
529 14th St. NW, #948
Washington, DC 20045
202/662-7323

National Network of Minority Women in Science
c/o American Association for the Advancement of Science
1333 H St. NW
Washington, DC 20005
202/326-6677

National Optometric Association
1489 Livingston Ave.
Columbus, OH 43205
614/253-5593

National Organization for the Professional Advancement of Black Chemists and Chemical Engineers
525 College St. NW
Washington, DC 20059
202/667-1699

National Organization of Black Law Enforcement Executives
908 Pennsylvania Ave. SE
Washington, DC 20003
202/546-8811

National Organization of Minority Architects
120 Ralph McGill Blvd. NE
Atlanta, GA 30308
404/876-3055

National Pharmaceutical Association
c/o College of Pharmacy and Pharmaceutical Sciences
Howard University
Washington, DC 20059
202/328-9229

National Society of Black Engineers
1454 Duke St.
Alexandria, VA 22314
703/549-2207

National Technical Association
PO Box 7045
Washington, DC 20032
202/829-6100

National United Affiliated Beverage Association
7141 Frankstown Ave.
Philadelphia, PA 19139
215/724-7585

National United Law Enforcement Officers Association
256 E. Mclemore Ave.
Memphis, TN 38106
901/774-1118

National United Licensee Beverage Association
7141 Frankstown Ave.
Pittsburgh, PA 15208
412/241-9344

National Youth Employment Coalition
1501 Broadway, #1111
New York, NY 10036
212/840-1801

Negro Airmen International
PO Box 1340
Tuskegee, AL 36008
205/727-0721

Negro Trade Union Leadership Council
929 N. Broad St.
Philadelphia, PA 19108
215/787-3600

Opportunities Industrialization Centers of America
1415 N. Broad St.
Philadelphia, PA 19122
215/236-4500

Organization of Black Airline Pilots Inc.
PO Box 5793
Englewood, NJ 07631
201/568-8145

Professional Women in Business Networking Systems
20220 S. Avalon Ave., #188
Carson, CA 90746
310/542-7381

369th Veterans Association
369th Regiment Armory
1 369 Plaza
New York, NY 10037
212/281-3308

Trade Union Leadership Council
8670 Grand River Ave.
Detroit, MI 48204
313/894-0303

Trade Union Women of African Heritage
530 W. 23rd St., #428
New York, NY 10011
212/929-6449

Tuskegee Airmen Inc.
4217 American River Dr.
Sacramento, CA 95864
916/485-4731

United Mortgage Bankers Association
800 Ivy Hill Rd.
Philadelphia, PA 19501
215/242-6060

HEALTH AND SOCIAL SERVICES

HEALTH PROFESSIONALS

Canady-Davis, Alexa
Children's Hospital of Michigan
3901 Beaubien St.
Detroit, MI 48201
Physician, researcher

Carson, Benjamin
c/o Johns Hopkins Medical Center
600 N. Wolfe St.
Baltimore, MD 21205
Neurosurgeon, author,
motivational speaker

Clark, Kenneth B.
c/o University Press of New
England
17 Lebanon St.
Hanover, NH 03755
Psychologist, educator, author

Dee, Gerald
c/o McCreay Report
E. 67th St.
New York, NY 10021
Doctor, television personality

Gayle, Helen D.
c/o Office of Research &
Development
U.S. Agency for International
Development, #1200
Washington, DC 20523
Epidemiologist, AIDS researcher

Hicks, Ingrid
Department of Psychiatry
University of Wisconsin Medical
School
Milwaukee Clinical Campus
2000 W. Kibourn Ave.
Milwaukee, WI 53223
Psychiatrist, author, researcher

Leffall, LaSalle, Jr.
College of Medicine
Howard University
240 6th St. NW
Washington, DC 20059
Cancer researcher, educator,
physician

Massey, Walter E.
University of California
300 Lakeside Dr.
Oakland, CA 94612
Physicist, educator, researcher

Poussaint, Alvin
c/o Judge Baker Guidance Center
Harvard Medical School
295 Longwood Ave.
Boston, MA 02115
Psychologist

Reed, James W.
Morehouse School of Medicine
Atlanta, GA
*Chairman Graduate Medical
   Education, President
   International Society of
   Hypertension in Blacks, author*

Welsing, Frances Cress
7603 Georgia Ave. NW, #402
Washington, DC 20012
Psychiatrist, activist, author

HOSPITALS

Bethany Hospital
5025 N. Paulina St.
Chicago, IL 60640
312/271-9040

Charity Hospital of Louisiana
1532 Tulane Ave.
New Orleans, LA 70140
504/568-2311

Fairview Medical Center
2048 W. Fairview Ave.
Montgomery, AL 36108
205/265-7011

**George Hubbard Hospital of
   Meharry Medical College**
1005 Dr. D. B. Todd Jr. Blvd.
Nashville, TN 37208
615/327-6218

Howard University Hospital
2041 Georgia Ave. NW
Washington, DC 20060
202/865-6660

**L. Richardson Memorial Hospital
   Inc.**
Drawer 16167
Greensboro, NC 27406
919/275-9741

Mound Bayou Community Hospital
Drawer R
Mound Bayou, MS 38762
601/741-2113

Provident Medical Center
500 E. 52nd St.
Chicago, IL 60615
312/538-9700

Riverside General Hospital
PO Box 8128
Houston, TX 77288
713/526-2441

Roseland Community Hospital
45 W. 111th St.
Chicago, IL 60628
312/995-3000

St. Bernard Hospital
3265 W. 64th St.
Chicago, IL 60621
312/962-4100

**Southwest Hospital and Medical
   Center Inc.**
501 Fairburn Rd. SW
Atlanta, GA 30311
404/669-1111

HEALTH AND SOCIAL SERVICE ORGANIZATIONS

African American National Foods Association
c/o Cheryl A. Simms
7058 S. Clyde Ave.
Chicago, IL 60649
312/363-3933

American Black Chiropractors Association
1918 E. Grand Blvd.
St. Louis, MO 63107
314/531-0615

American Public Health Association Black Caucus
8281 Jackson Dr.
San Diego, CA 92119
619/285-6452

Association of Black Cardiologists Inc.
13404 S.W. 128th St., #A
Miami, FL 35186
305/256-9994

Association of Black Cardiologists Inc.
3201 Del Paso Blvd., #100
Sacramento, CA 95815
916/641-2224

Association of Black Nursing Faculty
5823 Queens Cove
Lisle, IL 60532
708/969-3809

Association of Black Psychologists
PO Box 55999
Washington, DC 20040
202/722-0808

Association of Hatian Physicians Abroad
60 Plaza St.
Brooklyn, NY 11238
718/783-0701

Association of Minority Health Professions Schools
711 2nd St. NE, #200
Washington, DC 20002
202/544-7499

Association of Social and Behavioral Scientists
PO Box 4371
Fort Valley College
Fort Valley, GA 31030
912/825-6211

Auxiliary to the National Medical Association Inc.
1012 10th St. NW
Washington, DC 20001
202/371-1674

Black Health Research Foundation
14 E. 60th St., #307
New York, NY 10022
212/408-3485

Black Psychiatrists of America
2730 Adeline St.
Oakland, CA 94607
510/465-1800

Inner-City AIDS Network
1701 7th St. NW, 2nd Floor
Washington, DC 20001-3508
202/287-0800

International Society on Hypertension in Blacks
2045 Manchester St. NE
Atlanta, GA 30324-4110

Magic Johnson AIDS Foundation
1888 Century Park E, #310
Los Angeles, CA 90067
310/785-0201

National Association for Sickle Cell Disease Inc.
3345 Wilshire Blvd., #1106
Los Angeles, CA 90010
213/736-5455

National Association of Black Psychologists
PO Box 55999
Washington, DC 20040
202/722-0808

National Association of Black Social Workers
1969 Madison Ave.
New York, NY 10035
212/348-0035

National Association of Health Services Executives
50 F St. NW, #1040
Washington, DC 20001
202/628-3953

National Black Alcoholism Council
1629 K St., #802
Washington, DC 20006
202/296-2696

National Black Association for Speech-Language-Hearing
PO Box 50605
Washington, DC 20004-0605
202/727-2608

National Black Health Planners Association
1660 L St. NW, 7th Floor
Washington, DC 20036
202/673-3679

National Black Holistic Society
St. Louis, MO 63169
314/382-5196

National Black Nurses Association Inc.
1012 10th St. NW
Washington, DC 20001-4492
202/393-6870

National Black Women's Health Project
1237 Ralph Abernathy Blvd. SW
Atlanta, GA 30310
404/758-9590

National Caucus and Center on Black Aged
1424 K St. NW, #500
Washington, DC 20005
202/637-8400

National Center for the Advancement of Blacks in the Health Professions
c/o Della McGraw-Goodwin
313/345-4480

National Coalition to End Racism in America's Child Care System
22075 Koths St.
Taylor, MI 48180
313/295-0257

National Council on Black Aging
PO Box 51275
Durham, NC 27717
919/493-4858

National Dental Assistants Association
5506 Connecticut Ave. NW, #24
Washington, DC 20015

National Dental Association
5506 Connecticut Ave. NW, #24
Washington, DC 20015
202/244-7555

National Dental Hygienists's Association
5506 Connecticut Ave. NW,
#24–25
Washington, DC 20015
202/244-7555

National Hypertension Association
324 E. 30th St.
New York, NY 10016
212/889-3557

National Medical Association
1012 10th St. NW
Washington, DC 20001
202/347-1895

National Medical Fellowships
254 W. 31st St., 7th Floor
New York, NY 10001
212/714-0933

National Minority AIDS Council
714 G St. NW
Washington, DC 20003
202/544-1076

National Minority Health Association Inc.
PO Box 11876
Harrisburg, PA 17108
717/234-3254

National Pharmaceutical Foundation
PO Box 5439
Tacoma Park Station
Washington, DC 20912

Planning and the Black Community
c/o Stephanie Williams
142 51st Ave. NW
Opa-Locka, FL 33054
305/687-3545

National Podiatrical Medical Association
c/o Raymond Lee
1638 E. 87th St.
Chicago, IL 60617
312/374-1616

PFB (Pseudofollicutis barbae) Project
c/o Robert B. Fitzpatrick
4801 Massachusetts Ave. NW,
#400
Washington, DC 20016
202/364-8710

Research Foundation for Ethnic Related Diseases
2231 S. Western Ave.
Los Angeles, CA 90018
213/737-7372

Sickie Cell Disease Foundation of Greater New York
127 W. 127th St., #421
New York, NY 10022
212/865-1500

Sisterhood of Black Single Mothers
1360 Fulton St., #423
Brooklyn, NY 11216
718/638-0413

FOUNDATIONS AND CHARITABLE ORGANIZATIONS

Africa Fund
198 Broadway
New York, NY 10038
212/962-1210

African Freedom Fund Treasury
PO Box 3439
Washington, DC 20010
202/529-3635

Africare Inc.
440 R St. NW
Washington, DC 20001
202/462-3614

Afro-American Social Research Association
PO Box 2150
Jacksonville, FL 32203

Associated Black Charities
105 E. 22nd St., #915
New York, NY 10010
212/777-6060

Association of Black Foundation Executives
1828 L St. NW
Washington, DC 20036
202/466-6512

Beaulah Youth Development Council
PO Box 7243
Columbia, SC 29202
803/771-4197

Black Focus
4115 Bridge Ave.
Cleveland, OH 44113
216/631-7660

Center for Urban Black Charities
630 20th St.
Oakland, CA 94612
510/465-1927

Cooperative Assistance Fund
533 S. Wisconsin Ave., #44
Washington, DC 20015
202/833-8543

E. Bushaua Foundation
809 Ranch Rd.
Florence, SC 29501
803/662-2579

Heal the World Foundation
1801 Century Park W
Los Angeles, CA 90067

Marcus Garvey Foundation
PO Box 4261
Philadelphia, PA 19101

Michael Jordan Foundation
c/o Pro Serv
1101 Wilson Blvd.
Arlington, VA 22209

Moore Foundation
8725 S. Shore State St., #3
Chicago, IL 60691
312/488-5552

National Black Survival Fund
PO Box 3885
Lafayette, LA 70502-3885
318/232-7672

National Black United Fund
50 Park Pl., #938
Newark, NJ 07102
201/643-5122

Whitney Houston Children's Foundation
410 E. 50th St.
New York, NY 10022

Whitney M. Young Memorial Foundation
100 Park Ave.
New York, NY 10017

Yeah Foundation
5555 Melrose Ave.
Los Angeles, CA 90039

FRATERNAL AND SOCIAL ORGANIZATIONS

African American Conference
PO Box 15819
San Diego, CA 92175
619/560-2770

African American Women's Association
PO Box 55122
Brightwood Station
Washington, DC 20011
202/966-6645

Alpha Kappa Alpha Sorority Inc.
5656 S. Stony Island Ave.
Chicago, IL 60637
312/684-1282

Alpha Phi Alpha Fraternity Inc.
2313 St. Paul St.
Baltimore, MD 21218-5234
410/554-0054

American Bridge Association
c/o Gloria Christler
2798 Lakewood Ave. SW
Atlanta, GA 30315
404/768-5517

Ancient Egyptian Arabic Order of Noble Mystic Shrine Inc.
2211 Cass Ave.
Detroit, MI 48201
313/961-9148

Benevolent Protective Order of Reindeer Grand Lodge 842
E. 28th St.
Wilmington, DE 19802
302/762-5880

Black Women's Network
PO Box 12072
Milwaukee, WI 53212
414/353-8925

Carats Inc.
6236 N. 15th St.
Philadelphia, PA 19141
215/424-2212

Chi Delta Mu Fraternity Inc.
1012 10th St. NW
Washington, DC 20001
202/842-1111

Chi Eta Phi Sorority Inc.
3029 13th St. NW
Washington, DC 20009
202/232-3858

Chums Inc.
8339 E. Beach Dr. NW
Washington, DC 20012
202/882-0857

Conference of Prince Hall Grand Masters
4311 Portland Ave.
South Minneapolis, MN 55407
612/825-2474

Delta Sigma Theta Sorority Inc.
1707 New Hampshire Ave. NW
Washington, DC 20009
202/986-2400

The Drifters Inc.
10 Chelsea Ct.
Neptune, NJ 07753
908/774-2724

Edges
c/o Amerada Hess Corporation
1 Hess Pl.
Woodbridge, NJ 07095
908/750-6408

Eta Phi Beta Sorority Inc.
16815 James Couzens Ave.
Detroit, MI 43235
313/862-0600

Federation of Eastern Stars of the World
1017 E. 11th St.
PO Box 1296
Austin, TX 78767
512/477-5380

Federation of Masons of the World
PO Box 1296
Austin, TX 78767
512/477-5380

Frontiers International Inc.
6301 Crittenden St.
Philadelphia, PA 19138
215/549-4550

Gamma Phi Delta Sorority Inc.
Alpha Omicron Chapter
1900 Campbell Dr.
Suitland, MD 20746

Girlfriends Inc.
c/o Rachel Norcorn Smith
228 Lansing Ave.
Portsmouth, VA 23704
804/397-1339

Groove Phi Groove Fellowship Inc.
PO Box 8337
Silver Spring, MD 20907-8337
202/543-8376

Ida Van Smith Flight Club Inc.
PO Box 361
Rochdale Village, NY 11434
718/723-3054

Improved and Benevolent Protective Order of Elks of the World
PO Box 159
Winton, NC 27986
919/358-7661

International Benevolent Society Inc.
837 5th Ave.
PO Box 1276
Columbus, GA 31902
706/322-5671

International Black Women's Congress
1081 Bergen St., #200
Newark, NJ 07112
201/926-0570

Iota Phi Lambda Sorority Inc.
1727 Chester St.
Savannah, GA 31401
912/236-0459

Iota Phi Theta Sorority Inc.
PO Box 7628
Baltimore, MD 21207-0628
301/792-2192

J.U.G.S. Inc.
(Justice, Unity, Generosity and
Service)
1965 Thornhill Pl.
Detroit, MI 48207

**Jack and Jill of America
Foundation Inc.**
c/o Violet D. Greer
PO Drawer 3689
Chattanooga, TN 37404
615/622-4476

Kappa Alpha Psi Fraternity, Inc.
2322-24 N. Broad St.
Philadelphia, PA 19132
215/228-7184

Lambda Kappa Mu Sorority Inc.
1521 Crittenden St.
Washington, DC 20011
718/282-8525

The Links
1200 Massachusetts Ave. NW
Washington, DC 20005
202/842-8686

**Modern Free and Accepted
Masons of the World Inc.**
PO Box 1072
Columbus, GA 31906
404/322-3326

Moles
1418 Floral Dr. NW
Washington, DC 20012
202/723-1678

**Most Worshipful National Grand
Lodge Free and Accepted
Ancient York Masons Prince Hall
Origin National Compact
U.S.A. Inc.**
26070 Tyron Rd.
Orangeburg, SC 29115
216/232-9495

**National Association of Colored
Women's Clubs**
5805 16th St. NW
Washington, DC 20011
202/726-2044

**National Association of Girls
Clubs**
5808 16th St. NW
Washington, DC 20011
202/726-2044

**National Association of
Neighborhoods**
1651 Fuller St. NW
Washington, DC 20009
202/332-7766

**National Black Women's
Consciousness Raising
Association**
1906 N. Charles St.
Baltimore, MD 21218
410/727-8900

**National Coalition of 100 Black
Women**
38 W. 32nd St., #1610
New York, NY 10001
212/947-2196

National Council of Negro Women
1211 Connecticut Ave. NW, #702
Washington, DC 20036
202/659-0006

**National Hook-Up of Black
Women**
5117 S. University Ave.
Chicago, IL 60615
312/643-5866

**National Housewives League of
America**
3240 Gilbert St.
Cincinnati, OH 45207
513/281-8822

National Neighbors Inc.
2000 M St., #400
Washington, DC 20036
202/785-4836

National Pan-Hellenic Council Inc.
Indiana University
Suite 30
Bloomington, IN 47405
812/855-8820

Omega Psi Phi Fraternity Inc.
2714 Georgia Ave. NW
Washington, DC 20001
202/667-7158

100 Black Men of America Inc.
127 Peachtree St. NE, 7th Floor
Atlanta, GA 30303
202/892-7111

Phi Beta Sigma Fraternity Inc.
145 Kennedy St.
Washington, DC 20011
202/726-5434

Phi Delta Kappa
PO Box 789
Bloomington, IN 47402

Phi Delta Kappa Sorority Inc.
8233 S. Martin Luther King Jr.
  Dr.
Chicago, IL 60619

Sigma Gamma Rho Sorority Inc.
880 S. Stony Island Ave.
Chicago, IL 60617
312/873-9000

Sigma Pi Phi Fraternity Inc.
69 5th Ave.
New York, NY 10003
212/219-1360

Tau Gamma Delta Sorority Inc.
2528 W. 74th St.
Los Angeles, CA 90043
213/751-7084

**United Order of Tents of J. R.
  Giddings and Jolifee Union**
1620 Church St.
Norfolk, VA 23504

Zeta Phi Beta Sorority Inc.
1734 New Hampshire Ave. NW
Washington, DC 20009
202/387-3103

Zeta Phi Delta Sorority Inc.
PO Box 157
Bronx, NY 10469
212/407-8288